D0717996

English Heritage

Book of

Roman Towns in Britain

English Heritage
Book of

Roman Towns in Britain

Guy de la Bédoyère

B. T. Batsford Ltd/English Heritage
London

First published 1992

Typeset by Lasertext Ltd, Stretford,
Manchester M32 0JT
Printed and bound in Great Britain by
BPCC Hazells Ltd
Member of BPCC Ltd

Published by B. T. Batsford Ltd
4 Fitzhardinge Street, London W1H 0AH

A CIP catalogue record for this book is available from the British Library

ISBN 0 7134 6893 9 (cased)
0 7134 6894 7 (limp)

Contents

Illustrations

Colour plates

VLPI
VS
SILVA
NVS
FAC
TVS
EMERI
TVS·LEG
II AVG
VOTVM
SOLVIT
ARAV

Introduction

The towns of Roman Britain have always attracted attention. From an early date they were exploited as sources of building stone and in the year 1201 King John began excavating at Corbridge in an unsuccessful search for treasure. Throughout the medieval period the Roman defences of many towns remained in use but at the same time the last vestiges of their ancient buildings were disappearing beneath new networks of streets or fields. By early modern times the few upstanding traces of buildings were difficult to understand but occasional discoveries of mosaics, or the spectacular exposure of the baths at Bath, showed that substantial pieces of the ancient towns were still waiting to be found.

The extensive excavations at Silchester in the late nineteenth century recovered much of the town plan and created a stereotyped view of Romano-British towns as open places with well-spaced stone houses and elaborate public buildings. It has only been during the last thirty years that the comprehensive, rather than extensive, work done at the open towns of Verulamium and Wroxeter has given us a much more balanced perception of urban development and decline. In major cities where modern development has proceeded apace unprecedented opportunities have occurred to recover a vast amount of evidence for the Roman towns that lie beneath. London is easily the most outstanding example and the net result is that towards the end of the twentieth century we are now better placed to understand the extraordinary period of urbanization which took place during the Roman occupation. This book draws together as much of this work as possible in accessible form and explores some of the different ways in which we can try to understand how Roman towns developed. Many problems of interpretation remain, particularly when dealing with what happened to the towns during the third and fourth centuries.

I am grateful to Stephen Johnson, Catherine Johns and Sarah Vernon-Hunt for their help and advice with the text, and Philip Clarkstone for preparing the author's photographs.

All drawings and photographs are by the author except figures **19**, **54**, **55** (British Museum), **36**, **75**, **99**, **100**, **101** (English Heritage); **69** (West Yorkshire Archaeology Service); colour plates **1**, **2**, **6** and **15** (English Heritage); **9** (Gloucestershire Museums); **11** (British Museum).

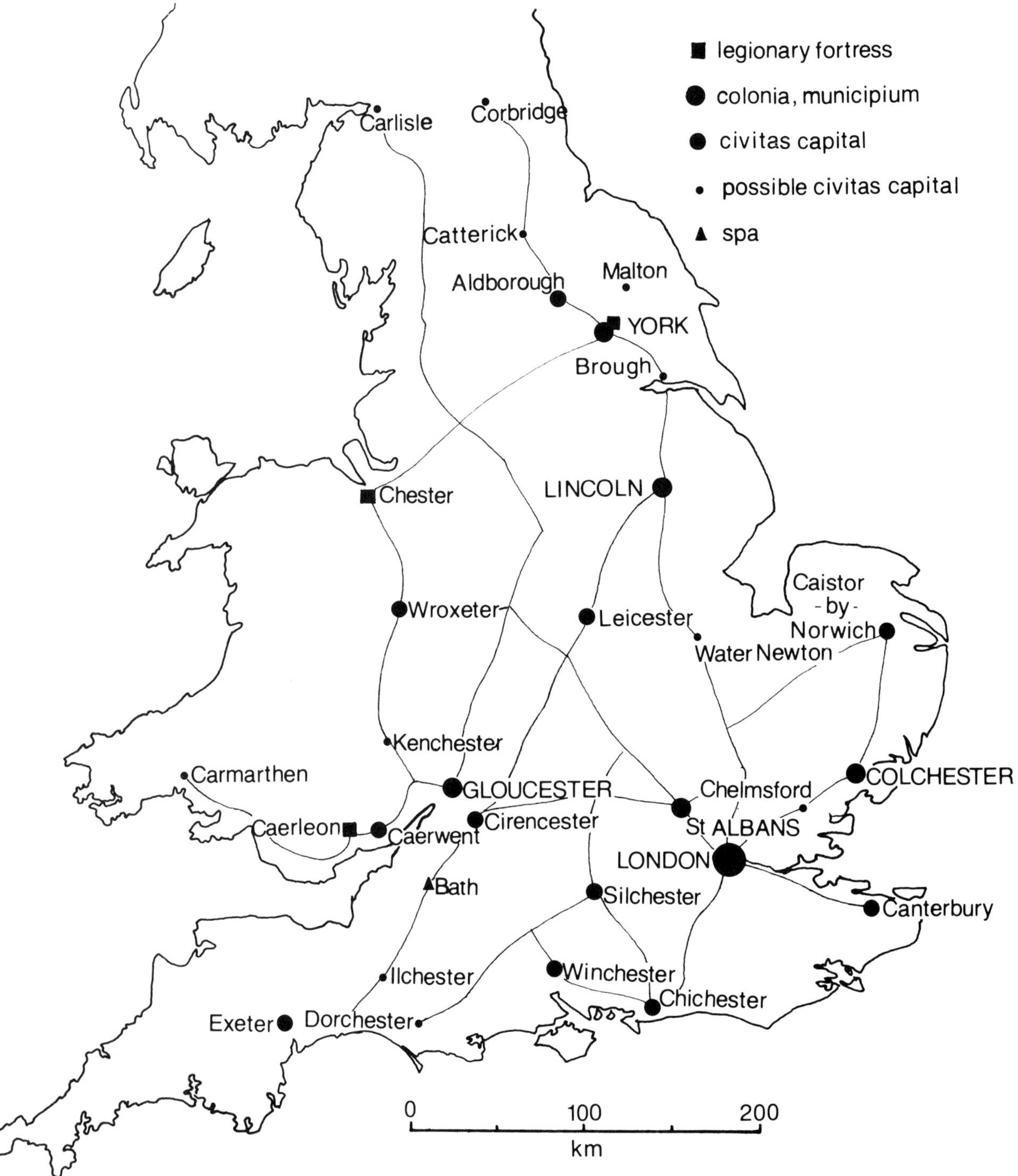
legionary fortress
colonia, municipium
civitas capital
possible civitas capital
spa
Carlisle
Corbridge
Catterick
Aldborough
Malton
YORK
Brough
Chester
LINCOLN
Caistor
-by-
Norwich
Wroxeter
Leicester
Water Newton
Kenchester
Carmarthen
GLOUCESTER
Chelmsford
COLCHESTER
Caerleon
Caerwent
Cirencester
St ALBANS
LONDON
Bath
Silchester
Canterbury
Ilchester
Winchester
Chichester
Exeter
Dorchester
0
100
200
km

1

The foundation of towns

Introduction

For each of us a town may mean one of many things. It may be a place in which to live and work, a place in which to buy and sell, or a centre of government and administration. We take these for granted, even more so in the late twentieth century when most of the modern British population live in a town of some kind. But what makes a town? Is it just a large group of buildings with a high street full of shops, a town hall, a swimming pool, a police station and a ring road? How do we distinguish a town from a village? Are towns just convenient facilities or are they more important than that? If a place is a town now, how long has it been one, what made it one originally and how long will it last?

We could ask many more questions than these, but already it seems that something which appeared to be crystal clear is not quite so well-defined. Archaeologists have found that deciding whether an ancient settlement was a 'town' or not is an excellent way of embarking on an inconclusive debate about the meaning of an apparently simple word.

In the Graeco-Roman world the concept of the town was a more basic part of society; in a way the town was synonymous with the community. Greece was ruled by city-states in which cities ruled their hinterlands. The city and its territory were effectively a single constitutional unit. Exactly the same was true of Rome. Rome had grown to be the dominant city in central Italy. It became immensely powerful because of its disciplined military force but no less because of its intoxicating sense of community, expressed both as *Senatus Populusque Romanus*, literally 'The Senate and People of Rome', and the way in which Rome was referred to as just *Urbs*, 'the City'.

The Roman government did not rule through the army, as is commonly believed; instead power was delegated through the government of the province to regional capitals which were modelled on the city of Rome itself. Each of these towns was responsible for administering the surrounding area on behalf of the state. In return it was granted formal status and financial support to give it the infrastructure, such as public buildings, to help it fulfil its role in the way that Rome herself fulfilled her greater role at the hub of the Empire (**2**). In the Roman world, therefore, the major town had a more sophisticated status and spiritual identity than modern towns. Throughout most of the Empire already existing towns were utilized to serve this purpose by being awarded official status, while others were founded where towns had not previously existed. Towns also grew up as a consequence of a thriving network of trade routes, usually at a place where roads met, or beside a bridge.

Britain presents a rather different picture. The existing communities which were conquered by the Romans did not generally have a tradition of living together in permanent

1 *Map showing the distribution of towns in Roman Britain with the most important ones named. There was a very marked bias to the eastern, central and southern parts of the province, reflecting the settled conditions and superior agricultural land. The 'Fosse Way', running between Lincoln and Exeter, provides a convenient approximate boundary. Note however that several areas in the south and east had few towns, e.g. the extreme south-east and south-west, and northern East Anglia.*

2 *The tetrastyle capitol at Dougga* (Thuggensis) *in Tunisia, north Africa. The pediment contains a relief carving of an eagle, symbol of Roman power. The temple dominated the town centre and is still impressive today.*

concentrated groups (usually referred to as 'nucleated settlements'); in other words towns, or anything resembling them, were not very common. The presence of the Roman army in forts may have encouraged the subsequent emergence of towns but a number of other factors could also lie behind the existence of any one town. Also, for every regional capital there were a number of smaller towns, many of which were no larger than something we would call a village. These small towns are not very well known but unlike the major towns they almost always lack any evidence for having been formally laid out, or for large buildings. This makes them especially difficult to understand.

Society and settlement in pre-Roman Britain

Legends on late-first-century BC and early-first-century AD British coins and their distribution show that the tribes were ruled by regional chieftains or kings who tried to assert their power through the successful pursuit of territorial quarrels (**3**). This evidence is complemented by Caesar's description of what he found in 55 and 54 BC, Strabo's writings, and by the accounts of the invasion campaign in and after AD 43 (Tacitus and Dio Cassius). This sustained confrontation would have provided a dynamic for society but in primitive communities subsistence is the first priority. Only when agricultural production becomes successful enough to produce a sustained surplus (when, for example, a family regularly produces more food than it needs) can the 'luxury' of a chieftain society with an upper tier of non-productive warriors be supported. The medieval kings and their barons are a useful parallel even if their disputes were generally on a larger scale.

In pre-Roman Britain society was primarily agricultural and sufficiently productive (though probably only just) to support the gradual emergence of an unproductive upper tier in society. Although mixed farming was both widespread and organized it absorbed the efforts of most of the community for most of the time, making significant production of manufactured goods like pottery only possible during slack periods in the agricultural cycle. But by the late first century BC Britain had goods to sell and there is an increasing amount of evidence for certain industries becoming sufficiently intensive to imply that specialist activities were involved, good quality pottery and salt production being amongst them. However it was the warrior aristocracy that appears both to have benefited from the trade in the form of imported manufactured goods, and probably controlled any domestic production.

In the year 43 there were no settlements in Britain which could properly be described as towns, even if some had similar characteristics. This is part of what made the Roman invasion such a radical event. It was far more than a military conquest. Much of the network of major towns in existence today was created by the Roman state out of the existing pattern of communities in the interests of effectively governing the new province. For sure there were places where large numbers of people had settled in close proximity. For much of the latter part of the first millennium BC the most conspicuous examples are the hillforts of southern Britain. A number of these, for example Danebury, appear to have grown at the expense of smaller neighbours but it is impossible to

3 *Gold stater of Cunobelinus of the Catuvellauni struck at the tribal capital of the Trinovantes at* Camulodunum *(Colchester). The magical beast and ear of corn symbolized strength and fertility. About* AD *10-40.*

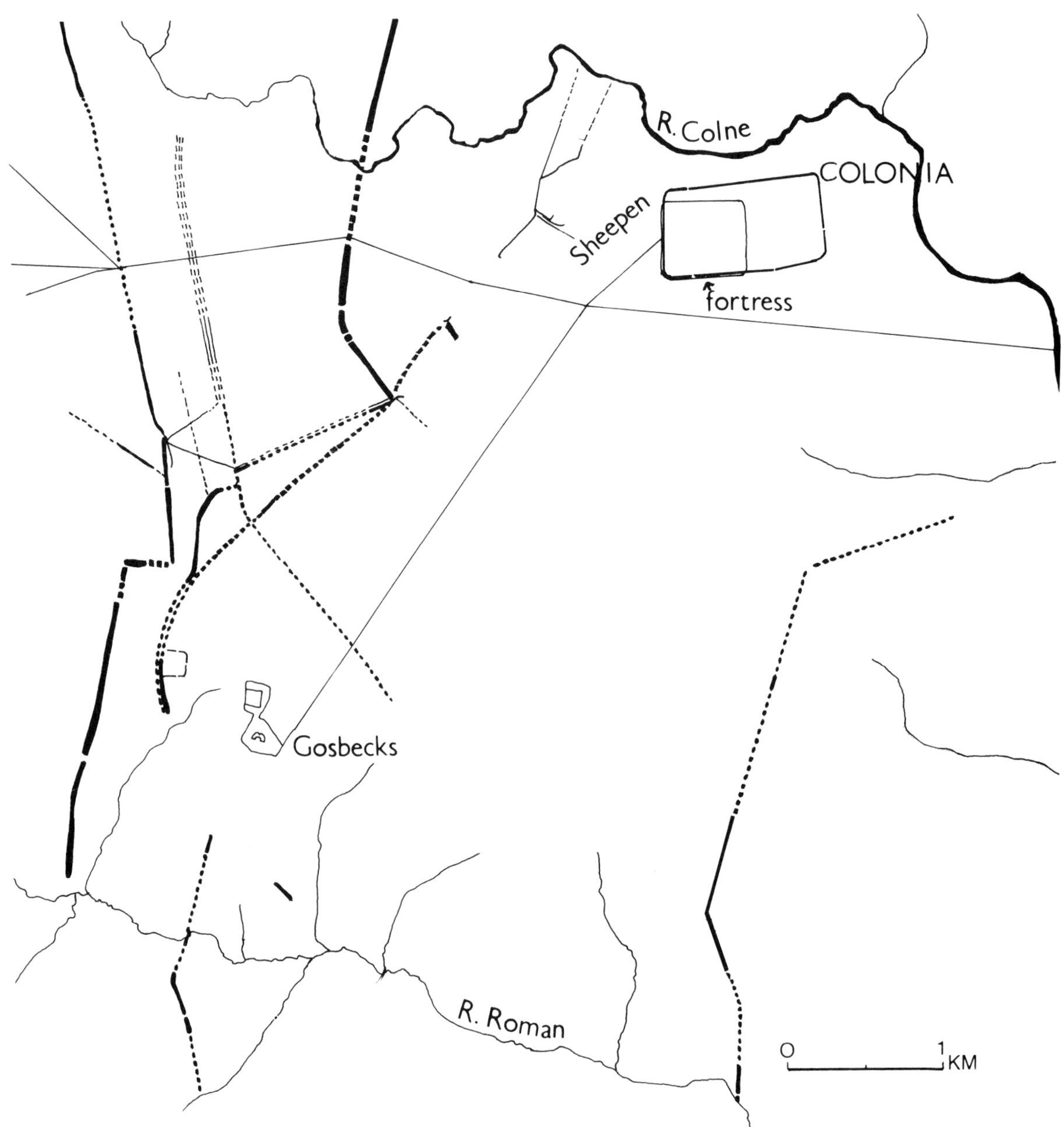

tell if this was a response to inter-tribal tension or social changes. In eastern Britain sites like Mucking seem to have developed into undefended village style communities from about 300 BC onwards.

By about 100 BC many hillforts had become disused and it seems that in south-east Britain in particular they were replaced with what classical authors like Caesar called *oppida*. *Oppida* were much larger and were located in more low-lying areas than hillforts. Their most

4a *The pre-Roman dyke system around Colchester forming the* oppidum *of* Camulodunum. *The lines of ditches seem to have acted as a boundary to the movements from the west enclosing a large area between the two principal rivers. Note the fort, of early date, beside the religious complex at Gosbecks, probably a focal point for the pre-Roman community. (After Hull.)*
b *Plan of the developed* colonia *at Colchester. (After Crummy.)*

obvious characteristic was the provision of substantial defences (**4**). But if the defences of hillforts and the dykes which marked the limits of the more low-lying and more sprawling *oppida* were fairly durable there is little evidence for any further permanence about them – any kind of buildings, for example, were rare (though this may reflect inadequate excavation), and apart from possibly acting as chieftains' strongholds they were not administrative centres. They may have been little more than elaborate, perhaps seasonal, bivouacs, though at Silchester a recent excavation on the site of the later basilica, despite being limited in extent, has shown that as early as the end of the first century BC a street grid of sorts may have been laid out and a number of rectangular buildings erected.

Strabo was emphatic in describing *oppida* as only temporary corrals for people and cattle, equipped with timber defences. This description compares well with Caesar's account of his assault on Cassivellaunus' stronghold which he said was protected by woods and swamps, though he also adds the general comment that the Britons built ramparts around their defensive settlements. This contrasts with towns in the Mediterranean world; at Pompeii the street grid contains traces of the layout of an earlier Greek settlement dating from at least as early as the fifth century BC. Like many other places in the Mediterranean world, Roman Pompeii was simply a development of a pre-existing town.

Amongst the *oppida* which have been discovered in Britain are Camulodunum (Colchester, see **4**), Prae Wood (by Verulamium) and Stanwick (North Yorkshire). Extensive areas were defined by lengths of unconnected ramparts which would have been ineffective against a concerted attack by a large body of troops, though they would have been useful in controlling day-to-day movements of people. They represent societies prepared to engage in substantial communal effort and this in itself implies centralization, or at least coercive leadership. Whether an *oppidum* was the focal point of the community in the sense that this was where the chieftain and his family lived, and from where he controlled his tribe and its territory, is not clear: archaeology does not generally provide evidence for this. It is doubtful whether an *oppidum* actually had much effective control over outlying communities. Caesar implies that

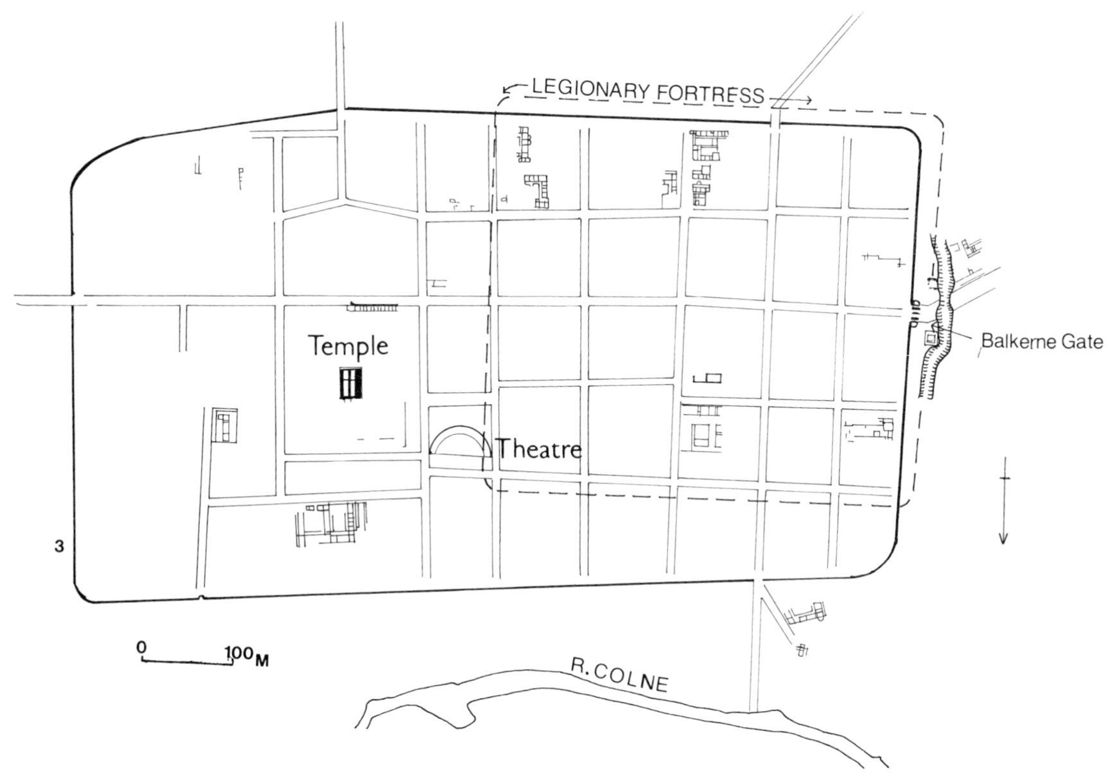

3

the stronghold which he attacked was that of Cassivellaunus. Even so, it is likely that the community rotated about the person of the chief rather than any particular place; his, or her, prestige would have been the foundation of power and influence. This was something that the Roman government exploited in the development of towns.

This situation played a crucial part in native resistance during the early years of the Roman conquest. Caratacus, son of Cunobelinus of the Catuvellauni, carried the war west with himself as leader of the opposition to the governor Ostorius Scapula (47-51). His prestige was considerable although he was betrayed in 51. Similarly, the Boudican Revolt a decade later shows how the personality of Boudica herself was the foundation of the revolt rather than a concerted defence of a particular settlement. The people followed her to the extent that the warriors brought their families too. So although this chieftain society was familiar with the concept of large-scale settlements they were not parallels with towns because they were not permanent, they were not administrative and, perhaps more importantly, they did not act as a symbolic centre of the whole community.

Understanding *oppida* has always been complicated by a lack of large-scale excavation. However, Sheepen, part of the Camulodunum *oppidum*, has been partly excavated. By the early first century AD it acted as a centre of industry and trade. Metalworking was going on as well as the importation of fine pottery from Gaul, and *amphorae* containing wines, oils and other foods. Despite this the impression is more of an *ad hoc* settlement rather than a co-ordinated and well-established one with a centralized administration. The buildings found were mostly wattle and daub circular huts and there was no trace of a layout of streets. Only the imported goods and the possible presence of a mint point to the site's importance.

The invasion of 43 and the founding of towns

The traditional view of Romano-British towns is that many developed as a result of civil settlement around an earlier fort. This is a perfectly plausible argument but while in some cases an earlier fort is a virtual certainty it has often been assumed that forts almost invariably preceded a town. This has even extended to 'inventing' forts where none has yet been found, usually on the basis of finds of pieces of early military equipment. These of course prove nothing, soldiers would have been permanently in transit as individuals and in units throughout Britain.

In reality towns might develop for many different reasons. Forts were undoubtedly one of these (for example the *coloniae*, or smaller places like Wall or Castleford) but others might be the presence of a local native settlement (which may well have been the initial reason for the fort, as at Colchester) or a place of special ritual significance (Bath), the presence of natural resources such as minerals (Charterhouse) or whether the site was incorporated into the communications system (London). Even at Cirencester, which is sometimes taken to be the prime example of a civitas capital which developed from a fort *vicus*, a native settlement lay only 5 km (3 miles) to the north at Bagendon, and it is almost certain that the *vicus* developed at least in part at the expense of the pre-Roman site (**5**). This is perhaps better interpreted as a localized movement of a centre of population than a whole new development. Where forts had been established it may seem strange that the civilians did not follow the army when it moved on, but if we assume that they were mostly local to begin with they were probably disinclined to leave.

The Roman world was held together as much by trade, a natural product of stability, as anything else. The presence of troops introduced people with earnings to spend, though there would have been other groups of people such as government officials and traders. Those who came to supply the military's demands had themselves money to spend, and so it went on. Towns had a crucial role to play in the circulation of goods and money and with the enormous expansion in trade which took place after 43 it is hardly surprising that they should have benefited; in a few cases, London being the best example, a town developed more or less entirely because it lay in a place of outstanding commercial convenience.

It would be foolish also to ignore the real needs which people have to come together to collectively express a sense of belonging to a community, or even to be drawn by the attraction of a community over which to exercise power and enjoy status. Equally, 'going to market' or attending ritual and social events

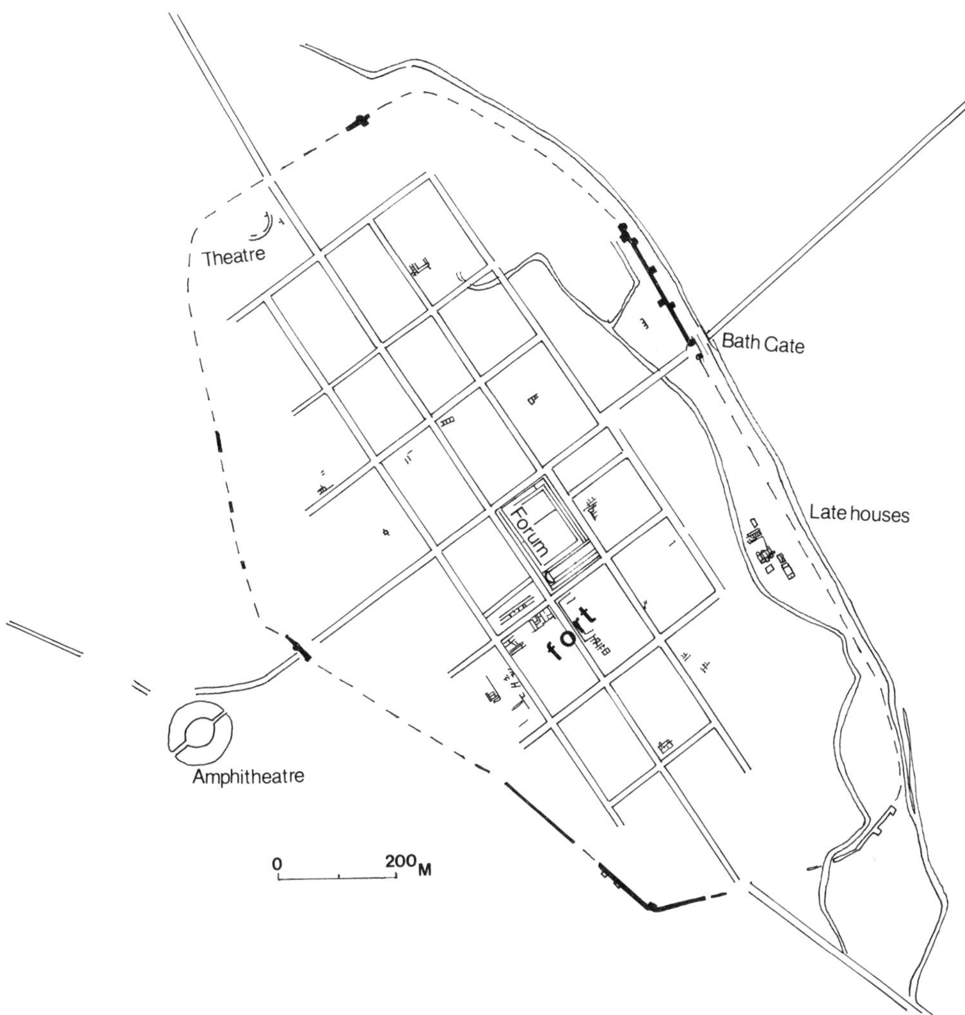

5 *Plan of the town at Cirencester showing the location of the mid-first century fort in the middle of the later settlement. The Bath Gate cemetery is discussed in Chapter 6, and the 'late houses' in Chapters 4 and 7. (Based on a plan by Cirencester Excavation Committee.)*

would have been an event to look forward to for those who lived outside a town. For those who lived within there would have been the appeal of being involved in all the petty pre-occupations of parochial politics and social relations. It is all too easy to forget such aspects of human society and to tend always to want to find obvious rational economic and physical reasons for places being where they were.

These are just general points and of course there are exceptions and many variations to these themes. Roman towns were not founded as fully developed institutions. Their development (or even lack of) was gradual, intermittent, individual and in some cases spontaneous. It would be wrong to imagine armies of surveyors, architects and builders moving into the allocated area and swiftly designing and erecting an instant Roman town complete with forum, basilica and baths while romanized natives loitered in colonnaded avenues discussing Virgil. It was often several generations later before such a town had all the necessary attributes of a miniature Rome, if even then. The main period of public building in Roman Britain lasted sporadically from the 60s and 70s right through to the mid-second century or even later. Throughout the province there were numerous small towns that have attracted limited archaeological attention and about which we know really very little. For the most part their origins and the roles they played in Romano-British society remain a mystery.

Towns in the Roman world

Roman towns fell into several different categories, some of which held a specific legal status and others of which had no significance beyond the fact that they existed. When Rome conquered territory in the eastern Mediterranean area she took control of peoples already accustomed to living in towns. In Asia Minor, for example, the great cities of Ephesus and Miletus had existed for centuries as Greek settlements. In the north-western part of Europe this was not the case, at least to anything like the same extent, and consequently there was no existing civilian government infrastructure which could be adapted to Roman rule. It was also the case that the army was perpetually confronted with the problem of having large numbers of soldiers who had come to the end of their 25 years' service.

The two problems were dealt with by creating colonies of retired soldiers, called *coloniae*. These colonies were founded in conquered territory by establishing and laying out a town together with a certain amount of land, *territorium*, around it. Britain had at least four: Colchester (see **4**), Gloucester, Lincoln (see **8**), and York. Each retired soldier was allocated a piece of land within and outside the town. He could therefore enjoy the benefits of Roman urban life and support himself and his family. This was as convenient for the government as it was for the ex-soldier. Not only was a trained reserve available but it also acted as an example of romanization to the conquered rabble. Not all colonies were settlements of ex-soldiers (who were also Roman citizens); sometimes towns and their inhabitants were elevated to the status as an honour, though instead of becoming full Roman citizens it was possible to grant them only the slightly lesser rank of Latin rights.

Much more common than the colonies were the regional capitals, or civitas capitals, *civitates*. Unlike the colonies, which were self-contained legal entities created by the Roman state, the civitas capitals were a formalized development of the existing tribal groupings. These special towns were not legally distinct from the tribal region in which they lay. In other words the Roman government took an existing tribal area, recognized it and imposed local government from a regional centre. In practice this was often around a fort which had been given up (but not always: no fort has been located at Silchester which became the regional capital for the Atrebates). Often the chosen settlement lay on or close to the principal former settlement of the tribe (for example Silchester and Canterbury).

Occasionally it was necessary to manufacture a tribal area where either a small dispersed population or a confusion over tribal boundaries made it impossible easily to exploit an existing arrangement. Winchester is an excellent example – its official name of *Venta Belgarum* merely employs the generic term for the people of south-eastern Britain, rather than an individual tribe. The fact that this was done emphasizes how important it was for Rome to be able to rule through self-governing local communities. Sometimes settlements within a tribal canton, apart from the civitas capital, were granted the formal status of *vicus* which allowed them to be self-governing units within the tribal area, though not separate from it.

The civitas capital was laid out on the model of a Roman town, generally with state assistance, but instead of being populated by Roman citizens it was left to the local inhabitants to run. This meant that pre-existing hierarchies within the social group were allowed to continue in a new, more easily manipulated, structure. Native laws remained effective and the inhabitants were not granted the status of Roman citizens or Latin rights other than in exceptional circumstances. The Roman government also had a vested interest in exploiting existing native social structures and customs in the interests of stable administration. If the existing élite could be allowed to continue to dominate the area in which they lived they would regard a burgeoning town as an advantage, and therefore tolerate their own subjugation. In a town they could retain status and have the opportunity to continue to exploit the local population. While there may have been opportunities for 'ordinary' people to live and work in towns we can be sure that the existing wealthy and powerful tribal aristocracy remained just that.

Occasionally a civitas capital was elevated to the rank of *municipium*. This is a word for which we have no convenient equivalent but we might almost consider these towns as honorary colonies. Like a colony a *municipium* would generally have its own allocated territory around it and its population were either made Roman citizens or enjoyed the slightly inferior legal status of Latin citizens. It is not entirely clear what a town had to do to achieve this status. Verulamium (see **7**) is the only town in Britain referred to in ancient sources specifically as a *municipium* (by Tacitus) but the reason is not mentioned and no inscription has been found which might be more helpful. It may simply have been a reward for exceptionally successful urban development or playing a significant role in a provincial crisis, perhaps the Boudican Revolt.

The various towns discussed above were all official in the sense that they held formal status and were founded by the state and recognized as being run by its delegates. They were all responsible for local government and were equipped with the facilities to do so. They were each governed by a town council, the *ordo*, which was theoretically made up of about 100 local worthies, each of whom had sufficient funds to satisfy the property qualification. The system therefore perpetuated the existing hierarchy and guaranteed that it would effectively be hereditary.

Although thousands of individuals would have sat on a town council during the history of Roman Britain almost none are known by name. This shows just how difficult it is for us to make direct connections between power, wealth and property in the province. Flavius Martius, buried at Old Penrith, was a councillor of quaestorian rank of the Carvetii (a tribe in the north-western part of the province), and had a romanized name which tells us nothing about his origins. Even the connection with Mars might mean a military or Celtic origin (many obscure local deities in the north were associated with Mars).

The members of this council then competed for the various magistracies which would further enhance their prestige and influence within the local community. The magistracies were also modelled on those at Rome. The main pair, equivalent to consuls, were known as the *duoviri iuridicundo* and were responsible for justice, supervision of the *ordo* and religious festivals. They were assisted by *aediles* who dealt with public services like the water supply. The colonies also had *quaestores* to administer public finance. Lesser towns with organized government had similar offices but they only had power within the town, rather than the civitas community, for example Marcus Ulpius Ianuarius, *aedile* at Brough-on-Humber in or around 140–4.

We can be sure that a small number of local families would have dominated the holding of office for generations, although we have no specific evidence for this in Britain. At Herculaneum in Italy the basilica, buried by mud and lava during the eruption of Vesuvius in 79, was found to contain statues honouring the whole family of one Marcus Nonius Balbus who had paid for the building to be rebuilt at an earlier date. He was of senatorial rank which meant that he was extremely wealthy and was a member of the Roman Senate. He had served as one of the two annually elected consuls in Rome. It is clear that this man used his prestige to hold great sway over local politics. By paying for the basilica's repairs he was investing in his family's future.

It is all very well listing off the various legal features of town status in the Roman world but it gives us little idea of what towns were actually like, and the roles which they played in the lives of their inhabitants and those who lived round about. Pompeii, also covered by debris from the eruption of Vesuvius, is of exceptional importance not just because so much is preserved but because the town was caught at a moment in time. It is easy to forget that archaeology is an imprecise discipline and it is almost impossible to say what the actual state of any building, and even less a town, was at any given moment. Pompeii, however, allows us to glimpse what went to make up a Roman town on one particular day. Of course it cannot be exactly representative because it lay in a rich part of Italy, close to the sea and was a relatively short distance from Rome. But we have nothing else like it. The better-preserved remains of nearby Herculaneum are confined to a small, predominantly residential, part of the town (**6**). At Pompeii it is still possible to make one's way from the forum to the amphitheatre past dozens of shop fronts, or alternatively explore the back streets of the older part of the town with its brothel and then enter the large houses of the well-to-do.

Everywhere in Pompeii are traces of the bustle of town life and the various comings and goings of people and their goods. At many

6 *A street in Herculaneum buried in* AD *79. Roman Britain's town streets in the first and second centuries would have looked similar – note the upper storey built with a timber frame and supported on columns.*

street corners the paving stones still bear the deep ruts worn by countless wagon wheels, sometimes up to 25 cm (10 in) deep. We know from Tacitus that in AD 59 the amphitheatre was the scene of a violent confrontation between locals and visitors from nearby Nuceria. The incident arose from an exchange of insults during a gladiatorial bout which degenerated into the drawing of swords. A number of people were killed and Pompeii was punished by being forbidden such displays for ten years.

This gladiatorial display was just the sort of event which would have been promoted by those seeking public office and one of the most interesting features of Pompeii is the lively range of election slogans daubed on walls. Most of them probably relate to the election which would have taken place in March 79 for the magistracies commencing on 1 July. In one instance the goldsmiths collectively recommend one Gaius Cuspius Pansa as *aedile*, though a more practical anonymous pundit prefers Gaius Julius Polybius because he supplies good bread. These are interspersed with advertisements for gladiatorial bouts and references to sexual prowess (or lack of). One accuses Colepius, keeper of the forum baths, of being excessively familiar with women.

Romano-British town life must have been just as frustrating and as vivid, but unfortunately pages of excavation reports listing broken pottery can sometimes obscure the reality of a human experience. We should always remember that concentrations of human beings invariably produce strains which can sometimes lead to disproportionate consequences, or at least disproportionate emotions. A shortage of bread at Aspendus in southern Turkey caused by stockpiling speculators led to a riot in which a crowd tried to burn a magistrate. A more innocuous frustration gripped Seneca in Rome and caused him to write his famous tirade against the noise he suffered by living over a public baths, particularly from the shouting of customers having hairs plucked.

The mechanics of laying out a town

In theory the first stage in founding a town was to lay out roads to create a series of rectangular or square areas known as *insulae*, or literally 'islands'. The two main roads which crossed in the centre of the town were known as the *Cardo Maximus* and the *Decumanus Maximus*. While the meaning of the latter is a little obscure the former means 'hinge' or 'axis'. This grid formed the skeleton of the new town though there were enormous local variations, taking account of contours, rivers and existing routes. Verulamium is a prime example; here the grid was laid out parallel to the banks of the river Ver. The road from London entered from the south at an unsympathetic angle but was accommodated by creating a number of triangular *insulae* (**7**). At Lincoln the town was divided into an upper and lower town. The lower town was laid out on the steep hillside below the upper town and had special staggered streets to allow wheeled traffic to tackle the slope (**8**). In small towns like Water Newton (see **71**) or Kenchester such planning never took place to any significant extent and instead the main road which runs through both merely formed a spine for the straggling streets leading off it.

Ideally a town was laid out with fortifications in mind and four gates would have been built, one at each end of the main streets. In Britain town walls were built later in the history of most towns and only in the colonies which reused the site of a legionary fortress were defences a part of the town from the beginning. An exception was Colchester where the legionary defences were demolished prior to laying out the new colony. Part of the consequence of this was that towns developed in a slightly random fashion with the result that the areas eventually walled (not necessarily the entire settled area) were very irregularly shaped. Surveying was more than just a technical exercise; it had great symbolic significance and there would have been foundation sacrifices accompanied possibly by the marking out of the boundary with a plough-team made up of a cow and a bull to symbolize fertility. Such a gesture, though official Roman state practice, would have probably been appreciated by the Celtic Britons, many of whose gods were identified with both particular places and fertility.

Public buildings

The visual impact of Roman public buildings was considerable anywhere and must have been especially so in an island where nothing like them had ever existed before. None survive intact so it is difficult to appreciate the powerful impression they would have created. At Sbeitla in Tunisia the *capitolium* survives in a remarkable state of preservation and although this was a remote provincial town the buildings show that one could be far from Rome and yet still sense her presence (**9**). At Pompeii a visitor is drawn to the forum by the way in which the roads appear to lead there. Despite individual variations all the public buildings of Roman towns were similar, something which becomes evident to a modern visitor fortunate enough to be able to explore several different examples. This was of great importance in the Roman Empire because it promoted the sense of institutional unity, a sense of belonging to a world which was familiar wherever one went. In a world where natural forces were less easily controlled the underlying feeling of stability which this created should not be underestimated. This was paralleled by the use of common coinage, the same laws and sworn allegiance to the emperor.

Areas were set aside for the principal public buildings during surveying. The grid itself had been derived from a fixed point in the centre of the future town with a device called a *groma*. This piece of equipment, a kind of primitive theodolite, allowed the sighting of straight lines over distances. The angles at which the lines intersected could be varied but were usually right angles. The fixed point from which the surveying was done normally marked the site of the future forum and basilica. That the site of this building was earmarked early on has been shown at Silchester where timber structures of early date resembling the later

7 *Plan of Verulamium based on excavations and aerial photography. The street grid is fairly regular apart from the entry of Watling Street from the south-east. The basilica (B) and forum (F) dominate the town centre with the theatre (Th) and its attendant temple (T;* **81***) a little to the north. Close by is* Insula *XIV (see* **13***) while in the southern part of the town the Triangular Temple (T;* **82***) lies at the point where Watling Street met the town grid. Within the third-century town walls is the earlier boundary known as the '1955 Ditch'; two arches (A) marked the former city limits (see* **26***). (After Niblett.)*

8 *Lincoln town-plan. There were two quite distinct parts of the settlement with the main centre at the top of the hill over-lying the former legionary fortress. The basilica (B) and forum (F) lie over the fortress headquarters building. W marks the site of the water cistern which supplied public baths. There were a number of burial areas around the settlement (C). Note the diagonal streets to aid wheeled traffic trying to negotiate the steep gradient, the contours (in metres) show the steep slope which the lower town was built on. (After Wacher and with additional information.)*

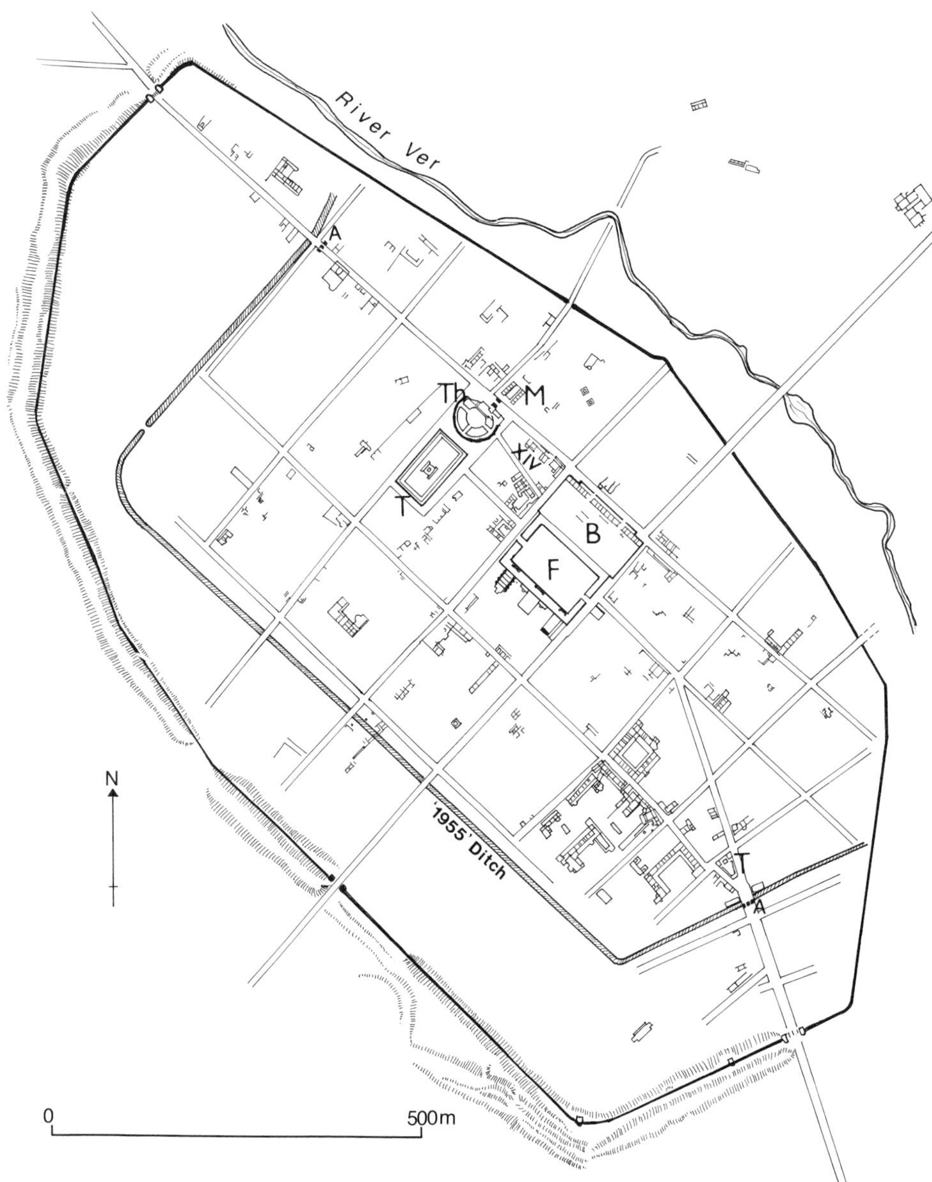

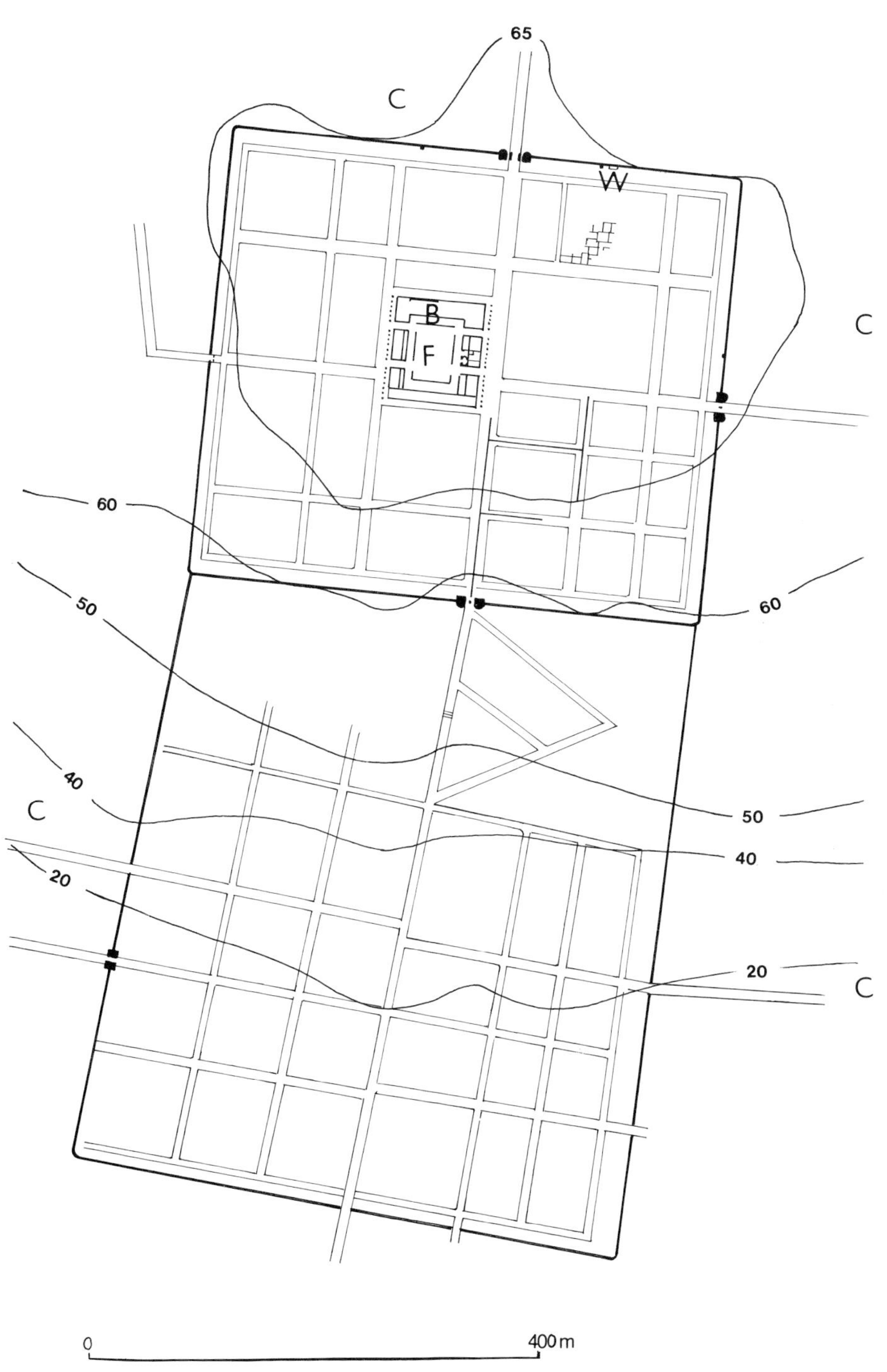
65
C
W
B
F
C
60
60
50
C
40
50
40
20
20
C
0
400 m

9 *The capitol at Sbeitla (*Sufetula*) in Tunisia, north Africa. There were three temples, probably dedicated to Jupiter, Juno and Minerva, overlooking the forum (only two are shown). The forum at Verulamium would have been similar (***colour plate 4***).*

stone basilica have been found underneath (see **16**). It was a good choice – although the site of the town is generally flat the forum and the basilica were placed at the highest point, particularly evident when viewing the town from the lower-lying south-east corner. Verulamium's theatre was not built until the middle of the second century but the plot in which it lies appears to have been vacant until that date, despite being a 'prime site' close to the middle of the town. As far as the rest of a town is concerned we know nothing about how land was allocated for shops, houses or temples in Britain. Much of it may have remained in the ownership of the town and was rented out.

Romano-British towns and the Roman world

As an isolated component of the Empire, Britain was regarded with a mixture of fascination and apparent indifference. Very few individuals of Romano-British origin, if any, made any great impact on the history of the Empire and often references to the province are little more than casual asides. Not surprisingly the towns of Roman Britain also feature little in these references though they were occasionally mentioned on inscriptions listing an individual's career which had included a spell in Britain.

In the mid-second century a geographer called Claudius Ptolemaeus, now known as Ptolemy, drew up a compendium of places in the known world and gave details of location by using a crude form of latitude and longitude. This provides useful information about which towns were the most important or whether they had some special reputation – Bath, for example, is named as *Aquae Calidae* which means 'Hot Waters'. However, he rarely gives details of a town's status and even omitted a few, like Gloucester. Many of the otherwise unknown names he listed are probably forts and cannot now be identified. Ptolemy probably drew up his information from a number of sources including old maps and verbal accounts from travellers – both prone to inaccuracy.

Ptolemy was trying to create an equivalent of a world atlas. Travellers would have found it of little value; instead they made use of route maps which listed the places to be found along a given road, a little like a modern schematic map of a motorway and its junctions. Armed with such a map a traveller knew where the next town was and how long it might take him to get there because details of distance were included. The best known is 'The Antonine Itinerary' which lists more than 200 roads and was based on a route map which may have been drawn up for the Emperor Caracalla in about 214. Fifteen Romano-British roads are mentioned and eight start from London. The details of distance, even though sometimes inaccurate, and intended ultimate destination have made it possible to identify many towns on the ground including a number of small ones. In some cases the civitas capitals are given their full titles, for example *Venta Silurum* (Caerwent) on Route 14, or *Venta Icenorum* (Caistor-by-Norwich) on Route 9, providing useful confirmation of a town's status and sometimes the only evidence for its existence. Other route maps are known, such as the *Tabula Peutingeriana* and the Ravenna Cosmography, but are either too incomplete or corrupt to provide anything more than supplementary material.

Romano-British place names were almost invariably pre-Roman in origin. We know from Celtic coinage that *Camulodunum*, *Verulamium* and *Calleva* were already the names for Colchester, St Albans and Silchester (in fact the Roman site at St Albans is still known as Verulamium today and it will be referred to as such throughout, as the site is actually quite distinct from the later settlement). Where names were purely Latin they were usually new sites, such as forts, with names that were nothing more than descriptive such as *Trimontium* 'Three peaks' for Newstead in Scotland. Even the Celtic word *Venta*, used for a number of towns, probably meant nothing more than 'Market'. This reflects social continuity from Celtic to Roman Britain, and also the island's isolation from mainstream classical society.

2

Conquest and colonization

Introduction

The development of towns was one of the first effects of the Roman invasion in 43 but the reaction of some of the indigenous population to military defeat and urban administration had been grossly underestimated. As a result the province was very nearly lost during the Boudican Revolt of 60. Our understanding of this early period is dominated by what we know about military activities. Dio Cassius, Tacitus and Suetonius provide a limited amount of material which describes the advance of the army both westwards and northwards across Britain.

The details are recounted in a number of modern works and need not detain us here. But, in brief, the invading force under Aulus Plautius consisted of approximately 20,000 legionaries of the II *Augusta*, the IX *Hispana*, the XIV *Gemina* and XX *Valeria* and a roughly equivalent number of auxiliaries. They landed somewhere in east Kent and made their way westwards crossing the Medway and eventually reaching the Thames somewhere in the vicinity of modern central London. Near here they split up. The II made its way towards the south-west, the XIV went across the Midlands towards central and north Wales, and the IX advanced north.

The XX, however, fell back on Colchester, or *Camulodunum*, one of the strongholds of the Catuvellauni which at the time was the dominant tribe in south-eastern Britain (**10**). Since the beginning of the first century, mainly during the reign of Cunobelinus (about AD 10-40), it had been expanding its power from a tribal area centred on Verulamium first at the expense of the Trinovantes to the east at Colchester and later, during the reign of Cunobelinus' sons

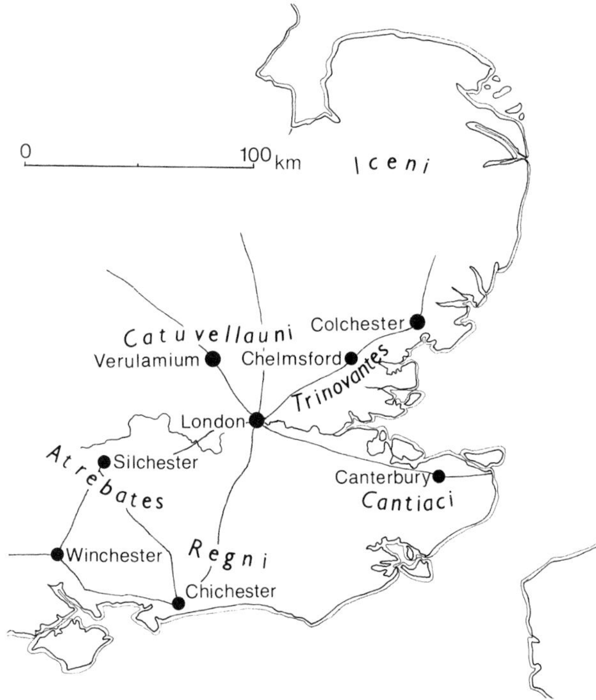

10 *Map of south-east Britain in the mid-first century showing towns which have produced evidence for some sort of urban-style occupation before AD 60, and the approximate distribution of tribal groups.*

Caratacus and Togodumnus, the Atrebates to the south-west at Silchester (*Calleva*). An Atrebatic king, Verica, sought assistance from Claudius and provided him with a convenient excuse to invade Britain. Therefore the invasion strategy seems to have been initially focused on defeating the Catuvellauni.

By 47 the XX legion had been despatched to fight in Wales. In its place a colony of veteran legionaries was established on the site of *Camulodunum*. Tacitus' description of this and the impact of the Boudican Revolt both here and at London and Verulamium gives us a vital glimpse of the Roman style of town life which had emerged in the few short years since the conquest. Archaeology has been able to supply us with more detail of how these towns grew up before they were destroyed.

The early province of Roman Britain was relatively small. Although the army advanced swiftly into Wales and south-western England only the south-east experienced civilian development before 60. Even this was very limited. Colchester was the first town but the Thames crossing was a focal point of communications, and the earlier stronghold of the Catuvellauni at Verulamium seems to have been an attractive site for early development. Further west the Atrebatic tribal area was merged with others to the south to create a client kingdom. It was ruled by a native called Cogidubnus with nominal independence. He may have been related to Verica. The arrangement was conditional upon Cogidubnus' unconditional loyalty. The major settlements within this area, Silchester, Winchester and Chichester, subsequently emerged as separate civitas capitals once the client kingdom was dissolved, probably towards the end of the first century after Cogidubnus' death (see **10**). They too show evidence for early urban development but as they were not destroyed during the Boudican Revolt this gives archaeology less opportunity to easily distinguish features which can be confidently dated to before 60.

Colchester before 60

The removal of the XX legion from Colchester meant that its earth and timber fortress was left vacant. Recent excavations have thrown light on the extent to which the new colonists utilized the redundant buildings. Instead of the fortress being completely demolished and a neat new Roman town built in its place, the transition was a much more long-term project. Even so there was extensive early investment in public buildings. The whole area of the fortress was surrounded by parts of the former Catuvellaunian stronghold *Camulodunum*, which before about AD 5-10 had been the Trinovantian tribal centre. Coins were issued in the name of Cunobelinus and bearing the mintmark CAMV (see **3**). At Sheepen, 0·8 km ($\frac{1}{2}$ mile) to the west, lay an important industrial and trading centre, while Gosbecks, 5 km (3 miles) to the south-west, seems to have been a farming and possible religious zone. An extensive series of dykes defined the whole area which was also enclosed by two rivers, the Colne and the Roman, which run parallel from west to east (see **4**). The fortress, which has only been discovered recently, was built on unoccupied high ground in the northern part of the area.

The new colony needed more land than the fortress supplied so the military defences were demolished in order to allow its annexe to be incorporated. A fort annexe was a kind of subsidiary defended area attached to a fort or fortress, used for storage and perhaps corralling animals. Obliterating the defences was a mistake because it made the town vulnerable to attack: colonies established later in the first century in the former legionary fortresses of Gloucester and Lincoln seem to have retained their defences. The new town was therefore easily attacked by Boudica's supporters in 60. Curiously, the street grid was laid out on a different alignment to that of the fortress despite the fact that a number of the old barrack blocks were adapted into living quarters. In most cases the centurion's house at the end of each block was retained as a house, but the soldiers' accommodation was sometimes demolished to make way for gardens or cultivation. This seems strange considering that colonists were generally awarded additional plots of land outside the town expressly for such a purpose. However, there are unlikely to have been many veterans at this stage so the population was probably much smaller than the 5000 or so of the departed legion.

The description of the sack of Colchester in 60 gives us an idea of what work had been done in only 13 years. Tacitus says that the town had a 'senate house', a 'theatre' and a 'temple'. Obviously the destruction of the town means that we have no idea of the extent to which these buildings had been completed but it is clear that Colchester was already emerging as a 'typical Roman town' in a province which had seen nothing like it less than a generation before. This reflects the colony's purpose as an example of civil and civic government based on law. These public buildings were sited in the former annexe though strangely the theatre, if

11 *Reconstruction drawing of the façade of the temple of Claudius at Colchester. This imposing monumental building acted as a provocative symbol of Roman domination to the dispossessed Trinovantians and it was destroyed during the Boudican Revolt. Although it may have been only partly completed by 60 it would almost certainly have been comprehensively rebuilt.*

the known remains of the later theatre lie over the theatre of 60, was built directly over the filled-in ditches of the fortress. Much the most imposing would have been the classical temple dedicated to Claudius (**11**) which, along with its precinct, was large and secure enough to have served as the last stand during the sack. In effect this created a kind of public building zone, isolated from the rest of the town rather than being in its centre. Perhaps it was felt that placing imposing new buildings in amongst the old barracks would have diminished their impact.

The new town was more than just a showcase of Roman public life. Its Roman inhabitants would have become swiftly discontented in their remote provincial exile if they had been prevented from living in the style to which they were accustomed. There would have been an influx of merchants and craftsmen eager to supply goods and services, and archaeology has provided much evidence for their presence, often in burnt layers which may be associated with the Boudican Revolt. Not only was there the well-known 'samian shop' which contained the burnt and fused remains of hundreds of fine red-slip wheel-thrown bowls, dishes and cups from southern Gaul, but also remains of a clay oil-lamp factory. Large quantities of perishables, such as wine and foodstuffs, would have been imported, as well as grown and traded locally.

Colchester at this time has been described as a 'boom town' and also as a 'converted army camp'. Both are true but the town was designed to be more than either. By being sited so close to the principal Iron Age settlement of pre-Roman Britain it may have been planned as the provincial capital with its official title of *Colonia Claudia Victriciensis*, following Claudius' triumphal entry to the town in 43 (**12**). However, Tacitus' description of the Boudican Revolt clearly implies that the procurator of the province Catus Decianus (the financial administrator, acting as deputy to Suetonius Paulinus) was based elsewhere. Unfortunately he doesn't say where (it may have been a fort rather than a town) but whatever the situation, it may have been decided that the town was too closely associated with the unacceptable sides of Roman rule to function as an effective capital after 60. The temple was regarded as the prime symbol of Roman power and Colchester's

12 *Brass* sestertius *of Claudius (41-54) struck in Rome. Actual diameter 36 mm (1½ in).*

colonists had been unduly harsh to the Trinovantians who lived around the town by summarily seizing their property. This was compounded by obliging some Trinovantians to serve as priests in the temple and enforce the handing over of even more goods as 'offerings'. This was correctly interpreted by the Trinovantians as a racket which left them nothing to lose by participating in an armed rebellion.

Verulamium before 60

Tacitus naturally concentrated on the dramatic and symbolic details of Colchester's destruction in the Boudican Revolt. We therefore know less about the other two principal towns involved: Verulamium and London. He said that the *municipium* of Verulamium suffered the same disaster as London and Colchester. What this also appears to tell us is that Verulamium had achieved the status of *municipium* by the year 60. As we saw in Chapter 1 this was normally only conferred on an already existing civitas capital. It seems unlikely that such an elevation could have taken place so swiftly. Tacitus may have been unintentionally using the town's title at the time when he was writing (around the beginning of the second century). But in the absence of a confirmatory inscription we have to take his reference on trust and assume that this was a possibility.

Unfortunately this brief reference is all we have. But if the town was important enough to attract the attention of the rebels, and also the provincial governor Suetonius Paulinus as he withdrew, it must have become a place of some significance. The area was already a centre for the Catuvellauni who issued coins in the name of the king, Tasciovanus, in about 20-15 BC. The coins were struck with the name of the settlement in various forms, for example VER or VERLAMIO. The exact location of the settlement is uncertain – it may have been on the higher ground to the west of the east-facing slope on which the Roman town was built, overlooking the river Ver. Subsequently Tasciovanus' son Cunobelinus extended the tribe's power eastwards to *Camulodunum*.

The situation became more confused during the reign of the Emperor Caligula (37-41) when Cunobelinus' son, Adminius, was banished. He surrendered himself to Caligula, an act which was conveniently interpreted for political purposes by the emperor as a gift of Britain to himself and therefore an invitation to invade.

Caligula's failure to fulfil this intention may be linked to the subsequent early development of the settlement as a Roman town as a way of making up and, more importantly, because Adminius would probably have been perceived as a useful ally amongst the British nobility. This is pure speculation and any connection is rather tenuous but there must have been a reason for the town's favoured status – it is after all the only Romano-British town we know was a *municipium* at some point in its history, and one of the earliest to have been equipped with masonry public administrative buildings.

Before 60 Verulamium had already been laid out with a modestly-sized street grid which ran parallel to the west bank of the river Ver (see **7**). It may also have been equipped with a defensive rampart and ditch, enclosing 47·6 ha (119 acres), about this time. This was exceptional for the period and it seems probable that the town had already been instituted as the *civitas Catuvellanorum*, though no inscription survives from the site which states this as a fact for any date (the well-known Agricolan inscription from the forum is incomplete in this respect).

It has been suggested that the town developed from a *vicus* that had grown up around an early fort on the site. The evidence for a fort is confined to traces of a rampart of only possible military origin and pieces of military equipment. Some of the latter were found in levels of later date, possibly having been disturbed in different building phases. The site is not a particularly suitable one for a fort because much of it is low-lying. The higher ground to the west or east would have made a better choice. We might then question whether there was ever really a fort here at all especially as no traces of barracks have been located. If there was a fort it was probably only occupied briefly and was therefore of dubious relevance to the subsequent development of the town. The fact that it lay on a major route and was already a prominent native centre was undoubtedly of greater importance and it is likely that the town benefited from the support of the local tribal nobility.

The main source of evidence for the early development of the town is the row of buildings in *Insula* XIV which fronted the main through-route from London (Watling Street). This elementary timber-framed construction, which resembles a barrack block, might have been built by soldiers using existing military timber components for the benefit of settlers. But almost all residential or small-scale industrial and retail units in the Roman world consist of variations of this style, at least as they appear in plan, so it is just as likely that it was a private venture (**13**).

More important than the origin of the building is that it existed at all. It appears to have contained a number of separate establishments whose occupants were engaged in various manufacturing concerns. Most of these involved metalworking including bronze, iron and gold. There may also have been an eating house or small inn. This is significant because it shows that at an exceptionally early date there was already business to be had in the manufacture and repair of goods which were not functional, for example bronze statuettes and gold items. That the buildings fronted Watling Street suggests that some of this trade was passing trade; after all there would have been a considerable amount of traffic connected with the advancing army. Clearly the traders, whoever they were, were making a living and we can assume that they represented not just a source of supply but also demand. There were similarities with the pre-Roman industrial and trading settlement at Sheepen (*Camulodunum*) but the *Insula* XIV shops differed in being buildings of a Roman type, and being sited beside a major road.

So at Verulamium we can tentatively identify the early stages of an urban economy based on the concentration in a small area of a group of people who were not primarily engaged in providing food for themselves, but had the income to allow them to buy it from elsewhere. This is the basis of all towns and depends on an agricultural economy with surplus. So long as this group continues to make a living from its trades then the town has life. There is nothing particularly profound about this but it is important to recognize that the group of shops in early Verulamium existed for some of the same reasons which lie behind our own urban society. It would be interesting to know whether the individuals concerned were operating independently or whether they were in some way tied to a master, Roman or native, who had financed their premises and exacted a tithe from their income. Although we do not have this kind of information Verulamium has

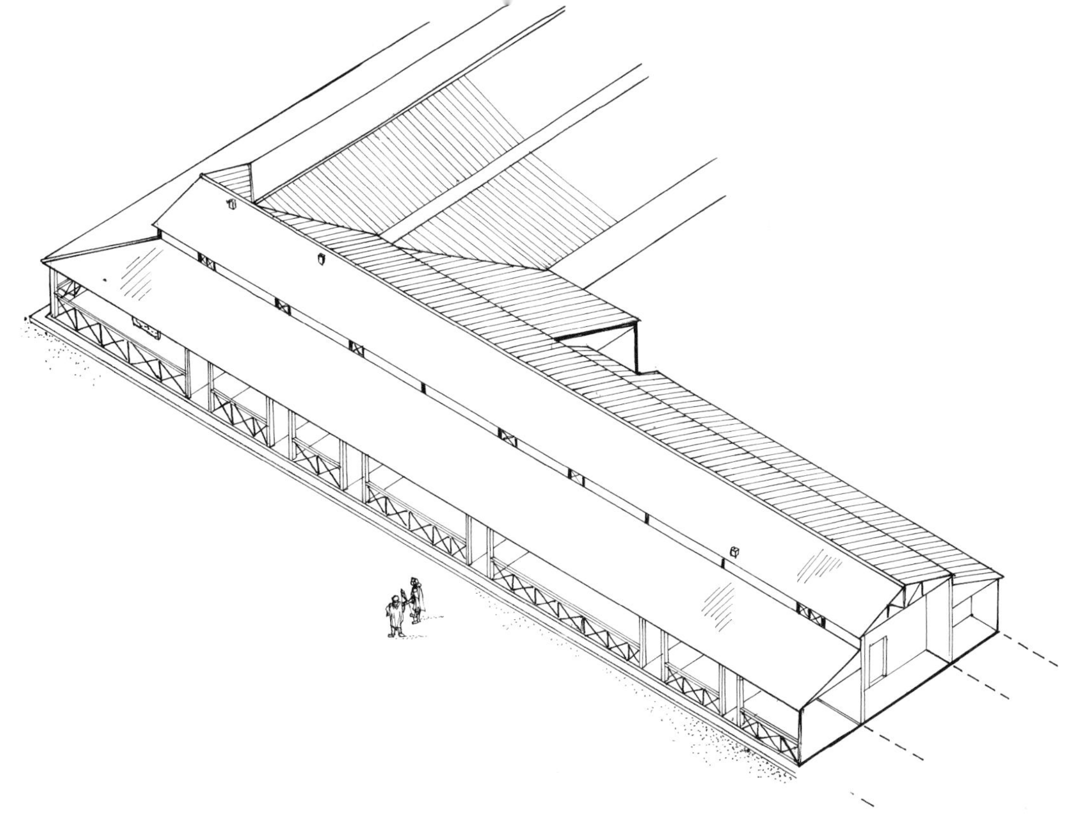

13 *Isometric reconstruction of the timber shops at Verulamium in* Insula *XIV as they may have appeared around the year* AD *60 before being burnt down, probably in the Boudican Revolt. The site remained in almost continuous occupation throughout the Roman period but went through many stages of reconstruction. It was typical of urban industrial and retail buildings in Roman Britain during the first and second centuries.*

provided an unparalleled body of archaeological evidence for pre-Boudican urban development, though the special circumstances of its location and historical background mean that it had advantages not always enjoyed in other places.

London before 60

While Colchester was certainly a town with official status, and Verulamium probably so, London was a town with no formal standing at all. Tacitus specifically says that while the settlement was not a colony it was already a very well-known and prosperous trading and business centre (**14**). This implies that it was effectively functioning with all the prestige and activity of a colony. It was even important enough for Suetonius Paulinus to consider making a stand against Boudica there. After the Revolt the new procurator of the province, Gaius Julius Classicianus, seems to have been based there instead of Colchester. His tombstone survives, found to the east of Roman *Londinium*.

The striking feature about this is that London had apparently developed almost in spite of official policy to found towns elsewhere. While the government was considering the political expediency of instituting civitas capitals and colonies, the underlying factors of trade and communications led to the spontaneous growth of a town where conditions were right. Until the conquest in 43 the river Thames had served as a tribal boundary and apart from isolated traces of native settlement in the area (for example the hillfort at Wimbledon and a concentration of Iron Age coin finds to the west of Roman London) no evidence has been found for a late Iron Age *oppidum*. The river will have already served as a communications route of course but the combination of the vast increase in continental and inland traffic under the Roman occupation and a politically neutral

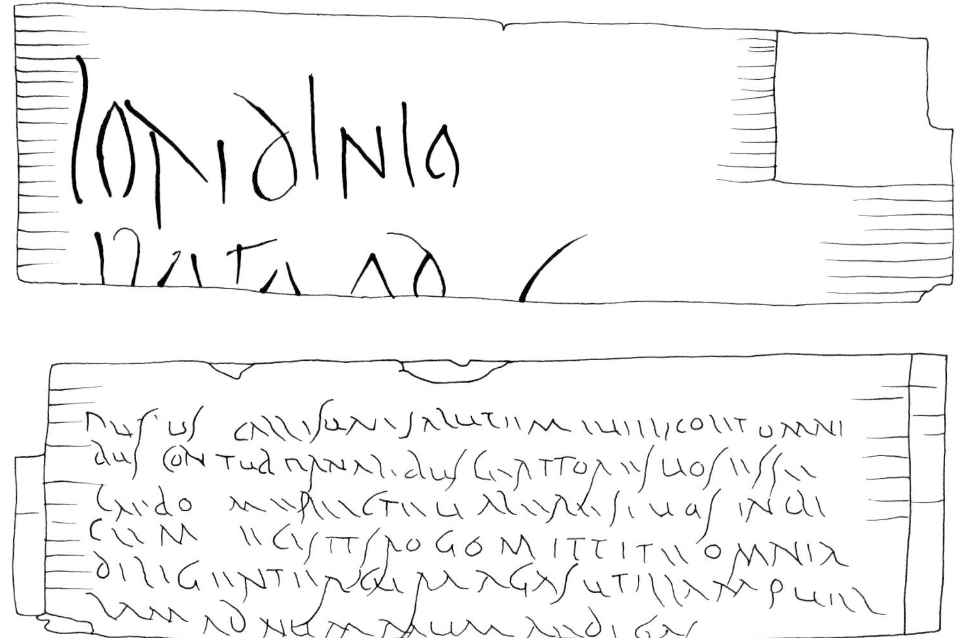

14 *Part of a wooden writing tablet addressed to somewhere in Roman London. The text records that the letter it bears was written by Rufus, son of Callisunus, to his servant Epillicus in order to discuss disposing of an estate. Found in the Walbrook, a tributary of the Thames that ran through the centre of the Roman town. (After Richmond.)*

location close to a convergence of a number of roads made it almost inevitable that it would attract settlement.

Excavations here have also yielded evidence for an early town with a thriving commercial base which was destroyed in 60. There is even less evidence here for a military presence before the town developed than at Verulamium. Traces of military-style ditches have been identified to the west of the town, by modern Fleet Street and also at Aldgate, but these cannot yet be attributed to a fort, and there is no concentration of early military artefacts. Another possibility is that there was a fort south of the river in Southwark where a number of military artefacts and coins dating to *c.* 40-65 have been found. So while there may have been a fort in the vicinity at some point, it is unlikely to have been connected with the subsequent or contemporary growth of London around an early bridgehead across the Thames.

The road network suggests that the traditional crossing of the Thames was about a mile to the west of the Roman town. Later the roads were diverted to converge at the Roman bridgehead. The trading settlement grew up on a site which was more suitable for development as a port, making a new crossing and later a bridge essential. The northern slope of the riverbank drops relatively steeply here and this would have made it easier either to avoid or limit the inconvenient beaching effect of low tides once a quayside had been built. Southwark consisted of a number of islands at this date. The most northerly was exploited to build the bridge at the point where the river was at its narrowest (**15**). With the communications network adapted, the settlement's development was assured and the situation has remained more or less unchanged ever since.

Considering its unofficial status it is perhaps surprising that the settlement seems to have been subjected to formal planning at such an early date. At least two roads were laid out running parallel to the north bank of the Thames, connected by a road which ran down to a possible bridge. The northerly road remained the principal east-west axis of the town. At the centre of this grid was an open gravelled space on what eventually became the site of the forum. It may be that here we have some of the earliest circumstantial evidence for public administrative buildings. Of course it may have been nothing more than a market place, or possibly part of an otherwise unidentifiable military compound, but its location and the later use of the site suggests something more significant.

By about the year 55 a number of rectangular timber-framed buildings were put up on the eastern side of the gravelled area. These extended to having some sort of frontage, resembling the 'shops' of *Insula* XIV at Verulamium (see **13**). However, no evidence was recovered to indicate what they may have been used for. There is plenty of other evidence for structural remains in London at this time, including stone foundations and traces of water-pipes and drains.

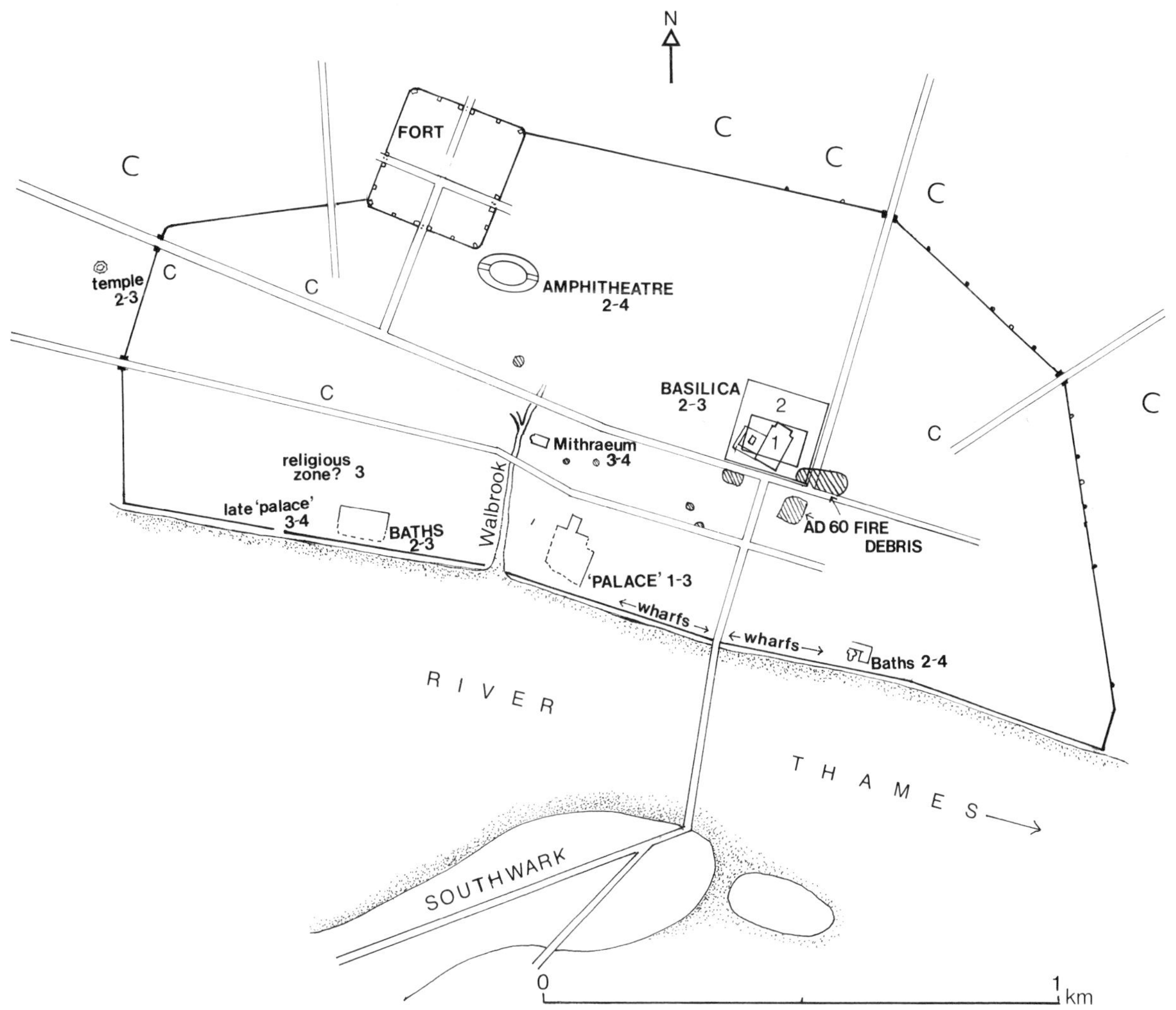

15 *Plan of London. Although a number of much later features are shown here various excavations have revealed traces of extensive burning dating to the mid-first century. These are often attributed to the Boudican Revolt. Traces of settlement of this date have been found all the way along the two main east-west roads. Subsequently the town was rebuilt with two successive basilica and forum complexes and is now known to have had an amphitheatre, perhaps associated with the second-century fort later incorporated into the third-century defences. 'C' marks the site of a cemetery, the smaller 'c' within the third-century walls denoting cemeteries associated with the first-century town. Approximate date ranges for buildings are indicated, e.g. 2-4 = second to fourth centuries.*

Excavations on the Roman riverfront have shown that by about 50 efforts were already being made to develop the north bank around the bridgehead, with timber being used to create revetments to serve as quays. Destruction debris from possible Boudican levels also indicates that trade was indeed thriving here with numerous remains of imported luxury goods. Evidence for metalworking has been found and even for the manufacture of engraved gemstones (intaglios) – a group of four from a pit included one which was discarded before being finished, implying it was made locally. At Colchester such comprehensive urban activity can be attributed to the presence of the ex-legionaries; in London it is less obvious who could have been responsible for what was obviously a centrally-planned and directed programme of land allocations and harbour development. It has been suggested that a body of Roman citizens, intent on making the most of the commercial possibilities in London, settled themselves there and set about the task of creating a trading centre. This is reflected in the distribution of settlement along the roads whose intersection at this place had created the catalyst for a town. However, it is equally possible that London was already being used by the Roman government as an administrative centre. This was certainly so later, but the town's convenience as well as its politically neutral location can hardly have gone unnoticed.

Chelmsford

Chelmsford lay in the heart of Trinovantian territory (see **10**). Little is known about its origin though it has been attributed to the presence of a fort and, perhaps, an attempt to create a tribal capital for the Trinovantes to foster an impression of Rome acting as a liberator from Catuvellaunian oppression. Its important sounding name, *Caesaromagus* ('Caesar's market place'), and the presence of early buildings destroyed in a fire associated possibly with the Boudican Revolt give this some credence, though we do not know when the town was awarded the name. It may have been granted during later re-organization of tribal government. Whatever the situation, however, Chelmsford did not develop into anything particularly significant. Tacitus and Suetonius do not mention it by name, and lying so close to Colchester may have deprived it of economic stimuli. Chelmsford is therefore an instance of a 'town' of sorts which did not develop swiftly in the years between 43 and 60 because it was neither originally an important native settlement nor did it have the advantage of lying at both a major road junction and river crossing.

The Boudican Revolt

The surviving accounts of the revolt supply us with valuable detail about some of the towns that were in existence at the time. The actual process of the Revolt and its put-down are outside the scope of this book but it is worth looking at how the Britons were portrayed as perceiving the towns. Firstly the towns of Colchester, London and Verulamium were clearly the primary targets. We are given the impression that once the native hordes had gathered they did not hesitate in making for Colchester. The temple symbolized their subordination and many of the Trinovantes had been dispossessed of their livelihoods by the colonists.

Thereafter they are said by Tacitus to have specifically avoided military installations, instead being attracted to the easy pickings of undefended towns. This led to the massacre of any remaining inhabitants, said to total between 70,000 and 80,000 though this is probably an exaggeration. While on one hand this gives us the idea that towns were developing swiftly and had attracted a substantial number of people, it also gives us an impression of a wider native population that was less than convinced. It would also be wrong to overrate the kind of towns that these settlements were. Rivet for example described Verulamium and London respectively at this time as being 'a straggle of shops and shacks' and the equivalent of a 'corrugated iron-roofed trading centre'. On the other hand to those who had never seen a town before they may have seemed exceptionally interesting and exciting or perhaps even intimidating places.

The other towns of early Roman Britain

The other principal settlements that have shown traces of early urban development are Canterbury, Silchester, Winchester and Chichester but these are of a completely different character (see **10**). Canterbury lay close to the place the Roman forces landed in 43 and was already a native settlement. It seems that some sort of street grid was laid out here shortly after the invasion and this together with fragmentary traces of timber-framed buildings indicates that the Roman authorities may have decided very early on to develop the place as the cantonal capital of the Cantiaci. Even so, some round huts of pre-Roman type appear to have remained in use for some time after 43 and there is as yet no evidence to suggest that any of the public buildings were begun at this time.

At Silchester the *oppidum* remained in occupation after the invasion. It was something of an ordered community because during the early first century AD a street grid was laid out and rectangular buildings erected, though evidence for this 'grid' is limited to two roads appearing to converge at a right angle (**16**). Finds of imported luxury goods also create an impression of a tribal chief trying to present himself as a sophisticated Roman-style ruler. Verica's mission to Claudius for help in the face of Catuvellaunian expansion reinforces the image.

The archaeological evidence suggests that the *oppidum* was re-organized as a more Romanized town in the 50s or 60s. No evidence for a fort has been found. A new street grid was laid out and we know that tiles were being manufactured in the vicinity during the reign of Nero (54-68) because they bear his name. This is an exceptional instance for Britain of a tile bearing an emperor's name in a civilian context and it is reasonable to assume that official resources were being supplied to the community in the interests of urban development. It may even have had a timber administrative structure in the centre, a site which was subsequently used for a Flavian timber basilica and later stone basilica. The recent examination of the amphitheatre has shown that the earliest phase, of earth and timber, may have belonged to this period. The town was known as *Calleva* in pre-Roman times and this was retained with the addition of the tribal name, making it *Calleva Atrebatum*. However, during the period concerned it was almost certainly one of the principal centres of the client kingdom of Cogidubnus, which would explain the apparently special treatment the town received.

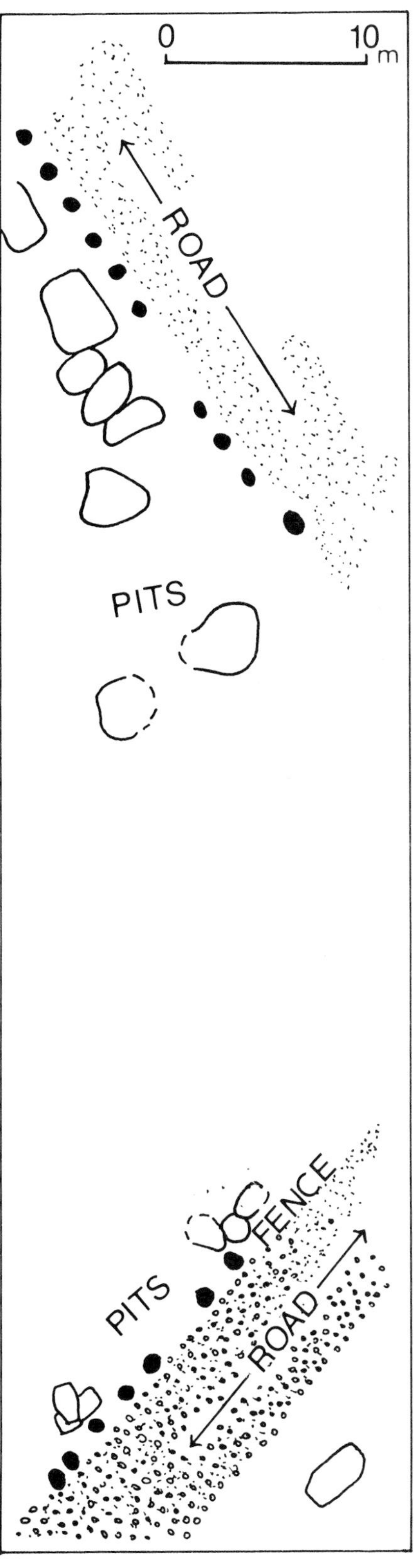

16 *Plan of the early first-century levels beneath the basilica in Silchester showing that a street grid had been established. (After Fulford.)*

Chichester is particularly interesting because an inscription found in the town names Cogidubnus as approving the dedication of a temple to Neptune and Minerva. The inscription is undated but must belong to somewhere between *c*.50 and *c*.80 and at least associates the king with an area, something Tacitus doesn't. As the town is now completely built over, excavation has been limited, but there was certainly settlement of a romanized nature at a very early date evidenced by the presence of metalworkers and potters, following the demolition of military style structures in about 50. A military presence is not certain but we do know that the army had a compound of sorts at nearby Fishbourne and the area may have formed part of a supply base for the II legion's advance to the south-west. A series of dykes to the north of the town may indicate the presence of an *oppidum* but no obvious centre has yet been identified.

More certain development as a town does not seem to date before the Flavian period but as Nero received a dedication from the town's senate in 59 we can assume that the settlement had received an official charter. It was probably not yet a civitas capital or else the inscription would have mentioned it. The town subsequently emerged as the civitas capital for the Regnenses, a tribe artificially created in the absence of any convenient grouping, but this probably belongs to the period after Cogidubnus' death. The same applies to Winchester which was made into the capital for the vaguely titled Belgae of the area (Belgae was just a general name for the peoples of south-east Britain). Like Chichester ambiguous evidence for some sort of early Roman presence has been found but nothing has been discovered to confirm if this was a fort, and whether it was associated with an as yet unlocated pre-Roman settlement still in occupation in 43.

Collectively Canterbury, Silchester, Chichester and Winchester are an interesting group of settlements. While they all emerged as conventional civitas capitals which never became especially prominent, at least three of them seem to have been the subject of early official attention. However, nothing has been located to indicate any of the thriving commercial activity so evident in Colchester, London and Verulamium. This may be a false impression because the latter three have benefited from enormous amounts of excavation in modern times, much of which has been published in a thorough and detailed form. Nevertheless the date 60 is useful because it seems to have been a point up to which urban development was piecemeal yet surprisingly intense in concentrations. We cannot attribute the various stages of later development in the towns to such a short period because we have neither the literary nor epigraphic evidence. Even so a picture has emerged of extensive and more consistent urban development in the rest of the province in the aftermath of the revolt, lasting from the Flavian period right through until the middle of the second century and later. The rest of the book explores this development through the various different aspects of the history, and commercial and religious life of the towns.

3

Reconstruction and growth of towns

Introduction

Although the northern part of Britain remained distinctly unsettled until the early part of the third century the southern part by the late first century had now entered a period when urban and rural life could develop reasonably peacefully. This was not an overnight activity; in the towns destroyed during the Boudican Revolt there is evidence to suggest that some sites may have remained vacant for ten or more years. But by about 75 there is a much more widespread impression of sustained urban development. Apart from the growth of the *civitates* two more colonies were created by the end of the first century at Lincoln and Gloucester. London also emerged as the provincial capital, if it was not already. The provincial council seems to have been established here by 100 and the provincial procurator, Julius Alpinus Classicianus, was working from London during the 60s after the Revolt. It may also have been elevated to *colonia* or *municipium* status.

This stability and its effects should not be underestimated. During the pre-Roman period most of the population would have been accustomed to almost perpetual insecurity. Tribal boundaries and fortunes fluctuated along with the rise and fall of the respective individuals who ruled them. This does not mean that the ordinary people lived in permanent fear of plunder and rape, huddled in corners of wattle-and-daub shacks; but that a great deal of economic and nervous energy was expended in the exercise of tribal rivalries and the pursuit of individual status. Tribal warfare was dependent on an economic surplus because the surplus fed the leaders and warriors. If inter-tribal warfare was terminated and armed resistance quashed the surplus could then be re-directed into supporting towns; similarly the members of the tribal élites would seek to assert their influence and power within the structure and offices of local government.

In almost all the major towns a long period of construction work began in the two decades after 60 and continued well into the second century. This picture has been largely created by the extensive excavations which have taken place in a number of the larger towns during the last thirty or forty years. The traditional reliance on Tacitus' description of Agricola's promotion of urban development between 78 and 84, and the chance survival of Verulamium's forum inscription from the same date originally created the impression that intensive urban development was concentrated in the Flavian period.

It now seems clear that while several towns like Silchester and Lincoln may have had early timber administrative buildings many of the more elaborate masonry forums and basilicas belonged to a much longer-term programme of building. The structures were the equivalent of medieval cathedrals in scale so they may also have taken generations to plan, finance and build. The difference of course is that, apart from the fact that the island was being ruled from Rome, we have no idea of where the money came from. We have very little epigraphic evidence for what has been described as the 'competitive munificence' seen elsewhere in the Empire whereby rich locals vied with one another to build the most lavish and generously endowed public buildings. This is a particularly interesting aspect of Romano-British towns which we shall examine in closer detail later.

The development of public buildings was

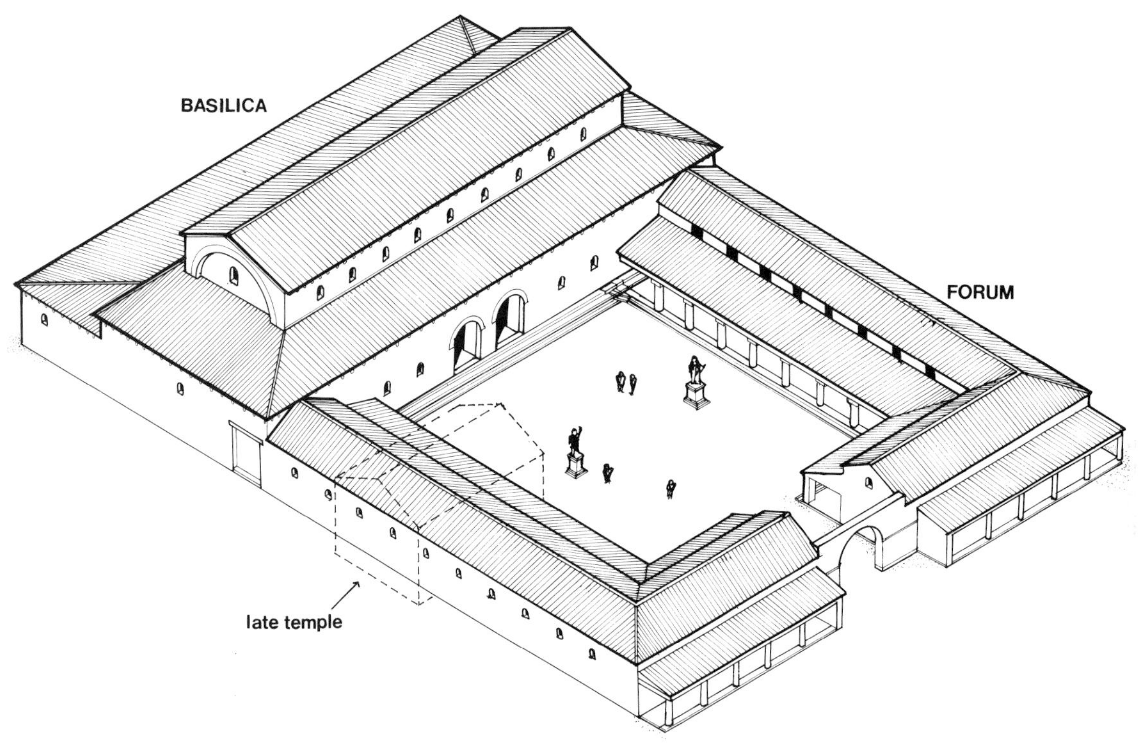
BASILICA
FORUM
late temple

followed by a marked general improvement in urban housing with a distinct move away from the congested commercial quarters of the first century. By the end of the second century widely-spaced stone housing was becoming normal. These houses contain evidence for an urban population which had surplus wealth to spend on decorations like mosaics and wall-paintings. The enormous quantities of archaeological material excavated from the late first- and second-century levels in towns show that the building programmes were matched with a thriving urban economy (see Chapter 5). By the third century, though, the energetic development of towns seems to have slowed. Whether this represents the onset of decline or simply a period of stabilization is a problem explored in later chapters.

The forum and basilica

A forum was an open square or rectangle, which in Roman Britain was surrounded by covered colonnades on three sides, with the basilica forming the fourth. Access was through a small number of entrances which would normally have excluded wheeled traffic (**17**, **18**). Very few Romano-British forums had temples incorporated into the structure, even though this was common practice on the continent. Only Verulamium seems to have been built like this (**colour plate 4**) while at Caerwent a temple was added later (**17**). London's modest first forum and basilica, built in the Flavian period, had a free-standing temple built in a precinct annexed to the forum. Perhaps the ill-feeling created by the Temple of Claudius in Colchester during the Boudican Revolt (it was perceived as a particularly potent symbol of Rome's domination) encouraged a low-key approach to enforcing official religion during the period in which the civitas capitals were being instituted.

The forum served as an open meeting place for the whole town. It was used as a market and as a gathering place for public pronouncements. It was an essential means of promoting a political and social sense of civic unity within the context of Roman town life. Consequently it was also a place where honorific statues of emperors or local worthies were erected, and also a place where religious dedications were made to the Capitoline Triad of Jupiter, Juno and Minerva (see **9**).

This is what we would expect on the evidence of other parts of the Empire. In Britain so little survives that we face a choice of either assuming that things would have been much the same, or suggesting that perhaps the lack of evidence implies that things were different. Suetonius commented in his *Life of Titus* (79-

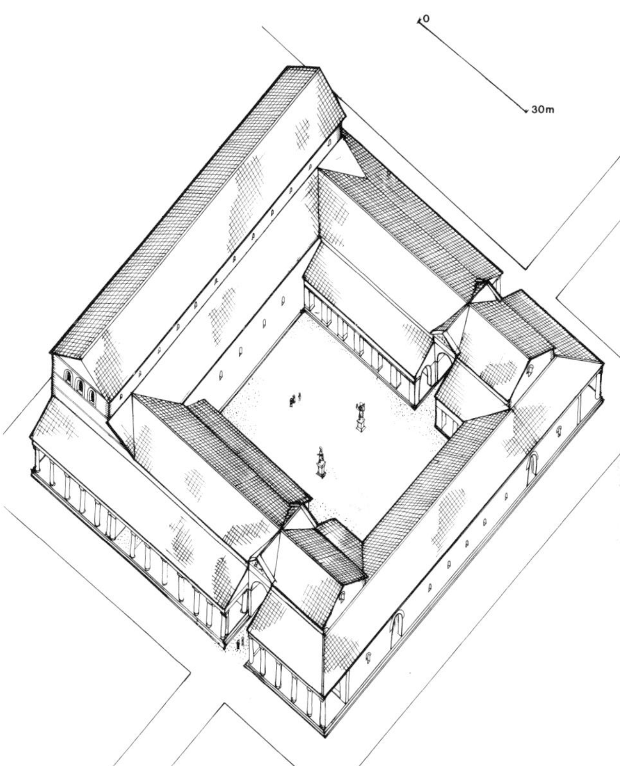

17a *Reconstructed isometric view of the basilica and forum at Caerwent. A plinth like the ones shown supporting statues in the piazza has been found in the vicinity. At a late date in the forum's history a temple was inserted in the nearest side wing.*

17b *The Caerwent basilica during excavation in 1991. The view is looking east along the north aisle with the nave to the right.*

18 *Reconstructed axonometric view of the forum and basilica at Lincoln. Part of the rear wall of the basilica has survived (see* **23***). The proportions were very compact with a relatively small piazza – contrast the piazza with London's (see* **21***) – and the basilica seems not to have had a rear aisle, though this is known to have been the case at some other sites like Exeter and Silchester.*

19 *Life-size bronze bust of Hadrian dredged from the Thames (height 41 cm (16 in)). It would have once formed part of a complete figure standing in a public building in London. (British Museum.)*

81) on how the emperor was so popular in Britain and Germany that statues and busts of him were plentiful in both provinces. Many of these would have been on public display in forums, dedicated by the *civitates* in the civitas capitals and the colonists in colonies. None survive but substantial fragments of monumental figures have been found, the most famous being the bust of Hadrian (**19**) found in the Thames in London which would almost certainly have come from the forum, and the bronze eagle from the basilica in Silchester (**20**). Other smaller pieces have been found in other towns, for example a piece of a bronze horse's mane from the Gloucester forum; this would probably have once been part of a statue of an emperor seated on horseback waving to the population, a stock posture.

The basilica was a long covered rectangular hall with nave and aisle(s), and with an apse at one or both ends (**21**). A number of Romano-British examples were built in a slightly curious form and had only a single aisle, for example at Silchester. The height of the roof was roughly equivalent to the width of the nave and one aisle added together (early churches of basilican type in Italy provide parallels). The roof was either supported by vaults or timber beams. It was here that the council of the *civitas* met, where justice was dispensed and where civic records and funds were stored. An inscription from Nomentum in central Italy tells us that one Gnaeus Munatius Aurelius Bassus spent part of his administrative career as a *censitor* (someone who looked after census records) at Colchester in the second half of the second century. He went on to work elsewhere in the Empire but during his time at Colchester he probably controlled civic records stored in the colony's basilica.

The basilica would have towered over surrounding houses. The site chosen in London would have been especially prominent. A road led up the hill from the north bank of the Thames to the forum, and the basilica would probably have been visible behind the forum's entrance all the way. Inside the basilica there

20 *Bronze eagle found in the basilica at Silchester during the Victorian excavations (height 15 cm (6 in)). It probably formed part of a much larger group of bronze figures which would have stood in the forum or basilica.*

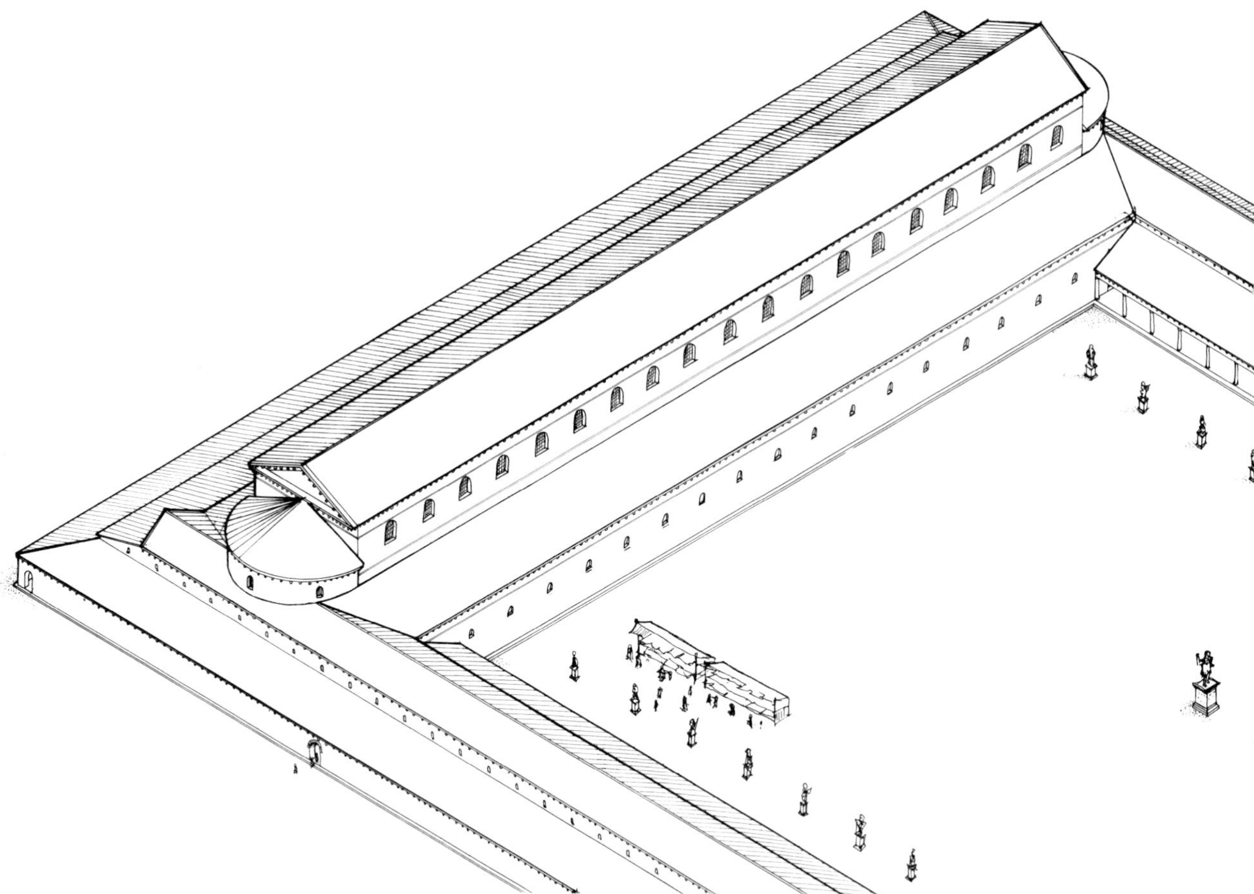

21 *Reconstructed isometric view of the monumental Hadrianic basilica in London. The building may never have been fully completed and is now known to have had at least two separate periods of construction, as well as superseding an earlier and smaller predecessor. The apse in the foreground is hypothetical.*

would have been some elaborately painted wall-plaster and a large amount of ornamental stucco and stonework. London was a special case, though. Excavations beside Cannon Street station have revealed traces of a monumental terraced complex which included an ornamental garden with a pool and a substantial hall. It has been tentatively identified as the palace of the provincial governor, built in the late first century. However, there are doubts about both whether the complex was all built around the same time, and also its function: it may have been the headquarters of the imperial cult in Britain or even a leisure complex with baths.

The forum and basilica site seems to have been set aside as an open area from an early date in many towns. Both London and Silchester, for example, seem to have had gravelled areas laid out before the Boudican Revolt. In both cases the sites were subsequently used for the forum proper so it seems likely that they were fulfilling some of the forum functions already. We know that Verulamium's forum had been officially dedicated by the year 79 (though this does not necessarily mean that it was finished). London's modest first stone forum and basilica appears to have been erected at a similar time. Although these were both masonry structures Silchester and Exeter appear to have had timber forums and basilicas built somewhere around 80-90 (with an even earlier phase at Silchester dating to about 60).

This is interesting because the remains belonging to Silchester's timber period have only recently been identified even though the site was cleared during the late-nineteenth-century excavations. Elsewhere most evidence points to masonry structures being erected in the early second century, as at both Leicester and Caerwent. An inscription from Wroxeter records that here a formal dedication did not take place until Hadrian's reign in the year 130 or 131 (**22**). It may be that these towns also had post-Boudican (or even pre-?) timber administrative buildings which have not yet been identified. Or, on the other hand, perhaps this essential component of Roman civic and provincial government was not automatically constructed in towns once the *civitates* were instituted. What we can be certain of is that from around the year 65 a long period of public administration building works was undertaken in Roman Britain with many not being constructed in stone until well into the second century.

The excavations on the site of London's second basilica in the mid-1980s showed that construction had involved at least two separate phases with the nave erected first, following the demolition of housing. The reason for the break, and its duration, are unknown but may have been connected with money and manpower. Whatever the circumstances it would obviously be wrong always to assume that these buildings were planned and built in an orderly and sustained fashion. It is also possible that some were never finished either inside or out.

London's second basilica and forum was enormous (see **21**). The basilica's nave was about 150 m (492 ft) in length, 14 m (46 ft) wide and would have been about 25 m (82 ft) in height. It would have been extensively decorated inside with carved stonework such as columns, capitals and architraves, and veneers made up from cut pieces of exotic stone like porphyry and marble, much of which would have been imported – assuming of course that it was completed and this was not necessarily the case. The basic fabric of the building was made up of fired bricks cemented together; this was common practice in the Roman world. Walls not decorated with stone veneers would have been plastered and painted – fragments of this have been found.

London was not unusual in these respects even though as the premier town in the province it was probably intended to be the most lavish. The modest basilica at Caerwent had decorated stone capitals, and others have been found at Silchester and Cirencester. As an early showpiece, Verulamium's would have been particularly interesting but the structure is almost completely inaccessible beneath a later church; and in any case we can be almost certain that any significant stonework would have been removed for use in constructing the nearby medieval abbey of St Alban. The only significant pieces of any Romano-British basilica surviving are part of the rear wall at Lincoln (**23**) and at Caerwent.

22 *Brass* sestertius *of Hadrian, struck in Rome about 129-38. Around this time many of Roman Britain's towns were having major public buildings erected. The reverse depicts a figure of Fortuna, a common motif. Actual diameter 29 mm (c.1 in).*

23 *The 'Mint Wall' at Lincoln, now known to have almost certainly formed part of the basilica's north wall, survives with a height of over 5m (16ft) and length of 21m (69ft).*

The macellum

The forum was not always sufficiently large to accommodate all the market activities that went on in a town. Sometimes it was supplemented with a *macellum*, a building that was really just a small version of a forum. Not very many have been identified in Britain but Verulamium, Leicester and Wroxeter **(24)** appear to have been equipped with one, though in no case is identification certain. Evidence from Pompeii suggests that while most of the booths were shops of various kinds there may have been a religious presence, perhaps in the form of a meeting place for priests involved in the imperial cult, or the cult of a *genius* (literally the spirit, or something akin to a patron saint) of a trade.

Verulamium's *macellum* had a long history. It enjoyed a central location, just across Watling Street from the theatre and close to the forum. It was originally built in the first century and consisted of two rows of nine 'shops' facing one another across an enclosed courtyard. It seems not to have been particularly well-used for it was subsequently reduced in size, though by the fourth century it had been completely rebuilt with a monumental facade. This is a rare instance in Roman Britain of what might have been the product of local competition for status. Perhaps the *macellum* was provided slightly unnecessarily by a wealthy man who wished to promote himself as a benefactor. The resulting over-provision of services or decline in demand led to its eventual reduction in size.

Triumphal arches

Triumphal, or monumental, arches were common throughout the Empire forming a kind of architectural statement representing power as well as acting as a symbolic point of entry into a town. In general they commemorated imperial military victories, so it is not particularly

24 *The* macellum *at Wroxeter, built into the* insula *which contained the main public baths. A number of small chambers, probably shops, were arranged around a small covered portico with an open central space. It was just across the main road from the forum (see* **52***).*

surprising that few are known in Roman Britain. In the late first century, the most likely time for them to have been built, they would have served as a tactless reminder of the obvious. Only four certain urban examples are known, three in Verulamium and one in Colchester. The latter, now known as the Balkerne Gate (**25**), was incorporated into the city wall at a later date and became the west gate. The Verulamium examples seem to have remained as markers of the town's early boundaries and were erected in the later second century, at about the same time as earthworks were being constructed to enclose a much larger area (**26** and see **7**).

Civic amenities

Of course there was more to public town life than purely administrative and honorific buildings and activities. Anyone who has visited the remains of better preserved Roman towns around the Mediterranean will have seen how the almost regimented format of town life was extended to all civic facilities and amenities. Almost every town had at least one theatre, a major bath-house and some sort of centralized water supply. In Britain we cannot say with confidence that this was the case in every town but the combination of literary, epigraphic and archaeological material gives us the impression that many would at least have aspired to emulating longer established continental towns.

25a *Reconstructed view of the Balkerne Gate at Colchester from outside the defences showing how an earlier monumental arch has been altered into a large gateway and incorporated into the city walls during the second century.*
b *The Balkerne Gate from within the town walls looking west. The visible stonework formed part of the southern tower and pedestrian passageway added to the original monumental arch. An arrow on* **a** *marks the point and direction from which the picture was taken.*

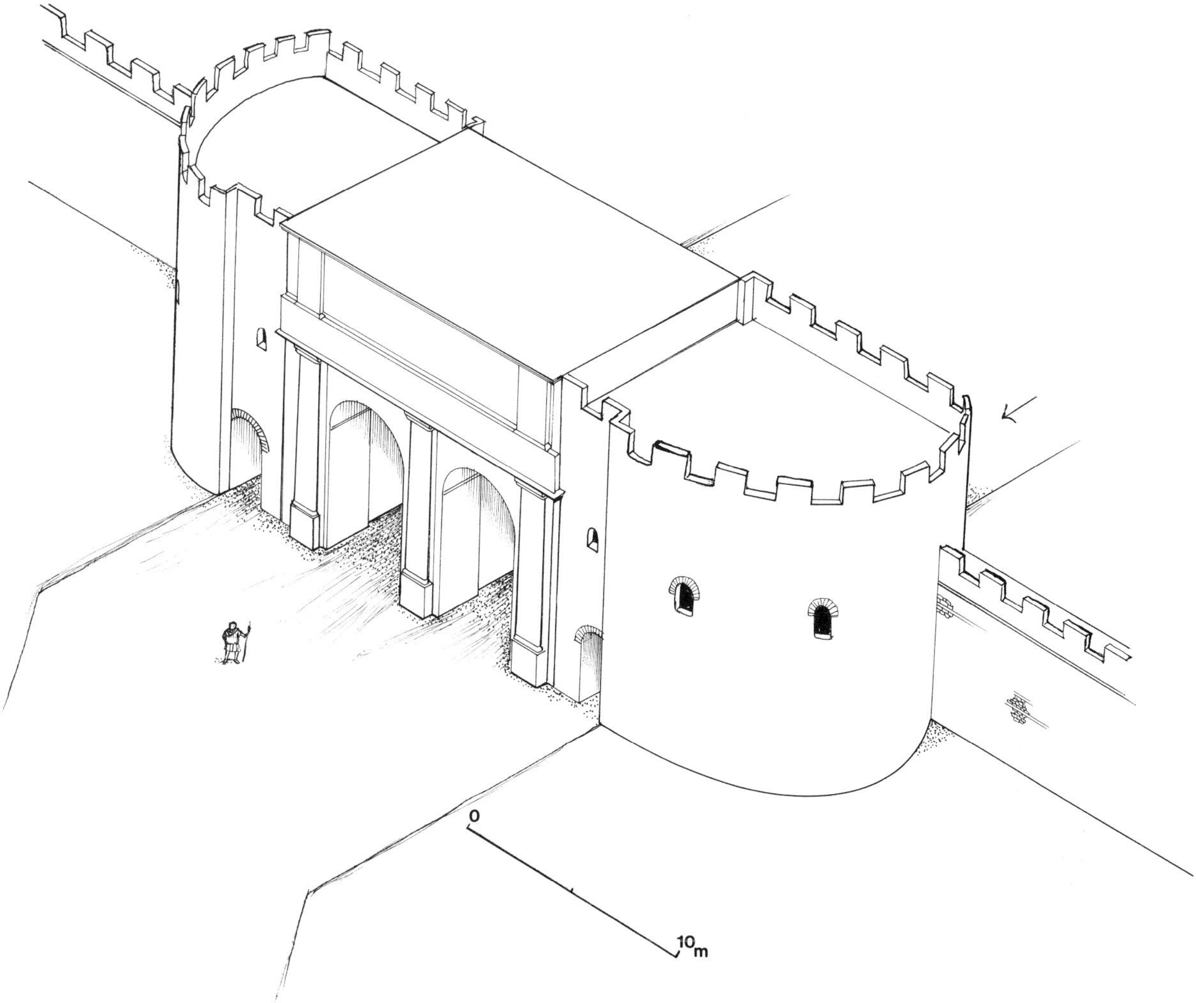

26 *Fragment of carved stonework probably from a triumphal arch in Verulamium. The arch was one of a pair which marked the town's earlier boundaries. Alternatively the stone may be from the nearby theatre.*

Theatres and amphitheatres

We have already seen that Colchester had a theatre by 60 (see p. 29-30). It may have lain beneath the later theatre known to have existed beside the precinct of the Temple of Claudius. No other literary references for theatres exist, but at Brough-on-Humber some time between 140 and 144 an *aedile* called Marcus Ulpius Ianuarius recorded his gift of a new stage to the town's theatre on an inscription which, in part, survives. This is interesting not just because as an inscription recording a personal gift of a civic amenity it is extremely rare for Britain, but also because Brough was a remote town which was not a civitas capital. If it had a theatre then we might reasonably suppose that all the major towns would have had one.

Curiously, however, this does not seem to have been the case. Wroxeter, Silchester and Caistor-by-Norwich were all civitas capitals that remain almost completely unbuilt upon. Silchester has been examined in great detail and was almost entirely excavated in the late nineteenth century. It has an amphitheatre, and a very early one at that, but apparently no theatre. Wroxeter and Caistor have not been extensively excavated but aerial photography would probably have revealed theatres by now; only a depression outside the south-east corner of the town walls at Caistor suggests that it may have had an amphitheatre of sorts. Even Verulamium's well-known theatre (**27**) is not a conventional Roman type; rather it appears to have been a modified amphitheatre, being not only more than semi-circular but also built out of raised earth banks.

Only Colchester and Canterbury certainly had theatres in the classical form, while traces of possible others have also been identified in Cirencester (see **6**) and London. Even Canterbury's was not built in more conventional stone classical form until the third century – before that earth and gravel banks built in the late first century had been considered adequate. Verulamium's site seems to have been reserved at an early date but it was not until well into the second century that it was put up; though even then despite extensive alterations it had fallen out of use long before the other civic buildings.

Does this mean that the Romano-British never really took to theatre-going? It cannot have been just a question of language: one of the most striking features of the Roman period in Britain is the rapid appearance of *graffiti* written in Latin and the complete non-appearance of Celtic as a written form. So many people would have been familiar enough with Latin to have enjoyed classical plays. Theatres were also far from being exclusively a place of entertainment – they played an important part in the enactment of ritual and myth and were often built close to or beside a temple as at Colchester, the nearby religious settlement at Gosbecks, Verulamium and probably also at Canterbury.

27 *The theatre at Verulamium looking south, built originally in the mid-second century. The remains of the stage are visible in the centre left. Four columns supported a cover for the stage and one survives. The seats were supported on earth banks which were revetted in stone. In the early fourth century a further external wall was built which allowed the auditorium to have additional rows of seats.*

There is certainly evidence that the Romano-British had some acquaintance with classical literature. Wall-plaster from the villa at Farningham in Kent bears a reference to Virgil's *Aeneid* and the mosaic floor at nearby Lullingstone bears an inscription also referring to the *Aeneid*. The small town at Baldock has yielded a fragmentary life-sized theatre tragic mask and pieces of others are known from London. While London would almost certainly have had a classical-style theatre, possibly even two (one being an 'odeon', used for literary readings and the like), Baldock probably did not. It may be much more likely that theatres were erected as temporary, maybe seasonal, structures out of timber. The Baldock masks may be the surviving traces of a strolling band of players who visited various settlements throughout the year. At Rome an inscription recording the events of the Secular Games for the year 17 BC mentions that Latin plays were to be performed

in the 'wooden theatre close to the river Tiber'.

Unlike their counterparts in the Mediterranean world, which consisted of a network of interlocking vaults surrounding an elliptical arena, Romano-British amphitheatres were not elaborate structures. Instead they were almost invariably built out of raised earth mounds around a sunken arena. Natural depressions were ideal, and so were Neolithic henge monuments (for example at Dorchester, Dorset, **28**). The earth banks were revetted with timber or stone. Of course this style of construction and the minimal use of masonry gives Romano-British amphitheatres a good chance of recognizable survival. They are often the only buildings surviving above ground level, for example at Silchester and Cirencester (**colour plate 5**), and even at the mining settlement at Charterhouse in the Mendips.

28 *Maumbury Rings amphitheatre at Dorchester, Dorset, built out of a Neolithic henge monument (a round or oval bank enclosing a ditch and central area) by lowering the central area to create an arena.*

Silchester's amphitheatre (**29**, **30**, **31**) has now been comprehensively excavated and has been shown to date from as early as the middle of the first century London's amphitheatre is thought to have been built around the beginning of the second century but it may overlie a timber predecessor. However, no artefactual traces of the kind of entertainments that went on were found (nor have they been at any other Romano-British amphitheatres). We can be sure that these would have included cock-fighting and bear-baiting, and probably extended to matched pairs of gladiators. A gladiator's helmet from Hawkedon in Suffolk may have come from a town originally but how it came to end up in the countryside is a mystery. Gladiators were certainly known of in Britain: one of the mosaics at Bignor depicts several pairs of cupids, dressed as fighting pairs; so too were wild animals: the Orpheus mosaic from the Woodchester villa is one of a number depicting exotic beasts like lions and tigers.

The third form of public entertainment building, the circus, was apparently absent from Roman Britain at least as a permanent feature

29 (Above) *The amphitheatre at Silchester following recent clearing and excavating. The earth banks once carried wooden seating in tiers.*

30 (Below) *Recess in the arena wall of the Silchester amphitheatre. See* **31** *for a reconstruction.*

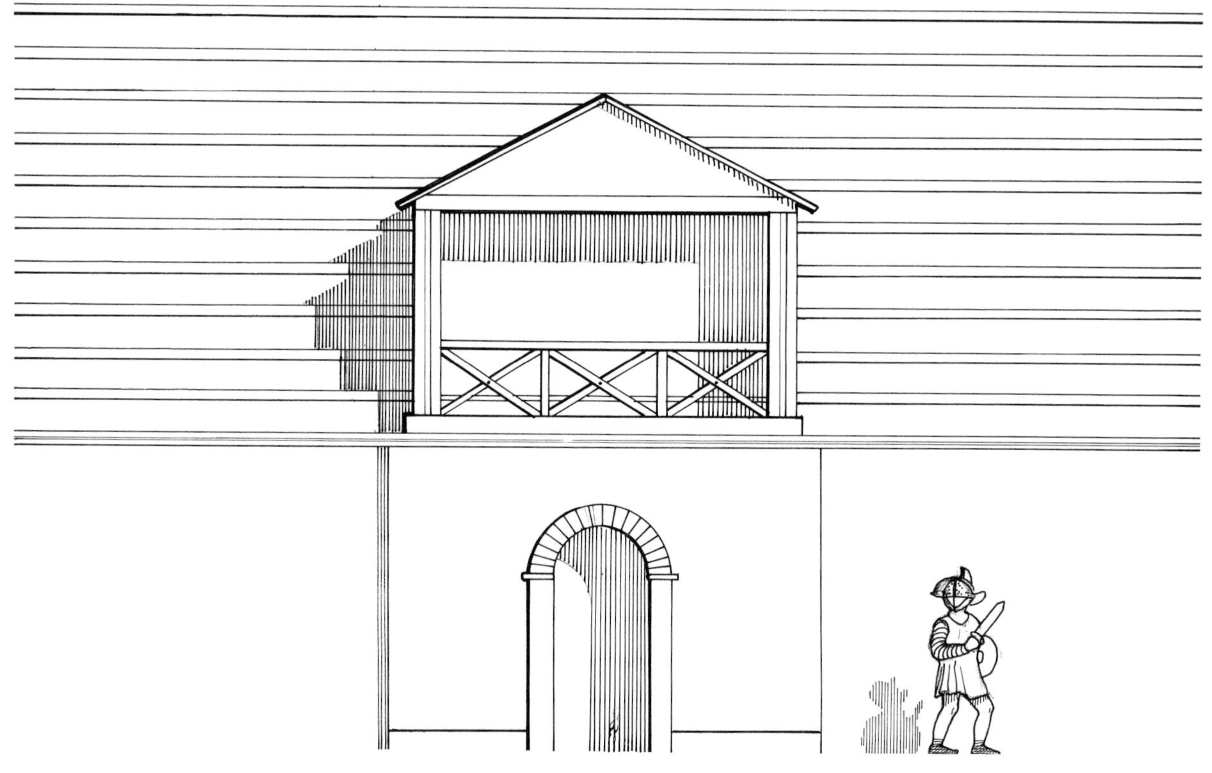

31 *Reconstructed view of the amphitheatre niche in* **30**. *It probably contained a statue and shrine to* Nemesis *(Fate) and supported a kiosk for civic or visiting dignitaries.*

of town life. None are known at all though this does not mean that chariot races did not take place. A mosaic from the house at Horkstow, South Humberside shows four chariots, each pulled by a pair of horses racing around the *spina* (central axis) of a circus. Whoever laid the mosaic was clearly familiar with the sport and the comparatively remote situation of the house suggests that therefore it must have been well known elsewhere in Roman Britain unless the owner had a specialist interest. If the towns had circuses these were probably laid out as temporary structures outside the confines of the settled area. On the continent circuses, unlike theatres, were not a universal addition to a town so the situation in Britain is hardly surprising.

Bath-houses

The town of Pompeii in Italy had at least three large public bath-houses; this was common for any Roman town. The pastime would have been entirely new to most of the British population and although it undoubtedly became widespread it does not seem to have been a major priority. Bathing was of course regarded by the army and other members of the Roman establishment as a vital and necessary activity so it is not surprising that fortresses and forts are the places in which we find the earliest and most elaborate bathing structures. Exeter, fortress of the II legion *Augusta*, was given over to the *civitas* of the Dumnonii around the year 85. The fortress appears to have contained only one stone building: a substantial bath-house with the full range of rooms: *frigidarium* (cold bath); *tepidarium* (warm bath); *caldarium* (hot bath); and, *palaestra* (exercise hall). It was built during the period 60-65 but after 85 it was demolished to make way for the civic basilica and forum.

It is interesting that what would appear to have been a desirable facility for the civil residents of Exeter was torn down. This implies a lack of enthusiasm about public baths which contrasts with Tacitus' description of the Romano-British being skilfully tempted into

Roman ways through such amenities. At Silchester the public baths were erected early in the town's history because they appear to be aligned on a street layout which had already been superseded by the end of the first century (**32**). Indeed its portico had to be demolished to make way for one of the streets of the new grid. Curiously, at Wroxeter public baths begun in the late first century were knocked down, while still incomplete, in order to make way for the new forum and basilica. Only subsequently were public baths provided in an adjacent *insula* during the second half of the second century (see **34** and **colour plate 2**).

Clearly we cannot draw any kind of general conclusion about the provision of public baths other than to observe that while in some cases they were provided early, they were not so important that they stood in the way of changes of civic planning; having said that, it does seem truly remarkable that a great deal of effort could have been expended on baths at Wroxeter which were then never used, and equally that Exeter's military baths were demolished, presumably making an expensive substitute necessary. Another interesting point is that while most of the towns have been found to have had public baths, very few seem to have had more than one main set and no inscriptions at all have been found which refer to them. Inscriptions referring to public buildings at all are very rare anyway but considering that almost every town had baths we might expect to have at least a semi-restorable example from somewhere.

This is even more curious when one considers that bath-houses had to have vaulted roofs if they were to last, because of the effects of heat and damp. This made them relatively massive and it was therefore inappropriate to build them out of timber, hence the Exeter legionary baths being the only stone building in the fortress, and similarly the Silchester baths at

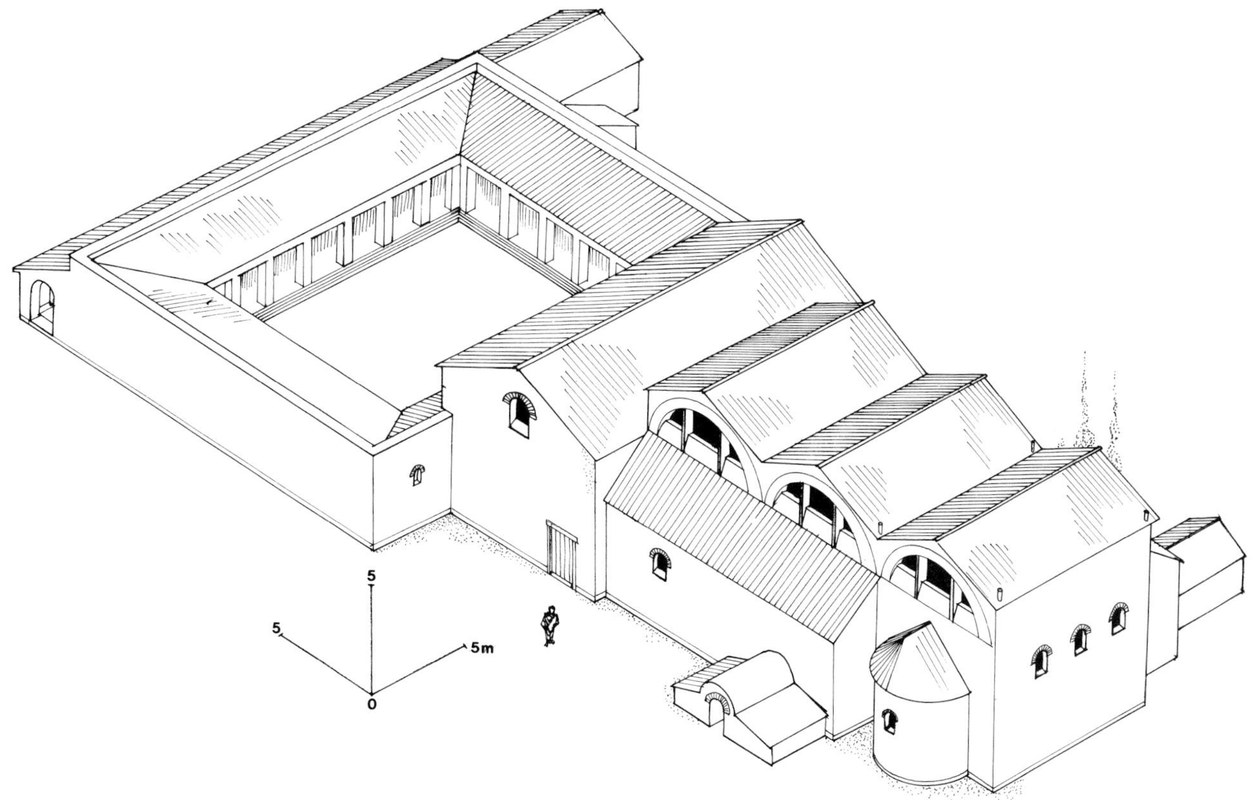

32 *Reconstructed isometric view of the baths at Silchester in their first-century phase. The open* palaestra *was a Mediterranean feature not often used in Roman Britain and resembles better-preserved examples still visible in Pompeii. The three vaulted chambers acted as the cold (*frigidarium*), warm (*tepidarium*), and hot (*caldarium*) rooms respectively while the larger roofed hall (*apodyterium*) was used for changing and preparation.*

a time when the basilica and forum were still built of timber. In addition, unlike the Mediterranean version where the *palaestra* was an open space, Romano-British baths often had covered exercise halls modelled on basilicas. The result is that where bath-houses survive their remains are usually quite substantial. At Leicester (**33** and **colour plate 8**) and Wroxeter (**34** and **colour plates 6** and **7**) sections of walls survive to a considerable height known as the 'Jewry Wall' and 'The Old Work' respectively.

Despite their scale and essential role in Roman life the urban bath-houses of Roman Britain have supplied little evidence either for internal decorations or for the kind of activities that went on inside. We know from better-preserved examples elsewhere that there would have been a complicated plumbing system using boilers, pipes and taps to carry water to the different chambers. In some, water would have been pumped into stone basins for washing, or into plunge baths. It is likely that the walls and vaults would have been decorated with stucco and painted wall-plaster. Furniture would have included benches and shelving for clothes and there would probably have been a number of statues and busts of deities.

We cannot be sure of the extent to which communal bathing became customary in Roman Britain but the fact that most town-houses in, for example Verulamium, did not have their own bath-suites at a time when rural houses were increasingly having them installed, suggests that public baths were relied on. Ironically Verulamium, despite lying mostly in open fields, is one of the few towns where a public bath-house has not yet been located.

No mention has been made of the monumental bathing establishment at Bath because this settlement forms a particular problem, being rather an elaborated shrine and attendant buildings, and is discussed in a later chapter.

33 *The 'Jewry Wall' at Leicester. Like the 'Old Work' at Wroxeter (see* **34***) this monumental piece of masonry formed part of the baths. The bottom of the doors marks the Roman floor level, beneath which was the substructure of the bathing establishment including drains (see* **colour plate 8***).*

34 *The 'Old Work' at Wroxeter. The masonry formed the south wall of the basilican* palaestra *(beyond) and at this point a doorway gave access to the* frigidarium. *Although severely damaged, the brickwork shows traces of three arches which would have formed part of the* frigidarium*'s vaults. The various small holes were probably left when scaffolding was removed after construction (see* **colour plate 7***).*

Water-supply and drainage

In Britain water supply is not generally a problem but public baths demanded large quantities which also had to be disposed of. The knowledge existed to supply water to residential areas. In Pompeii a water-tank, or cistern, was sited at the highest point of the town. From here water was siphoned throughout the town. Not only did it emerge in the various water fountains which stood at most street corners but was also pumped up into water-towers which stood on columns of bricks. From the towers it could be fed under the pressure of gravity to nearby houses. Drainage involved piping or channelling water away from houses into sewers which then ran into a river. There is very little evidence for such an elaborate system in Romano-British towns.

Supplying water in substantial quantities means coping with local topography. Britain is not particularly mountainous, but even the lowland zone can be described fairly as undulating. This presents problems with locating a water-supply at a point higher than the town and bringing it in. The solution was an aqueduct but these were only rarely built in the form of a channel or duct suspended on a row of arches. They tend only to appear in areas where water had to be brought from so far away that it was necessary to cross plains or deep valleys. Instead, the water was more usually carried in underground aqueducts or open channels which exploited natural gradients. An exceptionally fine example is known as the Eifel aqueduct near Cologne in Germany. Here a trench was dug and a brick conduit constructed with access manholes for maintenance placed at intervals. The trench was then backfilled. Even so aqueducts seem to reflect not just circumstances but also the preparedness of any settlement or individual to finance one.

Lincoln is an interesting example where local difficulties were met with different solutions. Much of the main part of the Roman town lay some 50m (165ft) above the surrounding landscape making the water available from the rivers Till and Witham at the bottom of the steep slope to the south as good as useless (see 8). The east range of the forum contained a well with a well-head which was such a serviceable public utility that it was still in use during the Middle Ages. There would have been many other wells but these were not enough. Water was also taken from somewhere to the north-east and carried into the town through an earthenware pipe supported on arches. This was not as simple as it sounds – one of the possible water sources is only about 1·8 km (just over 1 mile) away but is actually 21 m (70 ft) below the height of the town. So either it would have had to be raised under pressure, or alternatively water would have had to be tapped from much further away, up to 32 km (20 miles).

The arrangements clearly worked because the water was stored in a cistern built probably in the first half of the second century (which corresponds well with the evidence for provision of other civic amenities), the foundations of which have been found beside the north wall. From here gravity would have supplied the needs of the baths built in an adjacent *insula*. At Dorchester in Dorset an open conduit (a 'leat') cut into hillsides carried water over a distance of 19 km (12 miles) into the town.

Once in the town water was carried through lead, ceramic or wooden pipes to where it was needed. There is very little evidence for water being made available for use or collection by individuals in Britain apart from the Lincoln forum well, though at York, Catterick and Corbridge public (?) fountains have been found, the latter now visible at the site today. Elsewhere water seems to have been provided for a specific purpose. In the small towns this was typically for the baths of an inn (*mansio*; see below) and even in the major towns water pipes or aqueducts are normally only associated with baths. Most people would have been accustomed to taking water from wells and rivers.

Natural drainage would have taken care of much waste water and not all towns appear to have had some kind of sewer system, for example Silchester. York's sewers are the best known. Like the Cologne aqueduct they were built as masonry conduits under the streets and were fed by subsidiary conduits which ran down from adjacent buildings. The whole system was built with a slight gradient to ensure drainage. In many cases drainage may have depended on the streets. At Pompeii, where the streets are still in 'working order' it is clear from the crossing blocks for pedestrians that water ran away in the gutters.

Providing running water as a civic amenity symbolized organized Roman town life. Erecting public buildings was the thing, but with the provision of a civic water-supply and drainage system we can see the Roman town government at work in a practical day-to-day sense. This would have affected the life of every citizen and helped reinforce the sense of security and stability essential to maintaining the esteem of town life; just because we take it for granted we should not underestimate its effects on a less complacent society. It would have also helped create the feeling that town life was somehow superior to rural life, especially the Britons for whom such exploitation of natural resources would have been an extraordinary novelty.

Inns and staging posts

The Roman government could not possibly have ruled its provinces through towns without an effective means of communication. Roads are all very well but it was also necessary to make provision for food and shelter for those travelling on official business. This system was called the *cursus publicus*, literally 'public passage'. Along all major routes inns (*mansiones*) were established providing baths, food, a bed for the night and probably fresh horses. In his *Life of Augustus* the historian Suetonius said that the Emperor instituted the system so that a piece of official post or a message could be carried by a single individual all the way in order that he could be quizzed by the recipient for further details. Most known examples are found within towns but unlike other public buildings they appear to have been as much a feature of small towns and villages as they were of major towns.

However, not a single example of an inn in Britain has been recognized for certain; they have been identified purely on the grounds of their size compared to other houses in the towns, where they take the form of a substantial courtyard house. The principal differences lie in the fact that the individual room sizes tend to be small compared to the size of the building; they usually have a bath-suite (sometimes a pair, perhaps to allow segregated bathing), and occasionally have granaries.

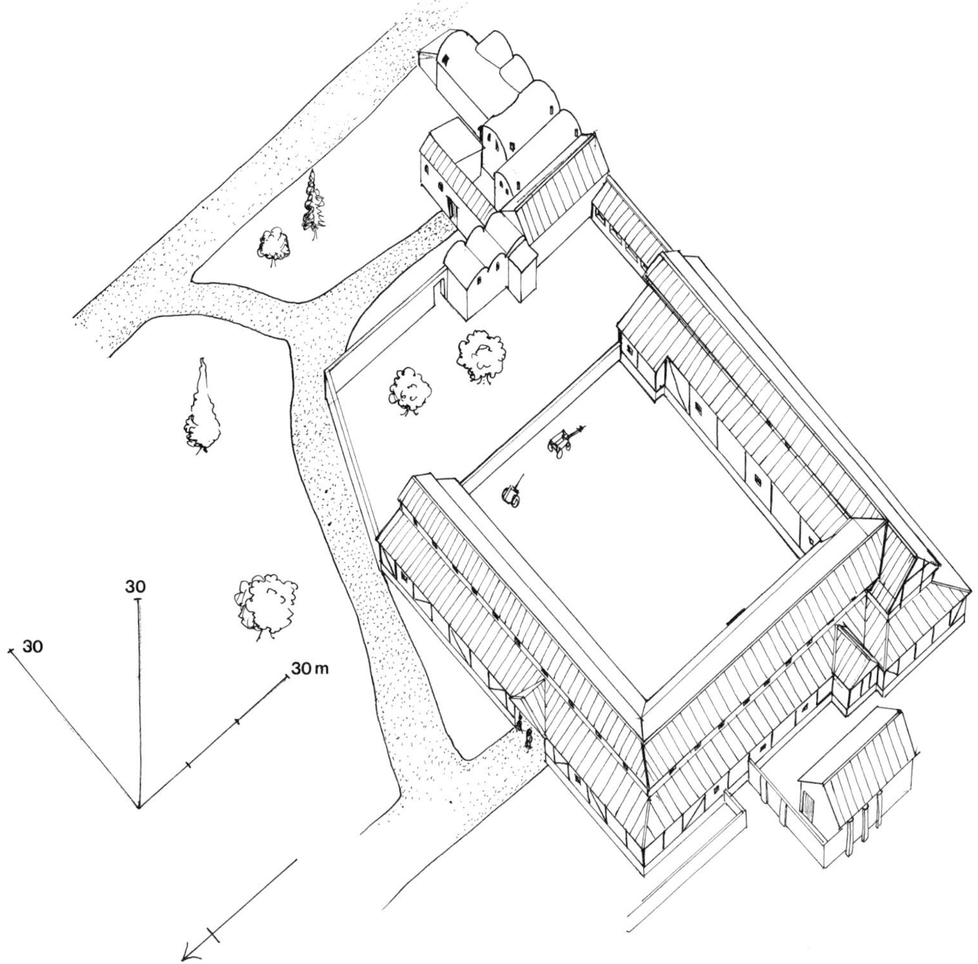

Although the examples known at Silchester (**35**) and Caerwent lie in peripheral parts of the enclosed area this probably reflects their comparatively unimportant role in towns which had local government buildings. Similarly a recently discovered possible candidate for a *mansio* in London of Flavian date lies in what was the straggling suburb of Southwark, on the south bank of the Thames (see **15**). In the smaller towns like Wall (**36**) they were more likely to occupy a central position and indeed may have been a pivotal feature behind a minor settlement's development but so little is known about most small towns that we cannot say. Even in a comparatively large 'small town' like Water Newton the only prominent structures are two central courtyard buildings one of

35 *Reconstructed axonometric view of the* mansio *at Silchester. The large building resembles a substantial private house but had the added features of a bath-suite (unusual for houses in towns) and a granary.*

which may very well have been an inn (see **71**).

At Godmanchester a small basilica-like structure in the centre was built around the early third century. It may have been used for local government but it was both dwarfed and preceded by a probable inn and baths constructed a hundred years earlier. At Wanborough near Cirencester a settlement grew up around a road junction during the late first and early second centuries. There is no evidence for the site having a pre-Roman origin and no structural

36 *The* mansio *or 'inn' at the small town of Wall (*Letocetum*) on Watling Street. A number of rooms were arranged around a small internal courtyard and the whole building was a few yards away from a substantial bath-house.*

evidence for a fort either. Even if there was a fort it has been suggested that the site owed its principal influence to the construction of an inn which has been identified from aerial photography. Excavation which has taken place in the town has shown that the roadside structures were small, simple and mostly made of timber. The substantial courtyard building is therefore quite conspicuously out of proportion to the rest of the settlement, though it has yet to be excavated. The problem with arguing that an inn could help stimulate a settlement's development is that it is clear from the *Letters* of the Younger Pliny that the costs of providing them fell on to the local communities and that he regarded them as onerous impositions. So possibly the presence of an inn in some minor towns may actually have ensured that they stayed as just that.

The funding of civic projects

Who paid for these public buildings? Tacitus says that Agricola provided official assistance for the building of forums, temples and houses. We must assume that this was either money or a workforce or both. The Verulamium inscription implies that this was not empty praise. In London tiles stamped P·P·BR·LON (*Procurator Provinciae Britanniae Londinii* 'the Procurator of the Province of Britain at London') are frequently found on the sites of major public buildings suggesting, but certainly not proving, that they were built with official funds.

Elsewhere in the Empire inscriptions are often found which record the munificence of local citizens who had contributed so much (sometimes the actual sum is specified) towards the building of a particular public amenity. The money could either be given during the benefactor's lifetime, or as part of his will. This is sometimes described as competitive munificence: wealthy individuals vied for status by advertising how much they had spent on public facilities. The town authorities could also finance projects in the name of the *civitas* from civic funds. This money was derived from official grants donated by Rome, local taxation, charging interest on loans, and from income raised by renting out public property or charging admission to public facilities.

Pliny the Younger's letters to Trajan in the early second century are particularly interesting because, as governor of Bithynia and Pontus, Pliny was plagued by the problems which resulted from civic building projects. The town of Prusa needed new baths which were to be financed by diverting funds and also calling in debts to the town government. Trajan approved this but only on condition that no new taxes were imposed and that no more money was re-allocated. This sort of rational arrangement was not always employed: at Nicomedia enormous sums were spent on two separate aqueduct projects, both of which were abandoned before ever being used. At Nicaea poor planning left a theatre subsiding and created a disorganized and potentially dangerous gymnasium, while at Claudiopolis baths were being built on an unsuitable site. Pliny paints a picture of disorganization, petty rivalries and hasty decisions and no doubt these were problems in Roman Britain too.

Comparatively few civic building inscriptions are known from Roman Britain, and even fewer name private individuals instead of the *civitas*. Verulamium and Wroxeter are the only places where forum dedications have survived and these name the *civitas*. Brough is the only place where a theatre inscription has been found, although this only refers to a new stage even if the work was performed at the expense of a private individual. A recent survey by Tom Blagg of similar inscriptions from the other provinces of northern Europe has shown that Britain has a far higher proportion of surviving inscriptions referring to the construction of religious buildings; and that, along with the province of *Gallia Belgica*, Britain's inscriptions record a higher proportion of dedications by 'corporate bodies' rather than individuals. This may mean that 'competitive munificence' was not really an issue in the province, perhaps because of a generally lower level of wealth and also because the preservation of a chieftain society had meant that a very small group of individuals had a stronghold on power and money in any one town. It was not therefore necessary or possible for large numbers of wealthy locals to publicize their generosity.

However, the intensity of post-Roman urban occupation in Britain has been so great that the chances of inscriptions surviving are small. Britain has probably the fewest upstanding fragments of Roman structures anywhere in the Empire so it would not be surprising if the numbers of inscriptions were small. The dedications from religious buildings are predominantly from northern Britain, a part of the province which had fewer towns and which has generally suffered less from destruction of Roman buildings. Moreover, and this is very important, we can see just how low the level of civic inscription survival is: the forums and basilicas for almost all the major towns have been located (12+), and the theatres (4+), amphitheatres (6+) and baths in a number have also been located (4+). It is certain that all of these would have been embellished with dedicatory inscriptions, yet only three are extant, one of those (Verulamium) consists of a few tiny pieces and the Brough theatre has not even been found. We can be sure that more of these buildings are yet to be explored – the public baths at Verulamium, Cirencester, Colchester and Gloucester, for example, have not yet been identified.

It is therefore impossible to draw meaningful conclusions about who paid for Romano-British public buildings from such a low proportion of what originally existed. As so often with Roman archaeology in Britain we are confronted with possibilities rather than facts. It is particularly interesting that some of the inscriptions that have survived record dedications to or by obscure individuals in relatively obscure places. The Brough theatre inscription is probably the best example, but an early-third-century statue base from Caerwent dedicated to a legionary commander and an arch in York (see Chapter 4) are other instances. Can it really be true that an *aedile* in Brough was unusual in having enough money to provide a theatre stage and recording it? Equally if the Caerwent community could fund a statue for one legionary legate surely they could afford it for other prominent locals. It seems much more likely that these are chance survivals of inscriptions which were once more widespread. Private gifts are recorded and so are those at the expense of the community, so we have to conclude that either were possibilities in circumstances where we have no specific information, and they may have been far more common than we will ever know.

Housing

Marcus Ulpius Ianuarius, the *aedile* in Antonine Brough, is a useful example of a man who had status in his local community and had enough money, inherited or earned, to sustain that status by contributing something to his town. He is representative of the upper tier of Romano-British urban society which had benefited from the Roman government's policy of exploiting existing social hierarchies in the interests of stable provincial administration. These individuals manned the town councils and we can be sure that they exercised lucrative controls over local land and trade; this was their reward. If the emergence of public buildings can in part be attributed to their philanthropic tendencies then the appearance of more solidly built and better-appointed houses in the second century can be attributed to a natural desire to enjoy their wealth privately as well.

Towns in Roman Britain were more than administrative or economic centres and as examples of romanization they would have had no purpose if none of the Romano-British had become accustomed to living in, and identifying themselves with, them. Once more we have to turn to Tacitus for the only instance where official policy is referred to. Agricola, he says, encouraged the Romano-British to build houses and the word he uses, *domos*, refers particularly to town-houses and in the sense of their being homes.

Excavations in towns have shown how buildings, apart from public works, seem to have been commercially orientated in the first century. Usually built from perishable materials and with a street frontage they often contain some sort of evidence for a trade or light industry like metalworking (see **13**). Only in the second century did significant numbers of stone buildings begin to appear. Their ground plans were usually more sophisticated and although solid floors and plastered walls were a common feature of earlier houses the new ones were much more likely to contain a mosaic floor or two and plastered walls painted with a colourful decorative scheme. Whether these houses directly represented family wealth accrued from earlier commercial activities we cannot say because the evidence does not exist for us to draw this kind of connection.

In their most elaborate forms town-houses might have several mosaic floors, out-buildings and an integral bath-suite though the latter was much rarer than in the affluent country villas (they were fire risks and public facilities were available). Much has been made of their ground-plans but these are for the most part no more than simple variations on rows of rooms and arguing for patterns of influence and development based on such elementary forms seems very suspect. Equally the idea that one can analyse social structures on the basis of room size and numbers seems hopelessly optimistic as we rarely have the slightest idea of what a single room was used for; and we have almost no knowledge at all of the nature or names of any house-owners in Roman Britain at any time. We need only consider the various different residents in a row of modern identical semi-detached houses to realize that we cannot make assumptions about who lived where.

No town-houses seem to have reached the extravagant heights of the great villas like Chedworth or Bignor; but then few town-houses in the last three centuries equal the extent and luxury found in the greatest English country houses. The wealthy have always tended to leave towns and invest their capital in rural seats; this removal to the countryside may have happened in Roman Britain too.

This perceived reduction in the urban population may have been paralleled by a decline in investment in public buildings (see also Chapter 5), perhaps further evidence of a withdrawal of the curial class from towns. There are problems with this theory (see Chapter 4) but the picture is a very difficult one to analyse. Excavations in towns tend to be piecemeal and the few towns that have been extensively excavated, such as Silchester (**37**) and Caerwent (see **38**), were dug at a time when techniques were unlikely to help locate structures made of wood.

Villas, or 'country houses' (usually farms), fall outside the scope of this book. While widespread in most of southern Britain they are rarely found very close to the major towns. This is almost certainly linked to ownership of land by the town governments or wealthier inhabitants (effectively the same anyway). However, it is not unusual to find a single villa within a short distance of the town limits. One such case is the villa estate at Gorhambury which lies about 1·2 km (just under 1 mile) from the north gate of Verulamium. Excavation on the site has shown that occupation within an enclosure dated from the Iron Age, and seems

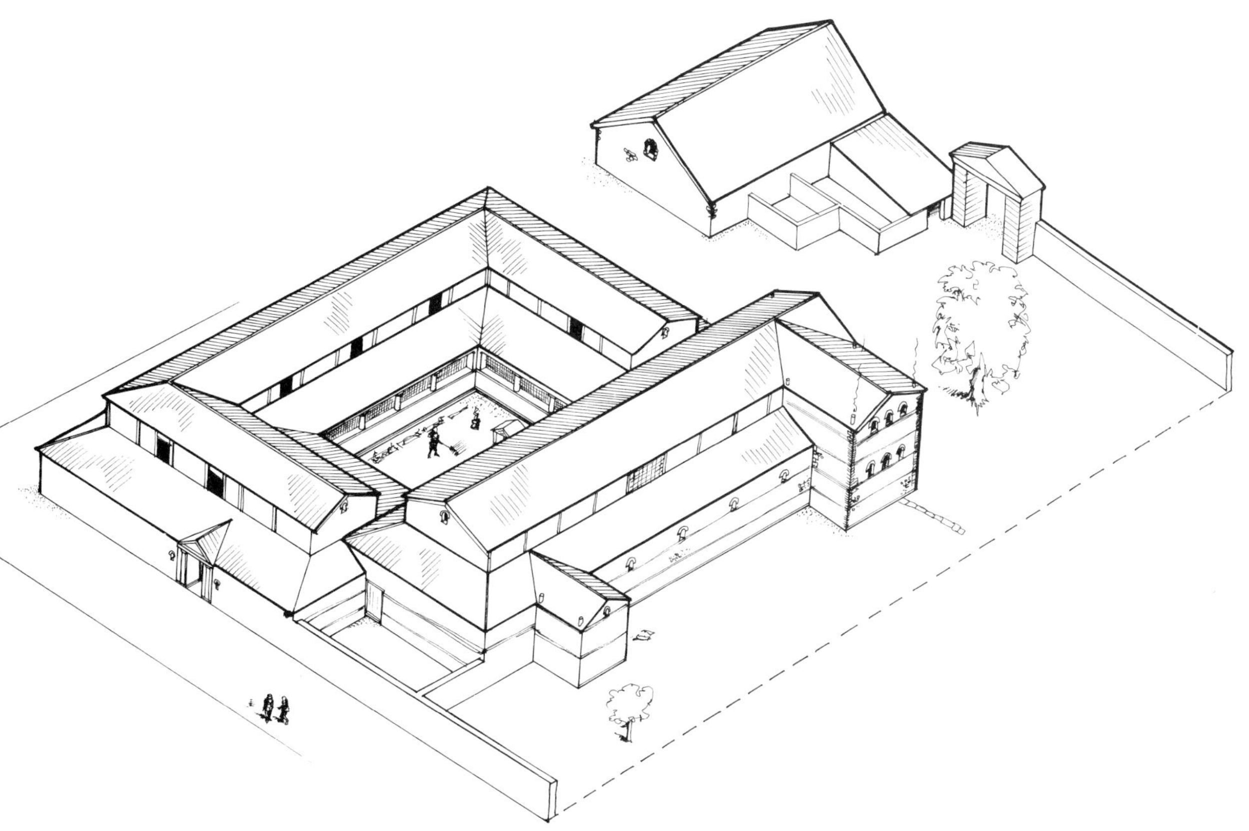

37 *Reconstructed isometric view of a substantial courtyard townhouse at Silchester (*Insula *XIV.1). Note the outbuilding, perhaps for livestock, and the gateway. The house may therefore have been involved with farming land outside the town limits.*

to have been linked to the dykes which formed part of the pre-Roman *oppidum*. By the beginning of the second century a stone house had been erected within the enclosure and it remained in occupation until the middle of the fourth century. In this case at least one plausible explanation is that the site belonged to an especially prominent family within the existing local tribal population and its members retained their status, and privileges, throughout most of the period, perhaps dominating the town government.

House-types

Not surprisingly town-houses resemble rural villas as structures. We do not have to assume that one derives from the other, or that both were derived from somewhere else. The idea of using rectangular or square rooms arranged in sequences was a relatively new one, but not unknown in pre-Roman Britain. Beyond that it is difficult to see what the alternative was to building in what were usually no more than two parallel rows. Anything wider would have required complicated roofing and made internal lighting a problem. Equally it is hardly surprising that larger houses made use of rows at right angles to one another. This minimized the distance a resident would have to walk to get from one room to another. The only alternative to a 'courtyard house' (see **37**) was building an extremely long row of rooms which would have been enormously inconvenient. This elementary observation makes the time-honoured series of classifications of house types a tool of dubious merit, apart from being conveniently descriptive.

In general, town-houses consist of nothing more sophisticated than one, two, three or four rows of rooms arranged at approximately right angles to one another. The observed series, though this need not necessarily be chronological, begins with the 'strip-house'. This type of building seems to have been typical of most towns that were thriving during the first two centuries. Verulamium and London have the best examples but other towns like Cirencester have been shown to have had similar buildings at about the same time. They were usually small rectangular structures built of clay and wood (a perfectly effective and quick way of producing a place to live), divided into several rooms and erected at right angles to a street. This feature maximized the number of establishments which had a street frontage and makes it likely that there was some sort of commercial activity going on.

Obviously we know nothing about land ownership in any one case but we might speculate that an entrepreneur could buy a plot of land and put up several of these buildings to increase his rent yield. This has been plausibly suggested as being the case at Verulamium's *Insula* XIV where a row of separate businesses seem to have been housed in a single, purpose-built, structure (see **13**). Despite the simplicity of the design the method was fairly durable apart from the need to replace ground timbers every 15 to 20 years or so and there is evidence from many sites, for example at Gutter Lane in London, that the owners were prepared to invest in painted wall-plaster and plain tessellated flooring or even mosaics.

The main problem was the risk of fire but it seems that at London and Verulamium it took serious conflagrations before more substantial house building in stone (or at least in part) took place. Both towns experienced fires that appear to have damaged extensive areas, in *c*.125 and *c*.155 respectively. The inflammable nature of the houses and the congested layout with narrow alleys must have made it easy for fire to spread swiftly (just as it did amongst the medieval houses in the London fire of 1666). Thereafter London and Verulamium appear to have joined a trend for better built and more widely-spaced housing which had already begun elsewhere, for example in Cirencester and Canterbury.

This must also reflect the fact that a proportion of the Romano-British urban population had accumulated sufficient wealth to finance such private projects. We need not assume that each house was individually owned and it may be that the people who were paying for the buildings were not very numerous. Even so, the largest town-houses were little more than elaborations of the strip-house which was easily expanded into a simple 'corridor house'. Here, slightly more rooms were accessed by a corridor which allowed both privacy and more insulation from the elements. The corridor types are all fairly simple and apart from a row of perhaps six to ten rooms usually vary only to the extent of having one or two flanking corridors, occasionally with an extra room, perhaps an outhouse, tacked on. If a larger house was needed then it made sense to build on wings. Instead of being symmetrical very few examples of winged corridor houses have matching wings; instead they were built according to requirements and convenience. They would have limited wing length and if additional rooms were needed then a fourth wing was also added to create an enclosed courtyard.

The principal exception to this rule is the Mediterranean type of house which is found in very limited numbers in Britain, apart from the legionary fortresses where they were used to house senior officers. The best-known examples have been found in Gloucester and Caerwent (**38**) where the proximity of the fortress at Caerleon, the colony status of Gloucester and an earlier date for the buildings concerned makes such a house style less surprising. The Mediterranean type of house is distinguished by being much more inward-looking. Almost invariably they consist of four compact wings packed tightly around a very small internal courtyard. Surviving examples in Italy show that the roofs were pitched inwards so that water drained off into gulleys around the courtyard. They were much more suited to a hot sunny climate so they were probably considered unsuitable for Britain and never became a popular alternative.

Many Romano-British houses were built with at least stone footings from the second century onwards; it is normally impossible to be sure whether the whole wall was made of stone or not unless a collapsed wall is found where it fell, for example at the Meonstoke villa. The thickness of the stone footings proves nothing either way; we cannot assume that all foundations were built exactly according to the precise structural requirements of the building and

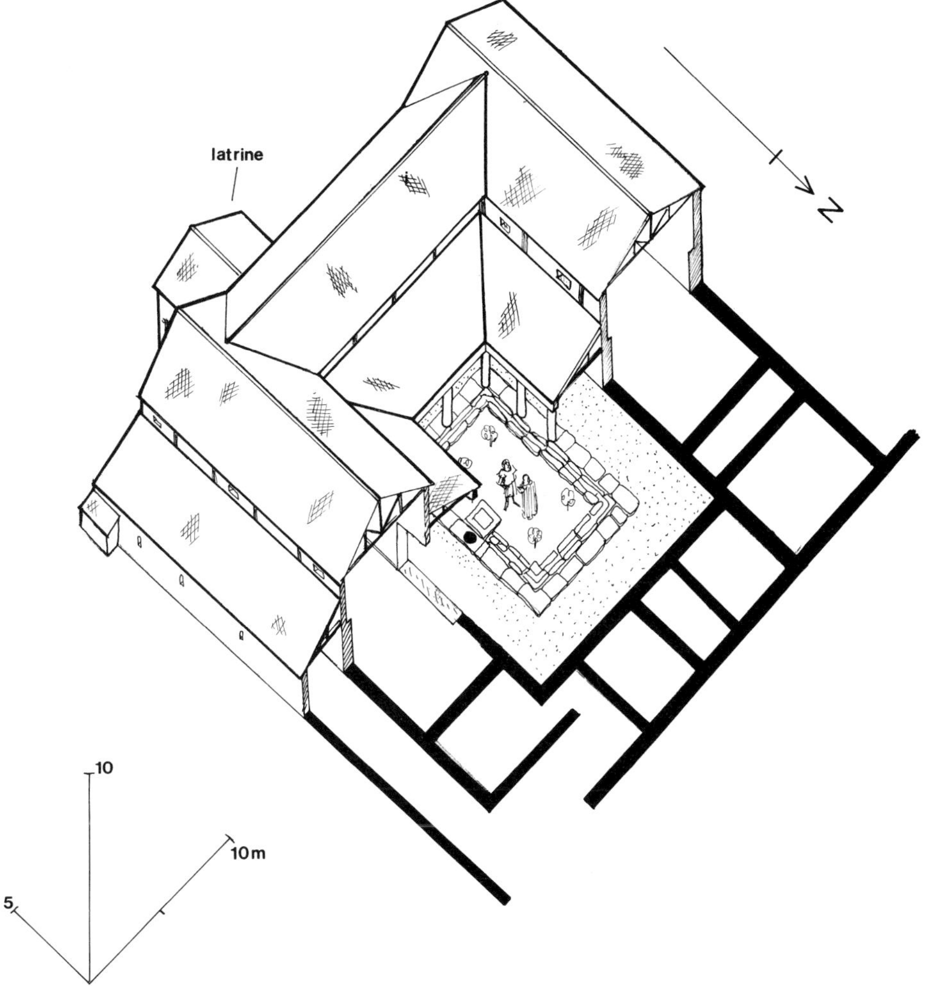

38 *Reconstructed 'cutaway' axonometric view of a Mediterranean style house at Caerwent (*Insula *IIIS). This compact and inward-looking design is rarely found in Romano-British towns.*

that the buildings were maintained properly either by their owners or landlords. There is plenty of evidence to show that this was far from the case, for example, the poet Juvenal cursed the way lives were placed at risk by appallingly botched repairs in Rome and the dangers to passers-by from falling tiles. All we can say is that houses would have been built either entirely in stone, entirely of wood, or a combination of both. All would have been completely serviceable on a day-to-day basis if constructed properly. The choice of building materials and whether to maintain them must have reflected costs and tastes, and greed, which must have been as prevalent then as it has ever been.

The relatively poor dating evidence from extensively excavated towns makes it difficult to be sure which houses existed at the same times as others. From the town plans it is possible to see that the *insulae* generally have from one to five significantly-sized masonry houses so that the spacing between houses had become much greater by the third to fourth centuries than in the 'boom' of the late first century, with interesting relevance to the discussion of population figures. There is a great contrast with most continental towns of the period which tend to be much more congested than the 'garden-cities' of Roman Britain. Only

Colchester remained relatively tightly-packed though some of the small structures within the same *insula* may be outhouses belonging to a larger house or an independent residence. A similar pattern is found at Verulamium, for example *Insula* III has a single courtyard house (the only one known in the town), while the adjacent *Insula* IV has what appear to be between four and five houses.

However, one house need not mean one family. We know from papyri in Roman Egypt that it was quite common for families or individuals to buy part-shares in property, or to rent rooms or suites within a house. These could include traders who wanted a room with a street frontage. Exactly the same arrangements are found at Pompeii, though here the *insulae* are rather more congested. In one, the *Insula* of the Menander, a number of traders were running businesses from shops that had once been internal rooms of the houses. The individuals probably lived in rooms above their shops. The buildings tightly hugging the eastern sides of *Insula* XXVIII at Verulamium (**39**) would, for example, have been able to offer prime sites near the forum. On the other hand, a single house might be only one home of a wealthy family which owned other properties within and without the town. From the evidence available to us from Britain, therefore, we have to recognize that we cannot assume a particular type of occupant for each type of house.

In addition to these considerations, the number of houses which had upper storeys has probably been underestimated, though for the structural reasons outlined above it is not usually possible to demonstrate exactly which ones did. The more solidly-built stone town-houses are more likely to have had an upstairs which would thereby have increased the amount of urban accommodation available than is apparent from the ground-plan. This is

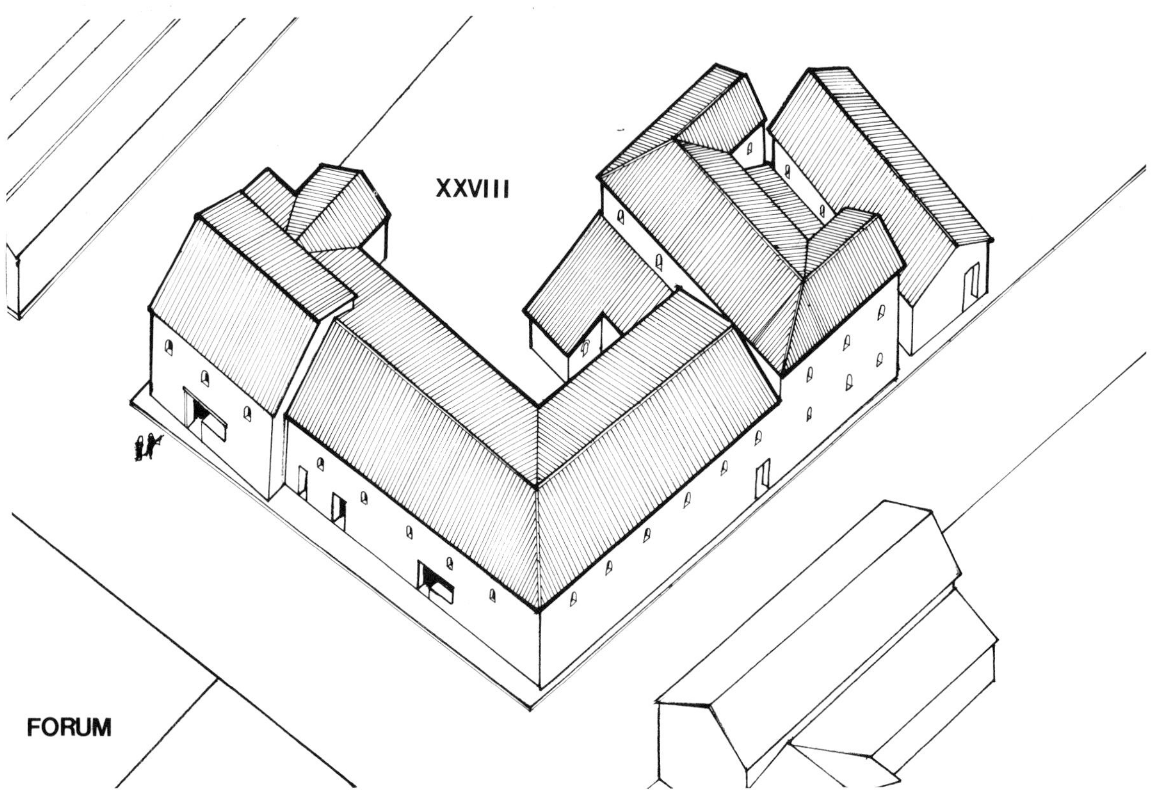

39 *Late-second-, early-third-century town-house at Verulamium in* Insula *XXVIII (axonometric reconstruction). Although a single structure the house appears to have had several components including various establishments on the street front including a latrine and a small eating house. These may have been individually owned or rented.*

40 *Centre panel of a mosaic from Verulamium depicting a sea god from a town-house (*Insula *IV.8). The mosaic was one of a number laid in the town during the second century. They were generally simple geometric designs but often contained more complex motifs or figures.*

certainly often found in houses at Pompeii, and more particularly at Herculaneum where the town was buried beneath scalding mud and lava. The conditions at the latter carbonized and preserved wooden structural components showing that many buildings had stone lower storeys but timber-framed upper storeys which were sometimes self-contained (see **6**).

Decorations

Above all other things the internal decorations of Roman houses, mainly wall-paintings and mosaics, are regarded as amongst the most distinctive features of the whole period. The evidence for them in Britain parallels chronologically the structural evidence for houses. But even in the most well-appointed houses mosaic floors were rarely installed in more than a small number of rooms and wall-paintings usually survive in much too fragmentary a form for us to have a detailed knowledge of them.

The earliest mosaic floors known in Roman Britain were those of Flavian date found at Fishbourne 'palace'. Some houses in London, destroyed in the fire of *c*.125, had mosaic floors even though they had timber walls. These may have been laid in the late first century and demonstrate an unsurprising trend in what must have been the most cosmopolitan town in the island. However, it is only at Verulamium that there is fairly general evidence for the laying of mosaics during the second century associated with the new houses put up after the fire of *c*.155. Like examples of similar date from Colchester, Silchester, Cirencester, Leicester and Aldborough they tend to be geometric with very little figure content. The scallop mosaic from Verulamium is probably the most abstract example but the Sea-God bust from another house shows that the skill existed to create quite effective, if simple, images (**40**). The mosaics were generally colourful and accomplished but reflect quite conservative and unadventurous tastes (**colour plate 10**). Some of the Romano-British mosaic artists were capable of more inspired work, the most striking of which is the head of Dionysus as Autumn from the Seasons mosaic from Cirencester

(Dyer Street; **colour plate 9**).

If many of the better-off households were finding they could afford mosaics at this time we can assume that they would also have been commissioning wall-paintings. Traces have been found in many Romano-British town-houses, especially at Verulamium (**colour plate 11**). The painters largely confined themselves to very conventional formats based on the standardized tradition of a dado a little under a metre in height (3 ft), a main area around 2·5 m in height (7-9 ft) and a narrow upper band. The main zone was usually divided into vertical panels which featured the main themes employed in any one room. These could be quite simple, for example imitation panels of polished exotic stonework, divided by imitation columns; or they could be more sophisticated attempts to exploit the medium's potential for depicting fantastic architecture and figures as in examples from Leicester. Ceiling paintings were more usually straightforward patterns based on hexagons, diamonds, circles and squares containing various motifs.

The mosaics and wall-paintings tell us more about Romano-British society than they do about themselves. Arguments about schools of mosaicists and artists are rather academic because we have no satisfactory evidence which reliably distinguishes the work of one craftsman from another. But what is clear is that by the second century polite Romano-British society was now prepared to spend significant sums of money on completely non-essential items. A decorative mosaic is no more functional than a simple tessellated floor and painted wall-plaster no more so than plain. The improvements in house structures which had taken place were much more functional in terms of simple comforts. What this means is that a portion of society now had surplus wealth, a wealth which supported luxury industries. Wall-paintings and mosaics were ways of displaying and enjoying that wealth and were an alternative to spending large amounts of money on public works.

4

Insecurity and urban decline?

Introduction

The third century in Roman Britain was a time when fewer public buildings appear to have been put up, apart from urban defences, and by when commercial quarters in towns had been replaced with more widely-spaced large houses. These apparent facts and the known history of disorder in Rome and wars on the continental frontiers have all contributed to a belief that this was a time for economic decline, or at best stagnation, and insecurity in Roman Britain, affecting public and private projects especially in the towns. However, interpreting archaeological evidence from this period has always been complicated by a marked reduction in the supply of coinage and easily datable pottery. Both these limitations in the evidence are now recognized as such, rather than necessarily meaning that there was an absolute decline in the amount of activity. Even so while changes in the character of Romano-British towns were undoubtedly taking place it is less easy to generalize about what was going on; instead local factors seem to have played an increasingly important part in the development of individual towns.

Britain ceased to be a single province and instead was divided into two, namely *Britannia Superior* and *Britannia Inferior*. This occurred around the beginning of the third century and may have been a consequence of the civil war of 193-7 during which the governor of Britain, Clodius Albinus, decided to participate in a tripartite struggle to become emperor. He failed but the attempt showed how powerful the governor of Britain could be, given the disproportionately large garrison of three legions and various auxiliary forces.

Whatever the reason, the two Britains now each had a governor and a capital. London remained capital of *Superior* while *Inferior* was ruled from the legionary fortress of York where the attendant civilian settlement was elevated to colony status around this time. A further division had taken place by 312 reflecting a contemporary policy of reducing the size of provincial administrative units across the Empire. *Superior* was divided into *Britannia Prima* and *Maxima Caesariensis* whilst *Inferior* was divided into *Britannia Secunda* and *Flavia Caesariensis*. The boundaries are unknown but it is generally accepted that *Maxima* and *Prima* were ruled from London and Cirencester respectively, and *Secunda* and *Flavia* were ruled from York and Lincoln respectively. These reorganizations will almost certainly have had implications for the status of the civitas capitals and lesser towns, but we do not know precisely what.

Literary sources more or less ignore the province for the period 212-86. This lack of known historical events has made it impossible to construct a chronological framework; this is in contrast to the first and second centuries in which it has been possible to associate a large number of sites with specific, dated, events such as the construction of Hadrian's Wall in about 122. This helps to date contemporary artefacts, mainly fine pottery such as samian ware (see Chapter 5), which in turn provide archaeologists with a tool to date other sites occupied about the same time. Unfortunately even samian ware ceased significant production by about the beginning of the third century and new pottery industries did not manufacture such distinctively styled or name-stamped products.

Britain was probably experiencing a protracted period of internal stability – the northern frontier seems to have been peaceful from the end of the Severan campaigns in 212 until some time close to the end of the century. This explains the lack of literary references, which traditionally only referred to Britain when wars or unrest had occurred. There are several inscriptions from a later date which show that some forts and their buildings on the northern frontier had been allowed to decay into ruin during the third century, rather than having been destroyed (if the inscriptions are truthful).

The only new forts that appear to belong to the first half of the third century were at Reculver in Kent and Brancaster in Norfolk. They may have been linked to a maritime threat from northern Europe but if so, they seem singularly inadequate, and any threat was not seriously dealt with until towards the end of the third century when they were incorporated into a more substantial chain of coastal forts known as the Saxon Shore system. We know little about how these forts were used but they were likely to have served as supply bases for troops dealing with sporadic coastal raids rather than the kind of inland incursions which would have threatened the towns.

Britain formed part of the breakaway Gallic Empire from 259 to 273 and acted as an independent province during the revolt of Carausius and Allectus from 286 to 296 (see **64**). Carausius was the successful commander of the Roman fleet stationed in Britain and the north coast of Gaul. He had been ordered to patrol the sea in search of pirates from northern Europe. He decided to capitalize on his popularity by setting himself up as another emperor, until he was murdered by his associate Allectus. Both episodes indicate the province's maturity and self-sufficiency. A panegyric to Constantius Chlorus who recovered Britain in 296 praised the island's resources and wealth; obviously the war of repossession had to be presented as having been worthwhile but there is likely to have been some truth or else Britain would indeed have been abandoned. The success of Carausius' enterprise gives no hint of domestic dissent at his seizure of power and he had fought off at least one earlier attempt to dislodge him.

Public buildings and temples

By the early third century the major towns of Roman Britain were equipped with the necessary public buildings to act as centres of local government. Urban inscriptions, rare at any time, are almost entirely unknown from this period and this has sometimes been taken as a mark of decline in the sense that no one was prepared, or able, to fund civic projects. But this is not quite as straightforward as it seems: a statue base at Caerwent was dedicated to the legate of the II legion at nearby Caerleon by the town council in the name of the *civitas* in 213 (see **102**). If they could afford to honour this man they could presumably have afforded other projects for which evidence has not survived. In other places, and London is the prime example, there is evidence for major building activity in the third century.

A number of milestones are known from the third century, for example one from Kenchester, a minor town in the *civitas* of the Dobunni ruled from Cirencester. The milestone is dated to *c*.283-4 in the name of the *civitas* and shows that the authorities were able to afford to maintain roads in a remote part of their sprawling canton. Even in the north at Brougham, in the *civitas* of the Carvetii, a milestone shows that in *c*.259-68 under the Gallic Empire this local authority was maintaining roads. However, the penal system provided for prisoners to be obliged to repair roads as part of their punishment, so this may not have been a particularly expensive activity.

Now of course roads are essentials and one might argue that these would be kept up come what may. But would it really have been necessary to embark on large numbers of extravagant urban public building projects at this time? The existing buildings would have served well enough unless they had been damaged by fire or structural collapse. They may have required maintenance and alterations, but as this would have affected the now almost universally absent superstructures it is hardly surprising that we have little evidence for this kind of work. It is even possible that they were still being built – it is important to remember that the very limited evidence that we do have, like the Wroxeter and Verulamium inscriptions, tells us nothing about what stage the work had progressed to. We need only to consider the medieval cathedrals to realize that the public buildings of Roman Britain could have been under intermittent construction for a very long time, like London's basilica (see Chapter 3).

There is some evidence for public projects going on very late in the second century, and into the third century. The forum fires at

Verulamium and Wroxeter in about 155 and 165 respectively were followed by repairs and reconstruction. The date ranges involved are not very precise but it does seem that there was no sign of gradual decline and work may have been in progress over many years. Canterbury was able to afford to rebuild its earth theatre in about 220. It was replaced with a monumental free-standing theatre of classical design associated with a temple precinct. Verulamium built two monumental arches on Watling Street to mark its earlier boundaries (see **7** and **26**). A further fire at Wroxeter in the late third century destroyed the forum but this time was not followed by reconstruction (the public baths appear to have become derelict at this time too).

Recent excavations in London and York have yielded traces of monumental buildings belonging to the third century. Mostly of a 'religious' nature, such as an arch in London thought to be an entrance to a temple precinct, and a temple in York, they indicate some sort of official cash injection which may have extended to secular buildings as well. A governor in mid-third-century London was able to finance the rebuilding of a temple to Isis which had collapsed (see **84**). Presumably this would have been difficult to justify if there had been more pressing requirements elsewhere. The York temple has been associated with the presence there in the early third century of the Emperor Septimius Severus and his family, between 208 and 211, during campaigns in Scotland. More specifically a priest called Lucius Viducius Placidus who worked as a pottery merchant recorded his own building of an arch and temple in York in 221 on a site granted by the town's councillors (Appendix 2).

Severus has also been tentatively linked with the London arch which may have acted as the entrance to a large complex of religious buildings in the south-west part of the town. The arch had been subsequently demolished and its blocks used in the town walls by the early fourth century, hence the lack of certainty about its function. Also, substantial alterations seem to have taken place on the 'palace' site to the east around the same time. London's riverside wharfs were extended by building new quays further out from the banks. Timber frames were erected on piles driven into the riverbed and the voids filled in with rubbish and rubble. This may have taken place as late as the mid-third century and suggests that commercial activity was far from dead, even if it was not as vibrant as it had once been.

Close to the probable site of the London arch the foundations of a major building have been identified on Peter's Hill. It has been attributed to the reign of the rebel emperor Allectus (293-6) on the grounds of tree-ring evidence from its timber piles. The site may have been intended as a prestigious palace for the short-lived regime. However, it is unwise to form such a precise historical association in the absence of a confirmatory inscription. Instead the timbers may have come from stocks of felled wood and the building may belong to the period following the rebellion. Even so it is an exceptionally interesting incidence of major construction work going on at a time when the basilica and forum of London seem to have been demolished. These two cases show that it is sometimes rash to make deductions about a town's fate based on the fate of individual structures. At Caerwent the basilica seems to have been repaired in the late third century – evidence for scaffolding has been found in the form of rows of post-holes, and the stylobates (column supports) appear to have been strengthened.

The basilica at Silchester has produced some very interesting evidence for the building being given over to metalworkers in the mid-third century. While this suggests that the administrative functions had been transferred elsewhere in the town (an enigma of its own) it hardly implies that there was a problem with manufacturing except a shortage of premises. So, together with the other cases mentioned, it seems a little difficult to conclude that there was some sort of widespread urban economic decline in the third century manifested by a lack of civic building projects. The situation may have differed from place to place.

The Silchester basilica raises the interesting question of whether the whole nature of local administration had changed in later Roman Britain, perhaps in itself diminishing the requirements for administrative buildings. This would help explain the abandonment of the forum at Wroxeter in the late third century, and the demolition of London's basilica and clearing of its forum somewhere around the same time. The so-called church which lies beside the forum at Silchester was probably built during the third century (see **87**). No evidence for religious activity was recovered and it is possible that small meetings of magistrates and councillors were transferred here. But other places, like Cirencester, have evidence for public buildings remaining in use throughout the fourth century. At the small town of Wall the *mansio* baths were reconstructed during this time (**41**).

41 *Isometric reconstruction of the baths at Wall in their final phase. The main rooms are indicated: H (hot rooms,* caldaria*); W (warm room,* tepidarium*); C (cold room,* frigidarium*); Ch (changing room,* apodyterium*). Note also the furnace (F) and the aqueduct outflow (A).*

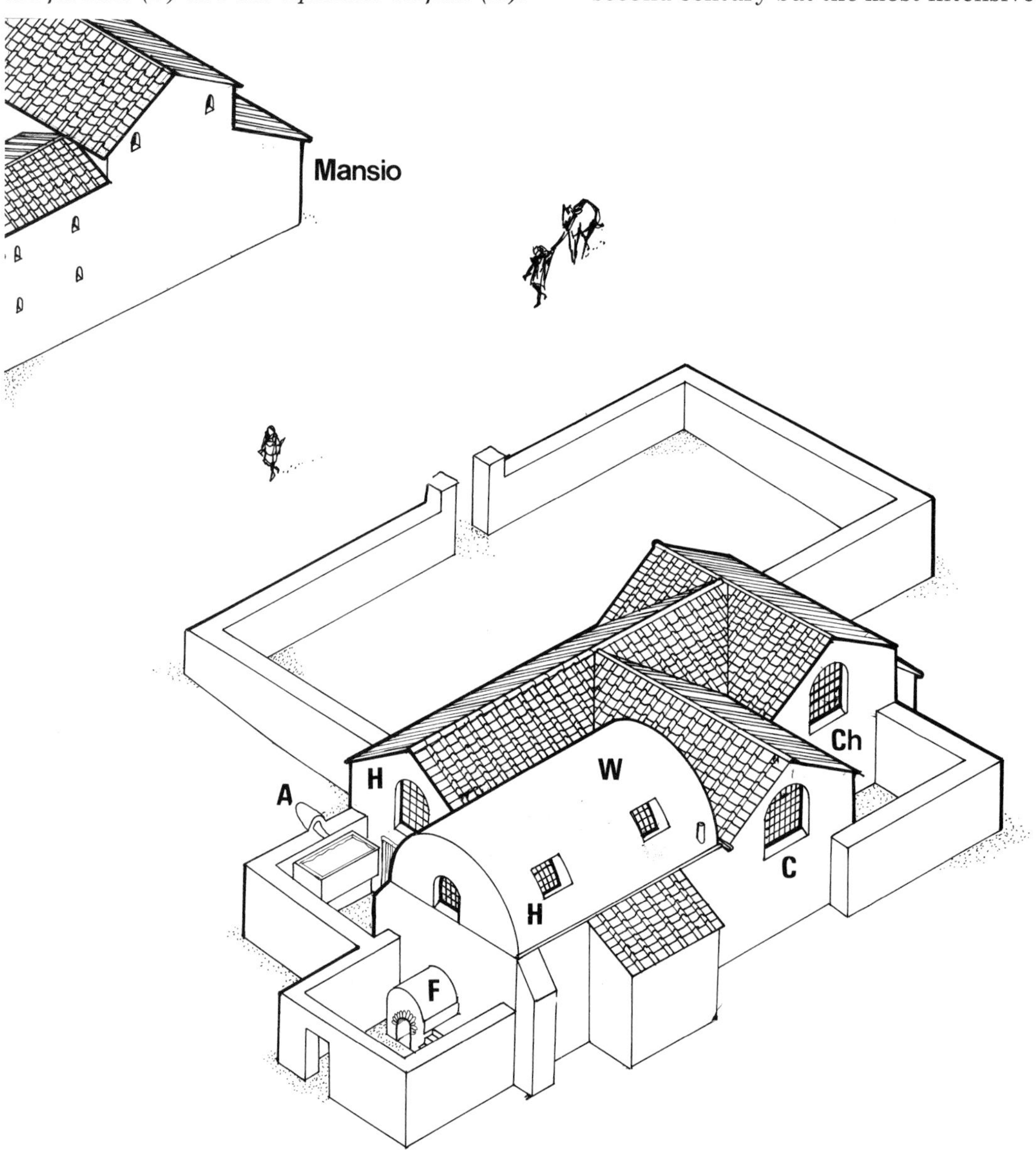

Defences

The question of economic decline and urban stagnation becomes even more complicated when we consider the appearance of circuits of earth and stone around the towns. The problem is to decide whether they were built out of necessity or choice, and when. The urban defences of Roman Britain form the most conspicuous visible remains of the province's towns – at Aldborough, Caerwent, Caistor-by-Norwich and Silchester, for example, almost nothing else can now be seen. Their history was a long one and goes back well into the second century but the most intensive phase of

their development was during the third century. A small number of towns like Colchester built defensive works in the first and second centuries. As a colony it was entitled to do so and so a free-standing masonry wall was erected in the early second century, incorporating the exceptional monumental west gate built around 100 (the Balkerne Gate, see **25**).

Verulamium was surrounded with a bank and ditch some time around the beginning of the second century, enclosing a smaller area than was subsequently enclosed by a masonry wall (see **7**). Apart from the other colonies of Gloucester and Lincoln (which utilized and added to elements of the legionary fortress defences, see **8**) the only other towns to have early defences were Silchester, Winchester and Chichester, where banks and ditches were put up in the first century. All three are thought to have been part of the client kingdom of the pro-Roman chief of the Regnenses, Cogidubnus. If so this would have exempted them from the legal restriction on defences for provincial towns which required the emperor's permission. The fact that Verulamium was apparently allowed to, emphasizes its special status as a *municipium*.

During the later part of the second century

42 *All that remains of the defences of the small town at Great Casterton, looking west. The wide ditch in the foreground was dug during the fourth century but the bank with a stone facing wall was erected around the beginning of the third century.*

many towns erected earthwork defences. This included the civitas capitals; Verulamium for example now enclosed a larger area than before, and a large number of the minor towns scattered about the province such as Alchester and Great Casterton (**42**). During most of the third century many towns proceeded to consolidate their defences by cutting into the outer face of the earth banks and building stone facing walls (**43, 44**). In some cases, including Verulamium's London gate and very probably the western gate of London (Newgate), these new walls incorporated stone gateways which had previously been a free-standing part of the earth defences. London's new walls also incorporated a small fort which had been built during the second century (**45**). Much later, around the latter part of the fourth century, some of these stone walls were augmented with external stone towers (**46, colour plate 13**) though at Verulamium these were part of the original scheme.

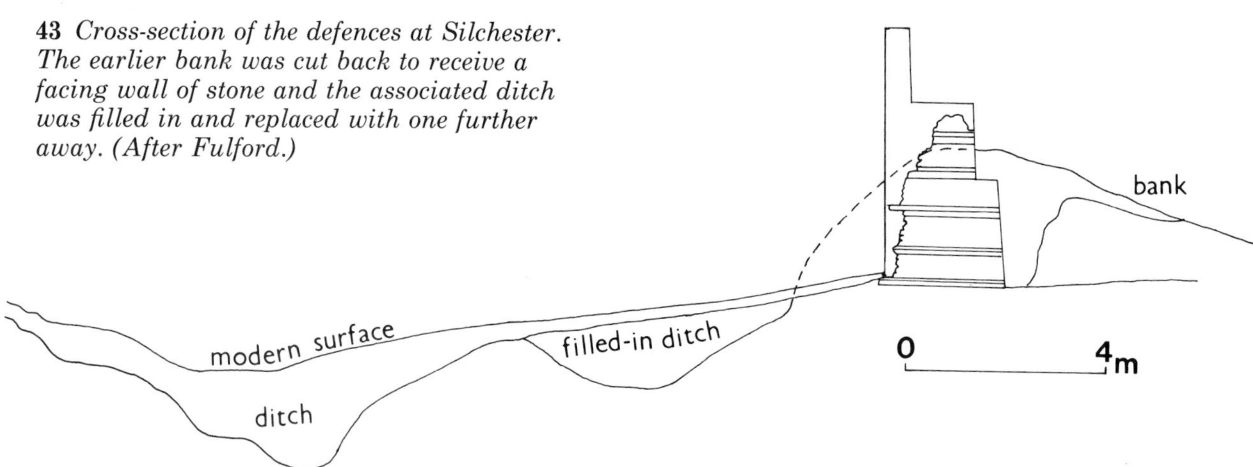

43 *Cross-section of the defences at Silchester. The earlier bank was cut back to receive a facing wall of stone and the associated ditch was filled in and replaced with one further away. (After Fulford.)*

The town gates formed impressive entrances to the towns though few survive in recognizable form today (**47** and **colour plates 3** and **12**).

These are the facts, derived exclusively from archaeological evidence. Defences are not a fruitful source of firm evidence and only at London and Verulamium have the recovery of coin hoards in a gate-tower and an interval tower given a *terminus ante quem* ('time before which') for the erection of the stone curtain. These are approximately 235 and 273 respectively, a range not contradicted by the less precise evidence of pottery and stray lost coins located in recent excavations on the defences at Silchester. Evidence for the late-second-century earth banks is dependent on the dating of features buried by the banks and waste material contained within them. Obviously the latest date of the latest object is the earliest date for the work, a rather vague and unreliable method. Apart from the fact that building these defences would have technically required the emperor's approval we know absolutely nothing else about them. No inscriptions have been found and no literary sources refer to them but we can assume that the towns (or exceptionally wealthy individuals) financed their own projects.

Debate about Romano-British urban defences has concentrated on trying to decide if the late-second-century earthworks and the third-century walls form part of a concerted programme in response to a centrally planned initiative. The truth is that while this is likely we do not know why, though it is clear that the work was monumental in scale. One possibility is that they were an attempt to meet a perceived threat – the forts at Reculver and Brancaster have already been mentioned. The problem with this solution is that we have no knowledge of any particular crisis which can be easily linked to the new walls, except the brief and unsuccessful attempt by the governor Clodius Albinus to become emperor between 193 and 197, but this is much too short-lived an event for a plausible association. He is unlikely to have expended resources on a protracted project which would have only had any value had he been forced to fall back on Britain.

44 *View of the defences at Silchester today in the south-east sector. The facing stones have been robbed but the levelling courses of tiles can be seen. The church (left of centre) lies within the town walls on the site of three temples.*

45 *The south-west corner of the second century fort in London. The fort was incorporated into the third century defences and the junction can be seen in the upper left part of the picture where the much thicker town wall abuts the fort's curved corner (arrowed). Compare with the London plan (see* **15***).*

An alternative scenario is that defences were a retrospective precaution following disturbances on the northern frontier around 184. In most cases the new defences were erected over long periods of time and enclosed a space which contained the most concentrated area of settlement (there were exceptions like Caistor-by-Norwich but the contraction here is merely further evidence for the town's generally retarded development). At Verulamium the new earthworks at this time almost doubled the size of the town and were eventually abandoned, the third-century stone walls only following their alignment in part. The fact that here there was money and time for monumental stone gateways, and triumphal arches to mark the town's earlier limits, hardly smacks of a crisis, military or economic.

London's early-third-century landward walls are particularly difficult to reconcile with a crisis. Here the riverfront formed something like a third of the town limits, yet remained unprotected for the meantime (see **15**). The

46 (Above) *The south wall of the third century defences at Caerwent, the best-preserved urban defences of any Roman town in Britain. The projecting bastions were built at a later date, probably during the fourth century.*

47 *Lincoln's south-west gate. Built in the fourth century as a simple archway it was subsequently re-modelled with two projecting towers. The towers were built partly out of re-used stonework and a large carved piece can be seen in the plinth. It may have come from a demolished temple or other public building, or was simply an odd piece which happened to be available following an earlier site clearing.*

landward wall had neat rows of squared facing stones broken by carefully laid levelling courses of tiles, surely not the product of a hasty attempt to protect the town. It enclosed virtually all the area known to have been settled and incorporated the second-century fort. The public building works now known to have been going on in London around this time reinforce the idea that carefully considered projects were under way.

Yet towards the end of the third century we find that a massive wall was erected on the riverfront, possibly augmented by watchtowers downriver looking out over the Thames (one has been located at Shadwell 1·2 km (¾ mile) east of the town defences). There are at least two possible reasons: the Saxon Shore fort system appears to have been in operation to defend the south-eastern coasts from raiders and London would have been susceptible with its exceptional frontage on a major tidal river; and secondly London fell to Constantius Chlorus in 296 during recovery of the province after the rule of Carausius and Allectus, either of whom may have seen fit swiftly to provide London with more defences in an effort to create a stronghold.

There were two distinct styles of construction used in the new London riverside wall. The eastern part, attributed on dendrochronological evidence from the foundation piles to the late third century, seems to have been built in a competent manner but only a small part has been located. The western part, of which much more is known, was entirely different to the earlier landward wall, having elementary foundations of blocks and making much use of stone taken from demolished buildings of second- and third-century date. We do not know whether they were demolished expressly for this purpose but it seems likely. It is noticeable that towns in Gaul seem to have remained unwalled until after a massive raid across the Rhine by the Alamanni (a German tribe) in 276. Subsequently walls were built but this usually involved significant contraction of the settled area, and the extensive reuse of masonry from demolished buildings. What all this means is that in London we have an instance of a late riverside wall which bears the hallmarks of being a response to some critical situation, whereas the main sequence of earlier town walls, including London's landward wall, seem to be the product of a careful and leisurely programme.

This still does not explain the main programme of defences. It would have been responsible for diverting resources which might otherwise have been spent on building more numerous and luxurious public buildings. In other words it seems that a choice was made, permission was sought to go ahead and this was duly granted. Possible reasons may have been a desire to impress, to tax the coming and going of goods more easily and control land rents more effectively, or even to restrict access to towns in order to keep undesirable elements out. It may not be coincidence that the walled towns of the third and fourth centuries seem to have been dominated by large, well-appointed town-houses, with a virtual absence of the congested artisan and commercial quarters so characteristic of the earlier period.

We know so little about what went on in Roman Britain at the time in terms of how the curial classes controlled their position and the politics of town management that we do need to consider all of these as plausible reasons for choosing to concentrate on walls rather than buildings. It may have simply been a regional custom, in the sense that building impressive defences was perhaps the Romano-British way, and needs no more profound explanation. There is also the possibility that it was considered necessary for town governments to be seen to be spending accumulated reserves on projects intended for the public good. In the absence of any confirmatory evidence we will have to content ourselves with recognizing a range of possibilities.

Houses

The stone houses built in the second century in many of the towns would have had long lives, even if they were substantially altered. So it is hardly surprising that there is less evidence for house building in the third and fourth centuries for the simple reason that demand would have diminished closer to replacement levels once the housing stock had been built up. The house known as Building XXVIII.1 at Verulamium seems to have been built around the beginning of the third century on a site abandoned after the 155 fire. Occupation layers from the basement contained coins running right up to around the mid-fourth century which suggests that the house was in use until at least then and very probably later (see **39**). A house in Lower Thames Street in

London with its own substantial bath-house (possibly run as a business) seems to have been built in the late second century and was still in use up to two hundred years later.

There appears to have been quite a dramatic decline in the number of sites in London that were occupied as dwellings from the later second century on. New houses were larger but fewer and many sites seem to have fallen vacant with a layer of dark earth, possibly agricultural, burying them. This picture could be partly due to a reduction in the supply of coinage, a decline in imported datable pottery, and destruction of upper Roman layers during the medieval period. All of these could combine to make it hard for archaeologists to recognize occupation from the later second century on. However, it is difficult to avoid concluding that there may have been a change in the type of town London was, reflected in other major towns.

Perhaps London had become a kind of garden city lived in by the well-to-do who liked the peace and quiet but also the prestige of being in the capital, instead of other busier commercial centres. Certainly there is evidence that the provincial economy was becoming more self-contained during the third century, and one in which a major port would have had less of a role to play. This transition is often perceived as representing some kind of urban failure whereas instead, if it did occur, it is just as arguably evidence for provincial maturity and self-sufficiency no longer dependent on massive imports. Also, as we saw in Chapter 3, house ownership was a complex matter in the Roman world. Just because there were now large houses more widely spaced need not necessarily mean that London's population had radically declined even if the nature of the town had changed. The construction work involved in the new public buildings and defences would have involved large numbers of workers. In any case excavations on the wharfs have shown that commercial activities were continuing, though at a reduced level, with imported pottery still arriving at quayside warehouses in the mid-third century.

If the dark earth in London was due to the farming within the town walls we have no actual evidence for it, but two fourth-century houses (*Insula* XII.1/2) in Cirencester were connected by a wall and had a number of associated structures including a possible barn (**48**). Nothing had ever been built on the site before and as the layout resembles a villa it has been suggested that this was a farm perhaps working land immediately outside the town walls. There is also evidence for other trades in late towns, working from houses rather than shops. A fourth-century house in Dorchester at Colliton Park seems to have had two separate components. The north wing had a mosaic in almost every room while the south wing seems to have been designed around a trade which involved the removal of water, perhaps fulling (**49**, **50**), suggesting a thriving local cloth trade.

Conclusion

So the Romano-British towns of the third century and, as we shall see later during the fourth century also, present us with a complicated and variable picture which is difficult to interpret. It does seem, however, that we cannot necessarily conclude that the whole province and its towns were experiencing a downturn in their fortunes. Stagnation and depression are terms often used to describe the period but it is just as reasonable to interpret what we see as stabilization and transition. London shows this in particular, while a change in function for a town's basilica may have been no more than a matter of local conditions and convenience. A failure to rebuild one burnt down is as likely to have been linked to local quarrels about who was going to pay for it, leading to civic inertia, as it is to have resulted from impoverished civic finances.

There has always been a tendency to start with the observation that Roman town life more or less disappeared during the fifth century and work backwards, looking for signs of gradual deterioration from up to two hundred years or more earlier. The truth is that conditions in the fifth century were a great deal different to anything that had gone before. Conditions in the third and fourth centuries may have been different to those in the second century but the towns were still functioning within the unifying and stabilizing influence of the Roman world. Trapped within the vagaries of archaeological evidence it is very easy to make generalizations which both exaggerate trends and ignore the probability that much of what we see was actually caused by the actions and decisions (perhaps misguided) of a small number of powerful people in each town. During the first and second centuries the Roman government would have been more influential

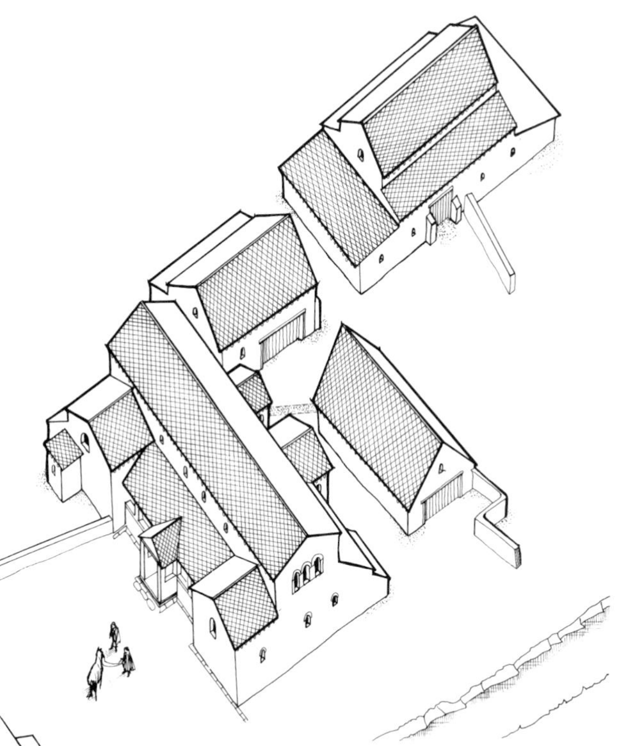

48 *Reconstructed axonometric view of a house in Cirencester (*Insula *XII.2). This building, closely associated with another nearby, was built in a secluded virgin part of the town between a river and the defences during the latter half of the fourth century (see* **5***). Excavation produced traces of metalworking and weaving tools and this along with the outbuildings has led to the suggestion that this was a farm, perhaps working land outside the walls.*

49 *Plan of a fourth-century house in Colliton Park, Dorchester, Dorset. There were two separate wings, one of which was apparently residential with a number of mosaic floors (M), while the other seems to have been concerned with a trade, perhaps fulling and dyeing (provision had been made for water drainage from floors). (After Selby.)*

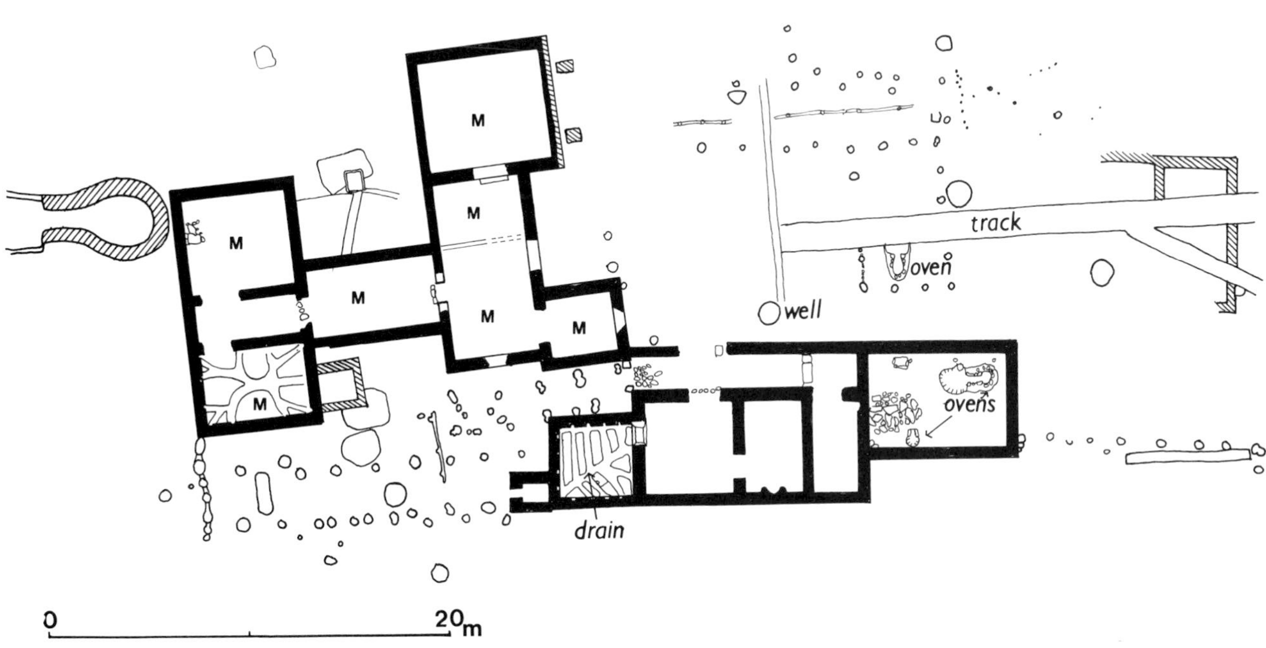

because the province was being built up. Official policy was being instituted in all the towns which is why we see a broadly similar pattern of development. Subsequently, as the province became more self-sufficient, and especially during the periods of independence, members of local town governments are likely to have had a more individual and perhaps idiosyncratic influence on a town's development.

It is of course a matter for infinite regret that we cannot know who these people were, but recognizing this possibility goes some way to explaining why we see so many different kinds of urban histories developing out of what was originally a generally similar set of beginnings. Assuming that localized instances of change necessarily reflect a general and protracted pattern of decline may be entirely wrong. Our inability to resolve this kind of problem from the archaeological record is one of the unpalatable realities of studying the period.

50 *View of the remains of the Dorchester house as it appears today (see* **49***).*

5

Trade, industry and urban economies

Introduction

The population of a town with a thriving economy usually expands and also enjoys an increased standard of living, while a town with an unhealthy economy experiences the opposite. All towns will tend to veer towards one or the other at different times. As we saw in the last chapter Romano-British towns are sometimes pictured as initially successful before going through a phase of stagnation and then declining, in one case being described as 'administrative villages', prior to being abandoned during the fifth century. But in an economic sense the evidence for this is non-existent apart from a reduction in imports, and the archaeological evidence for decline is at best ambiguous and prone to local variation.

Romano-British towns are a special case because there were none before 43. There is a difference between evidence for a town growing and expanding during a good period, and being built from scratch. Major building works in civitas capitals would take place in their early years because otherwise the towns would not have been able to function. Once built, only routine maintenance would be required unless they were burnt down. But, as the buildings no longer exist, apart from footings and foundations, we have no evidence for sustained investment of this kind unless an inscription is found recording repairs or occasional instances like the basilica at Caerwent. At the other end of the time scale Romano-British towns cannot be fairly regarded as 'failures' because, by and large, they did not survive as towns beyond the mid-fifth century. The whole basis of society had altered into one in which towns as Romano-British markets and administrative centres had no role to play.

Towns represented a 'surplus' because for every town dweller who was not working on the land (though some would have been) there would have been several people (at least) producing enough food on the land to support such a town dweller. This has only ceased to be true in the modern machine age. We don't know what that 'surplus' actually meant because we have no idea of prices related to earnings and the relative wealth of town and rural dwellers as a share of the 'Gross Romano-British National Product'. If we consider the case of the Roman army in Britain we can be sure that it would have taken all that it required, more or less regardless of how that left the farmers. In the same way it may be that towns existed as much as a result of coercion through local taxation in kind as the purchasing power of cash. Equally we have no idea of what the wealthy part of the community 'cost' the poor – in the nineteenth century for example this inequality was much more pronounced than it is now.

The distribution of towns certainly seems to reflect this crucial dependence on the availability of surplus food. A map of Romano-British towns (see **1**) shows that towns were distributed widely in the central and southern parts of the province. It can hardly be coincidence that this was also the part which was the most agriculturally fertile, or in economic terms, the least marginal. Here the land was generally good enough to allow the regular production of a surplus. In the north, west and extreme south-west this was not so true, though these areas were more productive than was once thought. Quite apart from that, these more remote areas were relatively unstable and while isolated villa estates existed, like Llantwit

Major in Wales or close to Durham in the north-east, nothing matched the density of rural settlement found in, say, the Mendips and Cotswolds (see **76**).

The villa estates reached their greatest density in the fourth century and many show that they earned sufficient surpluses to pay for the installation of mosaics and other luxury items at this time. Their clustering around major routes and towns makes it difficult to avoid the conclusion that their principal markets were urban populations (see **76**). Yet this is at a time when many archaeologists argue that towns had diminished populations with a very reduced level of commercial activity; an activity which would normally be considered necessary to pay for rural food production. These contradictions show how difficult the problem is for us to understand.

Clearly, as the towns were built and existed throughout the period they served some sort of purpose, and their populations were fed. The archaeological evidence is the only possible source of information but it provides us with instances and examples, not secure foundations for generalizations. It also, of course, necessarily tends to be confined to non-perishables, making the marketing of the most fundamental of all resources, food, largely a mystery. One exceptional instance has been found in London where a room in a building destroyed about the time of the Boudican Revolt had been used to store grain. On analysis the grain was found to have come from a country bordering the Mediterranean or in the Near East.

Goods in substantial quantities were shipped across from the continent during the first and second centuries. London has produced the largest amount of evidence but much is paralleled in the other significant towns like Colchester, Cirencester, Silchester and Verulamium. These trade routes were already functioning before the Roman invasion though for the benefit of a smaller part of the population. Most of the evidence for this survives in the form of ceramics, particularly fine wares and *amphorae*, deposited in wealthy graves. These routes extended as far as Italy as early as the mid-second century BC.

By the late first century BC a number of *oppida* in south-eastern Britain were receiving a wide range of goods from a number of continental and Mediterranean sources. So in some respects Romano-British trade and commercial activity was an extension of a marketing infrastructure which was already established and into which the new towns were absorbed. As the period progressed this cross-Channel trade became initially more extensive with what seems to have been a one-way trade in manufactured goods to Britain paid for by the exports of raw materials, though by the fourth century the province appears to have become much more self-sufficient in most respects. In economic terms the fourth century presents archaeologists and historians with enormous problems in trying to understand what happened to urban economies; some of the problems are explored in Chapter 7.

Population

As individuals the town dwellers of Roman Britain are only known to us through *graffiti* (**51** and see **67**) and tombstones (see **91**). While we can assume that the urban population was one which largely depended on the surplus agricultural production of the rural population we have no records of either the absolute or relative numbers of either. The relative numbers would be of more value because this would provide a basis for assessing the efficiency of the economy. As far as towns are concerned we have Tacitus' claim that 70,000 people died at London, Colchester, Verulamium and possibly other undefended settlements in the area during the Boudican Revolt. Even if he (or his source) was exaggerating we have no means of correcting him apart from looking at the sort of population the medieval towns and cities could support. In general these seem to range from about 1500 up to something in between 5000 and 10,000, no doubt varying according to the season and over the years.

It is possible that given the marginally greater likelihood of a Romano-British town having a better water-supply and drainage, the ancient populations could have been higher because the death-rate would have been a little lower. Unfortunately there is no reliable data which would allow an accurate figure for life expectancy in Romano-British towns to be assessed. Statistical models based on modern pre-industrial societies do provide a means of calculating a theoretical urban population for the province and these have been used to suggest a figure of around 240,000 plus or minus about 50,000. A recent estimate of about 3·3 million for the rural population is based on the

1 Wroxeter from the air as it may have appeared sometime during the third century, looking south. The view is based on excavation evidence and aerial photography. The town-centre is dominated by the forum and baths complex (see colour plate 2). (Ivan Lapper; English Heritage.)

2 Wroxeter town-centre from the air showing the second-century baths complex to the left with its series of vaulted chambers and covered exercise hall, and to the right the forum and basilica. (Ivan Lapper; English Heritage.)

3 Lincoln's third-century north gate as it appears today. The large arch was for wheeled traffic, the small for foot. The original gate would have had another pair of arches.

4 Verulamium from the air looking north-west across the first-century forum and basilica. In the distance the theatre can be seen. (The author.)

5 *(Above)* The amphitheatre at Cirencester looking north-east across the arena towards the town. Built from earth banks with timber, and subsequently stone, revetments the building remained in use throughout the Roman period.

6 *(Right)* Wroxeter *palaestra* (exercise hall) of the second-century baths complex. Part of the side wall survives today (colour plate 7). (Ivan Lapper; English Heritage.)

7 Wroxeter baths looking north across the bath suite towards the 'Old Work' which formed part of the south wall of the exercise hall. See also **34.**

8 Leicester baths looking across the baths suite towards the 'Jewry Wall' which formed part of the exercise hall. See also **33.**

9 *(Right)* Mosaic depicting Autumn *(Pomona)* from a house in Dyer Street, Cirencester. The mosaic was laid in the late second century and is an exceptional example of mosaic art in Roman Britain. It was clumsily repaired at a later date. (Gloucestershire Museums Service.)

10 *(Below)* The central part of the 'Hare Mosaic' from a house in Beeches Road, Cirencester. Laid in the fourth century.

11 *(Left)* Reconstructed wall-painting (by N. Davey) from a second-century house at Verulamium (*Insula* XXI.2). The division into three horizontal zones was a standard feature of Roman wall-painting. (British Museum.)

12 *(Below)* South gate of Caerwent from within the town. The gate was probably built during the late second or early third century at the same time as the stone walls. It was subsequently blocked up and the filling has preserved part of the arch. Note the drain at the bottom.

13 *(Above)* Caerwent's south wall from the south. The north and south walls had bastions added to them in the fourth century and several can be seen here. The stone curtain is in a remarkable state of preservation and retains many of its facing stones.

14 *(Right)* Sherd of unused decorated samian ware from the Roman foreshore at Billingsgate, London. The bowl was made at the beginning of the second century in central southern France by a potter called Drusus and was probably broken *en route*, or in a warehouse by the wharfs.

15 *(Left)* The *vicus* outside the fort of Vindolanda in Northumberland. This straggling settlement was typical of numerous other examples which grew up around a fort and developed into small towns. (English Heritage.)

16 *(Below)* Bath temple precinct as it may have appeared in the fourth century looking past the altar towards the temple of Sulis-Minerva. (The Author.)

51 *Elegantly incised graffito on a flagon from Dorchester, Dorset reading Nutricis, meaning '[property of] Nutricis'. (After Tomlin.)*

density of known sites and together with an army of about 125,000 (including dependants) suggests a total population of somewhat under 4 million. It therefore took something like thirteen or fourteen members of the rural population to support a town dweller. By way of comparison we can take the Domesday data for 1086 which suggests a population of about 2 million, but it was distributed very differently (south Sussex, south-east Kent and central East Anglia being especially conspicuous concentrations). Cemetery evidence (see Chapter 6) has provided perplexing evidence for a significant bias towards adult males in the urban population (see below, pp. 117-18).

It would be wrong to assume that people who lived in Romano-British towns always lived there, and had no interests in the countryside, and that therefore rural and urban populations were two exclusive groups. The lack of villas very close to major towns has already been commented on in Chapter 3 and this suggests that some town dwellers were farming land outside their settlements. Some villas were probably owned by people who lived in the countryside during the summer and in a town during the winter, employing staff to look after each property while they were away. The villa at Lullingstone in Kent was a modest but well-appointed establishment in a charming location which would have probably been inadequate for protracted stays. The recovery of two marble busts of obviously cultivated individuals, and carved in the late second century, has led to the plausible suggestion that the house was a country home of a man involved in provincial administration in London, which is less than a day's journey away. A writing tablet bearing a text recording a dispute over the ownership of a tract of land somewhere in Kent in 118 has been discovered recently in London. A man called Lucius Iulius Betucus was claiming that the land, *in civitate Cantiacorum*, was his. Of course he may have come to London to sort out the dispute but equally he may have been one of many Roman Londoners who also owned rural estates.

Communications

A town needs to be supplied with food and goods which are not manufactured locally. In turn it needs to supply its own products effectively. Verulamium grew up around a road which was one of the first features of Roman life to appear in the valley of the Ver. London was the product of its location and communications. Caistor-by-Norwich was a civitas capital built in what amounted to a regional dead-end and therefore could not benefit from through-traffic arriving from a number of different directions. This is almost certainly one reason for its modest development. We do not know the extent to which Roman roads were built along existing trackways, though this certainly occurred. As many towns, particularly the civitas capitals, lay on or close to the sites of native settlements it may well be that much of what passes for a Roman system of communications was actually pre-Roman.

So Roman towns may have been capitalizing on existing trade routes and patterns of local markets. This helps to explain why towns that grew up around early forts sited close to native settlements tended to remain in existence once the fort was given up, instead of their populations following the soldiers. As such they were an adaptation of what was already there, with the forts providing an impetus to move locally because they provided security as well as customers. People are much more likely to come to trade in a place used for generations, than to accept new routes and new markets imposed by a coercive authority.

Markets in towns

Although we know about buildings which acted as markets, mainly the forum and the *macellum*, it is not surprising that we know almost nothing about the markets themselves. A rare instance is the forum at Wroxeter which was wrecked by a disastrous fire during the second half of the second century (**52**). Subsequent repair work buried the shattered remnants of temporary stalls in the portico where they had fallen (**53**). Some of the non-perishable stock was recovered during excavations. This included a substantial quantity of samian ware from East and Central Gaul, both plain and decorated, mixing bowls (*mortaria*) manufactured in Britain and whetstones.

Imported ceramics

We know that shipping merchants called *negotiatores cretarii* (literally 'pot dealers') existed, like Lucius Viducius Placidus from Rouen who probably shipped goods from northern Europe to York in the early third century. We might imagine that the Wroxeter stall owner had bought his samian from someone like him. Much of the large quantity of samian excavated along the riverfront in London appears to be in 'as new' condition, which suggests (not

52 *Column bases from the portico of the forum at Wroxeter which was damaged during a disastrous fire in the late second century. Although it was repaired it seems to have been disused by the fourth century.*

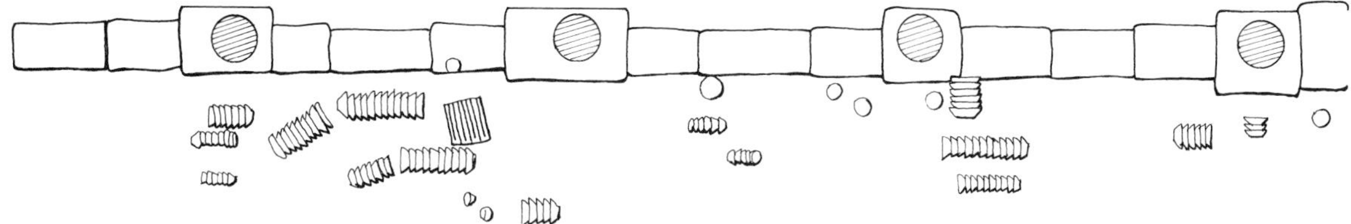

53 *Plan of the Wroxeter forum colonnade showing the stacks of samian bowls where they had fallen during the late-second-century fire. (After Atkinson.)*

surprisingly) that this was one of the major ports of entry for the commodity. At least two late-second-century ships bringing samian into London seem to have been wrecked on the Pudding Pan Rock of Whitstable in Kent.

Samian is found almost everywhere in first- and second-century Roman deposits in western Europe (**54**, **55**, **colour plate 14**); *amphorae* were almost as common in towns and are found over a longer period of time and were probably distributed in a similar way. The amphora was the universal method in the ancient world of storing foodstuffs and liquids for long-distance transportation. They were usually cylindrical with a cone-shaped terminal or spherical in shape, and in both cases had necks and rims and a pair of handles. The most common sources for those found in Roman Britain were southern Spain, southern Gaul and Italy and they generally contained (on the evidence of painted inscriptions) varieties of fish products, wine, or oils (**56**). An example from Spain found recently in London records the contents as being 250 measures of green olives transported by a merchant, whose name is abbreviated to G.L.A.,

54 *Samian Form 29 bowl, made in southern Gaul about 55-70 by the potter Celadus. Samian was manufactured in Gaul during the first and second centuries* AD *and is a common find on town sites, sometimes being found in large concentrations where warehouses or shops have been destroyed. (British Museum.)*

56 *(*Below*) The most important varieties of amphora:* a *southern Spain, contents usually olive-oil, first to third centuries;* b *also Spain but first century and usually containing fish sauce;* c *Gaul, containing wine, first and second centuries;* d *Gaul, for liquids, first century;* e *Italy, containing wine, first century*

55 *(*Above*) Samian Form 37 bowl made in central Gaul in the mid-second century by the potter Casurius. See also* **54**. *(British Museum.)*

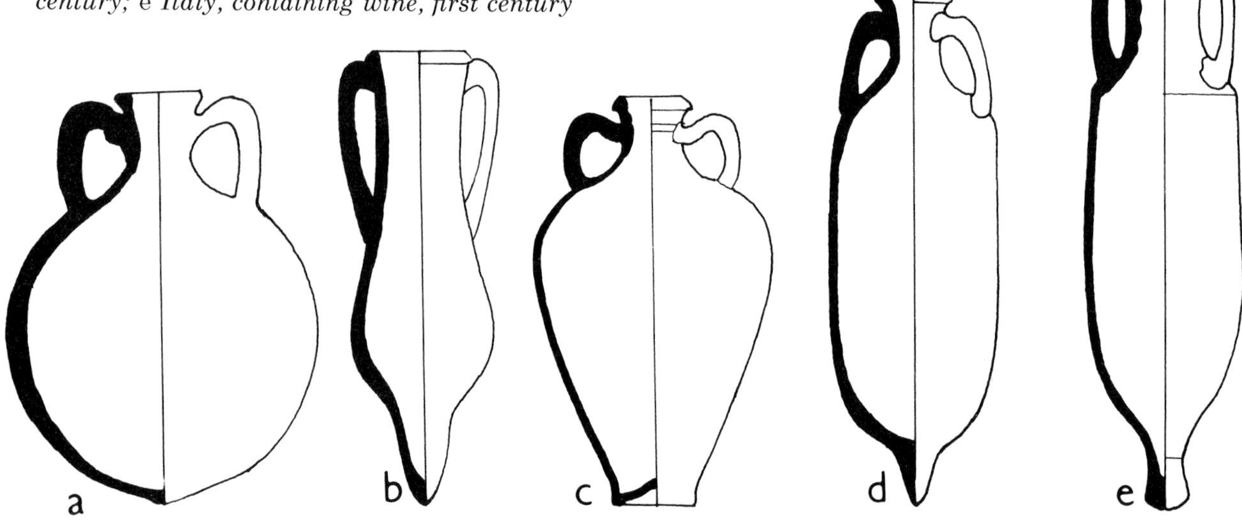

on behalf of someone called Avernus who may have been the owner. Some were still being imported during the fourth and fifth centuries from as far away as Palestine.

There were other sources of imported ceramic goods, for example the cups and beakers manufactured in the Cologne area (**57**), Italian and Gaulish oil-lamps (**58**), and the pipe-clay 'Venus' figurines from Gaul or Germany (**59**). Together with the samian and amphorae they form an enormous body of evidence from the port of Roman London for the massive levels of trade during the first and second centuries. Other evidence such as the Black Burnished kitchen ware industries of Dorset and the Thames estuary shows that within the province at this time some goods were being moved considerable distances. The army on the northern frontier seems to have been the main source of demand, and indeed may have provided the main impetus for some continental goods arriving via the towns before being shipped north and westwards during the first and second centuries.

During the third and fourth centuries the character of trade appears to have altered

57 *Some of the most important types of good quality pottery (known as 'fine wares'):* a *glazed flagon made in Gaul between 43 and 70;* b *and* c *cup and beaker made in the same area as some samian ware during the mid-second century but with a black slip;* d *beaker made in Cologne, Germany in the late first and second century (similar products were made in the Nene Valley near Water Newton);* e *beaker made in Trier with a slogan 'DA MERVUM' which means 'Give me more wine';* f *flagon made in the Verulamium area about 70-130;* g *flagon made in the Verulamium area about 120-160.*

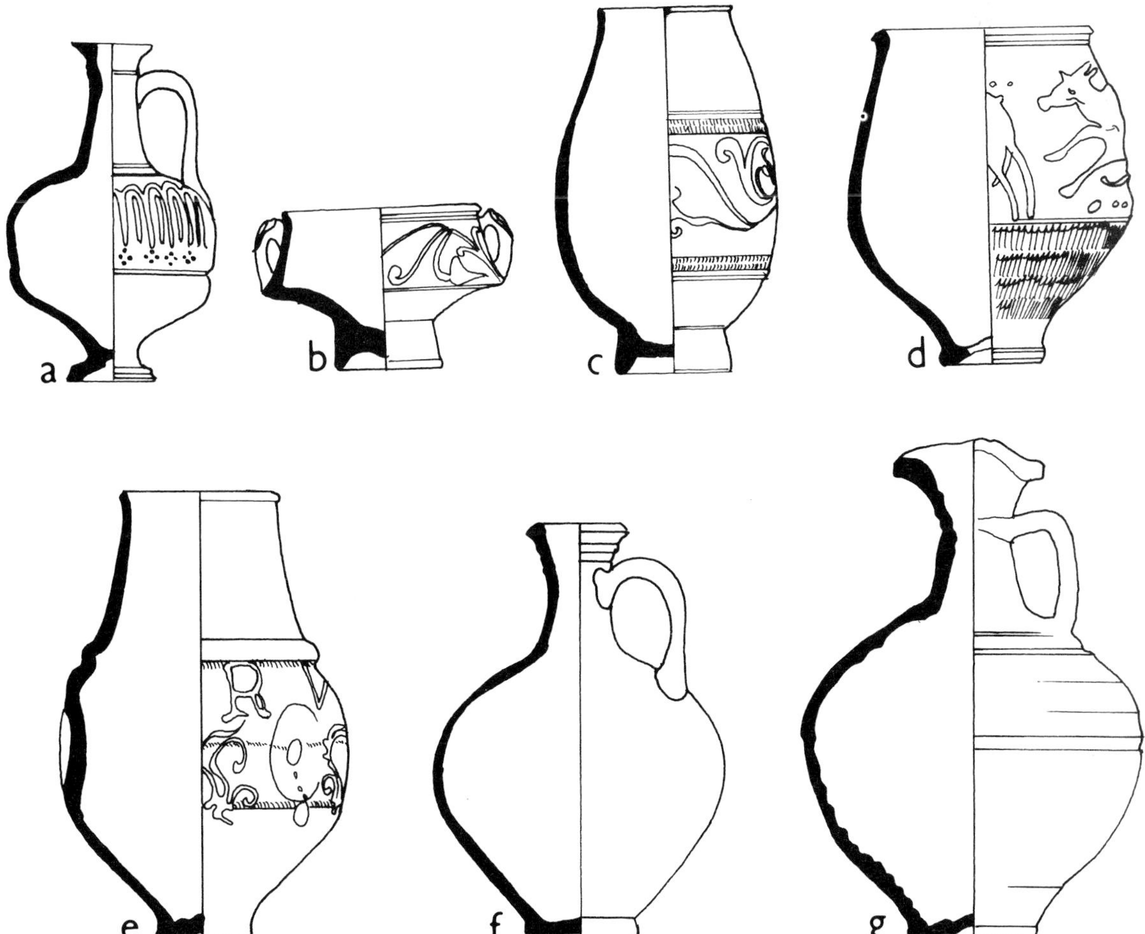

58 *Oil-lamps, both first century types, which were imported into Roman Britain from Italy and Gaul. The example on the left is plain but the right-hand one has a design on the* discus *(the lamp centre) depicting a rural animal scene. Lamps burnt olive-oil which was imported in* amphorae *and because of the expense of transporting the oil the lamps are only commonly found in towns or forts (see* **56***). (Lengths 94 and 114 mm (4 and $4\frac{1}{2}$ in).)*

radically in favour of 'home industries', reflected in a reduction in the amount of imported ceramics recovered from London's wharfs. Most fine wares in use in Roman Britain at this time were made in the Nene Valley (**60**) and Oxfordshire with lesser sources in the New Forest and in the north at Crambeck. These were moved widely around the province showing that goods could be dispersed to almost anywhere, though there is almost invariably a bias in favour of towns which were easily accessible. The Oxford potteries for example had easy access to London down the Thames, whilst the New Forest industries did not and this is reflected in the distribution pattern. The kitchen ware potteries at Alice Holt near Farnham came to dominate the market for cheaper pottery in the south whilst Crambeck took a similar role in the north.

59 *Part of a moulded white 'pipe-clay' female figurine made in Gaul and imported into Britain (a number were found in quayside debris in London). The figure is sometimes described as Venus but may have been a more regional fertility deity. (Height when complete about 15 cm (6 in).)*

Coinage

Roman coins are common finds in Britain so we tend to assume that the Romano-British economy relied on them as a medium of exchange. Buried hoards of coins only show that they were regarded as a convenient means of storing wealth (**61**). Instead we have to rely on coins which appear to have been lost in the normal day-to-day mêlée of minor urban transactions. There are plenty of these but they present an archaeologist with many difficulties. Sometimes they are hard to identify, but more important is trying to decide what they can tell

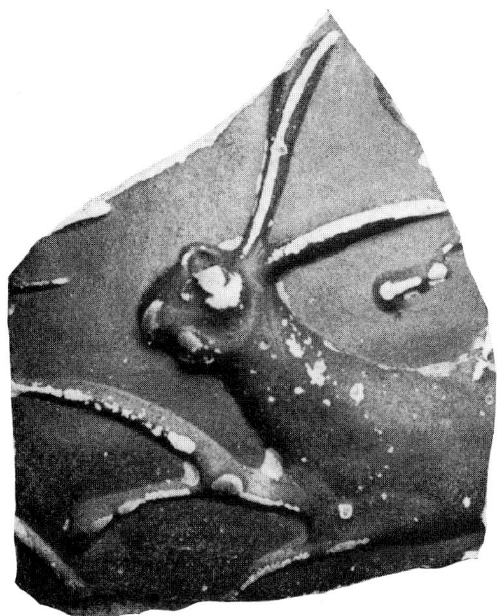

60 *Sherd from a beaker made in the Nene Valley (or possibly the Rhineland) in the late second or early third century, decorated with an animal scene in a style known as* barbotine *(liquid clay trailed onto the vessel). From London.*

61 *Silver* antoninianus *of Gordian III (238-44), said to be from the Dorchester South Street hoard of 1933 when nearly 21,000 silver coins dating between 193 and 260 were found in a pot. The hoard, deposited probably between 265 and 285, was almost certainly the result of saving relatively good metal at a time when base metal versions of the same denomination were being issued (see* **65***). The reverse depicts a figure of Laetitia (Joy). Actual diameter 25 mm.*

us about how coins were used in towns.

Most recent studies have concentrated on trying to build up a statistical base and so far these have shown that coins were supplied very erratically. As a result the coins of some reigns, for example Vespasian (69-79), Domitian (81-96) and Hadrian (117-38), are found significantly more frequently than others. Because this phenomenon is reflected in finds of coins in towns almost everywhere it is unlikely that there was an upsurge of economic activity at these times. Rather, it means that because there were more of these coins they stayed in circulation longer, had a greater chance of eventually being lost and therefore obviously will feature more frequently as finds. At times of poor supply there were occasional outbreaks of local copying of coins, similar to the 'token' coinage of the late eighteenth century which was a response by local firms to a shortage of official copper coins. In Roman Britain the main periods of such activity were between about 260 and 286, and on and off throughout the fourth century. Together with the sustained use of worn issues that derived from times of good supply, they imply that coinage was regarded as a vital component of Romano-British urban commerce.

A comprehensive survey of coins found in the sacred spring at Bath has shown that there were several low denomination coin issues, peculiar to Britain both in terms of type and date. Amongst these are the 'Britannia' *as* of Antoninus Pius of 154 and an *as* of Marcus Aurelius as emperor designate (heir apparent) for the same year (**62**) both of which are relatively common in Britain but rare elsewhere. River spoil at Billingsgate in London contained numerous coins of many dates but there was a particular group issued in the middle years of Domitian's reign. A number appeared to have

62 *(Above) Bronze* 'as' *of Marcus Aurelius as emperor designate, struck in the year 154 during the reign of Antoninus Pius (138-61), and of an issue only usually found in Britain. The reverse depicts a figure of Mars carrying a spear. (Actual diameter 24 mm (1 in).)*

63 *(Below) A pair of bronze* asses *of Domitian for the year 86, struck at the mint of Rome. The coins were struck from the same dies and probably represent part of a consignment shipped directly to London for provincial dispersal. The reverses depict Minerva carrying scales. (Actual diameter 26 mm (1 in).)*

been in 'as struck' condition, and several of these were from the same dies (**63**). They may represent a consignment of coinage shipped direct from the mint in Rome for official dispersal in London. This suggests not only that low value coins were distributed locally and tended to circulate locally but also supports the idea that supply was intermittent.

Some of the major Romano-British towns served as mints. In the western half of the Empire the principal source of coins was Rome until the middle of the third century when it became increasingly common for the government to issue coin regularly from other major cities like Lyons and Milan. In 286 the commander of the Romano-British fleet, Carausius, took power in Britain and a small part of northern Gaul. In order to help consolidate and advertise his power he issued coins, some of which carried mintmarks. Initially he seems to have contented himself with over-striking earlier coins with his image. This may only have been for a few weeks and soon new coins were being produced. The mintmark M L undoubtedly stands for *Moneta Londinii*, 'the Mint of London'. The mintmark C, or occasionally CL, may stand for a number of places including Colchester (*CamuLodunum*) and Gloucester (*GLevum*) or even Silchester (*CaLleva*). Both the former mints were kept open by Carausius' murderer and successor Allectus but after the latter's defeat by the Roman forces under Constantius Chlorus in 296 they were closed (**64**). The London mint was opened up once again by Constantine I in about 306 but by 325 it seems to have been permanently closed (see **96**), though the rebel Magnus Maximus (383-8) may have issued some gold from there.

These official or semi-official instances of striking coin in Romano-British towns were

64 *Bronze coins struck at the first Romano-British mints, and issued during the reigns of Carausius (286-93) and Allectus (293-96). The Carausian coin was struck at the 'C' mint, probably Colchester or Gloucester and bears a reverse depicting one of Carausius' war galleys (the mintmark reads CXXI – XXI being a mark of value); the Allectan coin was struck in London 'ML' = 'Moneta Londinii and bears a reverse depicting Pax (Peace). (Actual diameters 23 and 22 mm (just under 1 in).)*

not the only times that coin was manufactured. Forgers were active in a number of places. One of the gate-towers of the 'London gate' at Verulamium contained what seems to have been a forger's die for the reverse of a silver or gold coin of Hadrian. In London a tower on the wall contained clay moulds for producing forged copies of coins of Septimius Severus and his sons, with melted-down base metal coins found alongside the moulds. In the third century the basilica at Silchester was being used by metalworkers and this activity seems to have included producing copies of coins of the Gallic Empire's rulers: a mould for a coin of Tetricus I (270-3) was found amongst the metalworking debris (**65**). The location in this instance makes it likely that this was being done with local official approval, perhaps in an effort to supply coin to make it possible to buy in produce from the surrounding countryside because official supplies had dried up.

Industry in towns

Towns with a concentration of specialist skills generally supply services not easily provided in the countryside. There were sure to have been itinerant potters, blacksmiths and the like who toured the countryside seeking business, and some rural estates were bound to have been more or less self-contained. But for a craftsman or merchant an urban location allows him to store his tools, equipment and stock and also advertise his presence. A customer could visit a town and know that a number of jobs would be dealt with. We might imagine the villa owner or his foreman bringing his produce to sell and taking the opportunity to have a horse's harness repaired, a leaking bronze jug plugged, purchase imported wine and change some money into gold and silver to add to the concealed hoard at home. A weekly or monthly market would also have attracted the travelling tinkers to offer their services. This is not an idle fantasy – towns supply exactly the same sort of services today because without a rendezvous, trade and industry cannot function. Even the most self-sufficient villa estate would have needed an outlet for its produce.

Industrial activities were controlled both privately and publicly. There was a government weaving factory, *gynaecium*, at one of the Romano-British towns prefixed *Venta* (the source is not specific); it would have been used during the fourth century to supply the army. There is some evidence for the existence of guilds, known as *collegia*, in towns. An inscription from Chichester records a temple dedicated to Neptune and Minerva at the expense of a local guild of smiths (*collegium fabrorum*) some time around the middle of the first century (see Appendix 2). Other guilds are known from Silchester and near Verulamium but these are not specifically associated with any particular craft or trade. Some urban manufacturing was directly controlled by the civic authorities. The colony of Gloucester manufactured tiles stamped RPG for *Rei Publicae Glevensium* and named the magistrates for the year; in London tiles were made in the name of the provincial government. One site in London has also produced a number of tiles marked with a stamp of what seems to have been a private concern owned by two men who both had the same first name, Decimus (**66**). Another fragment of tile, inscribed before being fired, may record part of a London tile kiln work roster (**67**). Apart from stamping his product with his name a tiler might manufacture distinctive products like the Medusa tiles from Colchester (**68**).

65 *A base metal* antoninianus *of Tetricus I (270-3) similar to the types being produced in the basilica of Silchester during the latter part of the third century. (Actual diameter 19 mm ($\frac{3}{4}$ in).)*

66 *Impression of a tile stamp from Cloak Lane, London. The upper two lines are the initials of the manufacturing partnership: DMVAL (Decimus M....VAL...) and DMP (Decimus M....P...). The bottom line has been interpreted as an imaginatively abbreviated 'TEGVLAR[IAE]' for 'tiles', i.e. 'tiles (or tile [kilns]) of..'. (After Hale.)*

Metalworking

Other towns featured industrial activities as part of a rather broader spectrum of commercial activity. Verulamium is the best example of a town containing artisans making a living. This was mainly in the form of metalworking, fortunately the kind of activity which tends to leave identifiable traces in the archaeological record, like fragments of scrap, ceramic crucibles or moulds, and slag. Evidence like this has shown that a gold-worker was running some sort of business in the middle of London close to the later site of the so-called governor's palace in the Flavian period. Towards the end of the third century the basilica at Silchester seems to have become, at least in part, the workshop of bronze and iron smiths. The small town of Castleford, *Lagentium*, in West Yorkshire has produced a unique find of the remains of a manufactory for bronze and silver spoons: over 800 baked clay moulds have been found (**69**).

The small settlements at Nettleton and Camerton on the Fosse Way are known to have had facilities for casting tableware in pewter during the fourth century. There must have been numerous establishments like this in towns all over the province turning out small

67 *Fragment of tile from London inscribed before firing with a list (?) of names, perhaps tile factory workers. Here the name Titus is clearly visible, though this may be part of a longer and more common name, Potitus. (Actual diameter 47 mm (2 in). From Billingsgate, London.)*

68 (Above) *Moulded* antefix *tile from Colchester depicting a head of Medusa. The tile was inserted into the bottom row of roof tiles in order to provide a decorative trim. It was probably made in a local tilery. (Diameter 18 cm (7 in).)*

69 (Below) *Spoon moulds from Castleford* (Lagentium)*, Yorkshire. Part of a unique find of evidence for spoon manufacture. (Courtesy of West Yorkshire Archaeology Service, 1989.)*

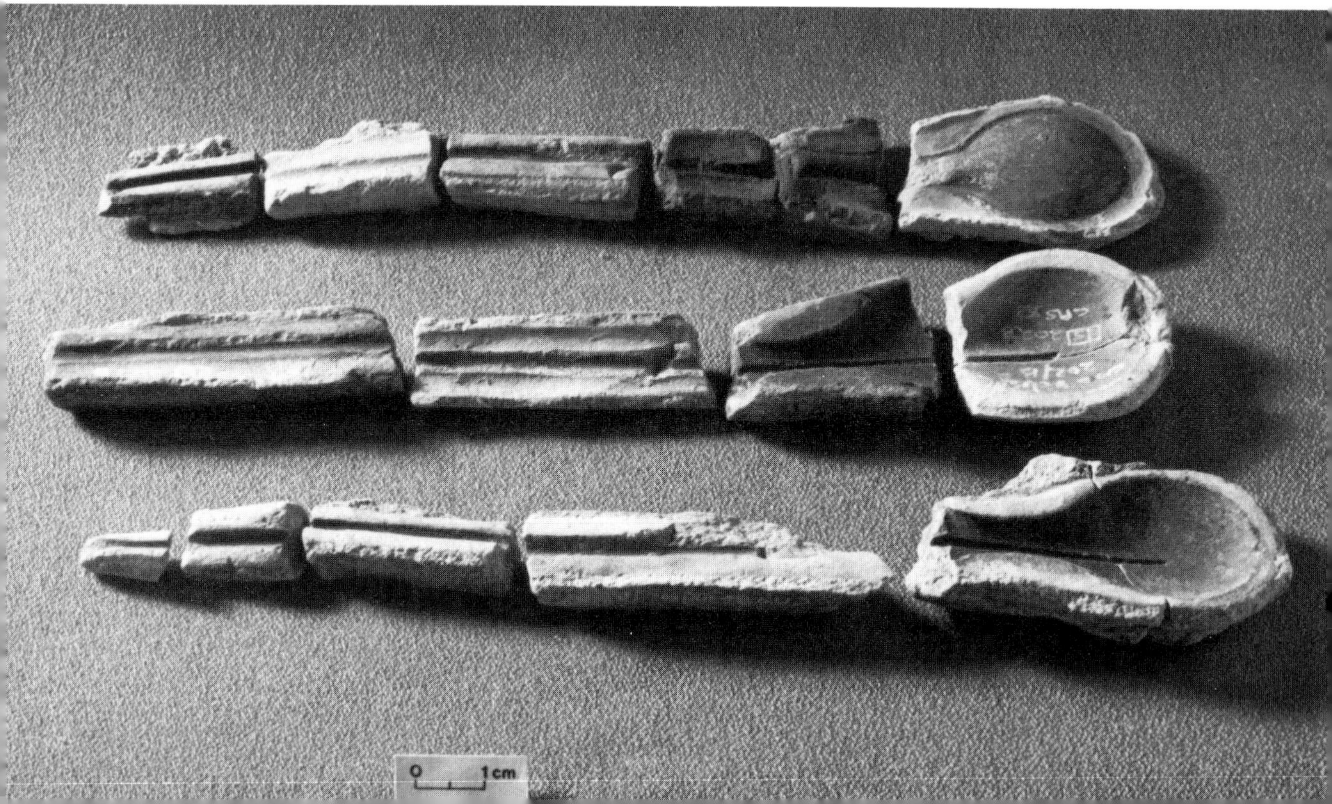

metal artefacts. Brooches, one of the most common finds from Roman sites, were almost certainly made in town-based factories as well as by itinerant craftsmen though evidence for all this is almost non-existent – only an unfinished brooch blank from the small settlement at Baldock points to a brooch-maker working there. A distinctive group of brooches with marked catch-plates has been identified recently as being distributed in and around Gloucester which was probably where they were made.

We can safely assume that almost all towns had some sort of metal industry though we know very little about the individuals. At Colchester an undated bronze plaque has been found which records a dedication to the god Silvanus Callirius by one Cintusmus the coppersmith (*aerarius*) (see **90**). He was probably someone who worked in the town. An actual establishment is testified in the *vicus* at Malton where a building stone, also undated, bore a dedication to the *Genius* of a goldsmith's shop (**70**). Knives and other utensils were sometimes stamped with a manufacturer's name, for example Basilis who probably made his iron-bladed knives in London.

70 *A building stone from Malton (*Derventio*) Yorkshire recording a dedication to the* Genius *of a goldsmith's workshop. It reads:* FELICITER SIT *(Happiness be...)*/GENIO LOCI *(...to the Genius of this place)*/SERVULE UTERE *(Young slave [be]..)*FELIX TABERN/AM AUREFI/CINAM *(...happy in this goldsmith's shop).*

Pottery manufacture

Metal of course retains some sort of value, whatever state it is in; pottery has virtually none unless it is complete or an expensive ware, considered worthy of repair. The presence of pottery is one of the most obvious clues to a site of Roman date because of the prodigious amount used, as opposed to the relatively small amount used before 43 and its almost complete disappearance during the fifth century. As a result, a vast amount of broken pottery was dumped throughout the Roman period and it can form an excellent, if limited, indicator of the kind of area over which a Roman town might have had an economic influence.

Almost every settlement in Roman Britain would have had a potter working at some time and a few places became the site of a major industry. Generally these were in rural areas where it was easy to obtain fuel, water and clay but which were also accessible by road or water. The pottery industry known as Black Burnished 2, for example, consisted of a number of dispersed kiln sites around the Thames Estuary. During the first and second centuries some of the major towns like Colchester had potteries situated in their outskirts. The industry which developed here was particularly important and it contrasts with the Romano-British pottery industries that developed in the third and fourth centuries which were almost entirely divorced from urban centres.

As a colony Colchester was largely populated from the beginning by people who had romanized tastes. Although this would have extended to as much of their way of life as possible, pottery is one of the few means which we can use to identify such habits. A great deal of pottery was imported during the first and second centuries with the fine ware component being dominated by Gaulish samian. However, potters identified a ready market in early Colchester and by the mid-first century colour-coated cups and beakers mostly modelled on examples made in Gaul were being produced nearby.

By the early second century the local industry had become more adventurous and productive, making a wider range of forms which were themselves being traded further afield in Britain, even reaching the northern frontier. Much the most distinctive are the decorated beakers but the potters were also manufacturing large quantities of the special kitchen mixing bowl, the *mortarium*. These were transported in large numbers to the military sites in the north until the early third century. Mortaria seem to have been made by potters who specialized in their production; at least two places seem to have developed into sizeable single-industry settlements around the kilns, at Brockley Hill near Verulamium and the Hartshill-Mancetter area in the Midlands (see **77**). These places were more industrial settlements than towns but they probably also supplied other town-like services to their hinterlands.

Around the year 160 a group of samian potters from East Gaul appear to have also identified Colchester as a good place to work, since they set up kilns close to the town. Their mould-decorated products, not surprisingly, resemble East Gaulish styles but were unsuccessful because while a great deal of debris, including fragments of more than 400 moulds, was found the pots themselves are barely known outside the vicinity of Colchester. The recovery of pieces of unfired pots suggests a swift termination to potting on the site but this could have been due to anything, perhaps frustration at inadequate clays or resistance from local vested interests, and there need be no sinister connotations. Curiously the other well-established parts of the local industry seem to have also had trouble keeping customers and eventually many of their markets (especially the army) seem to have had to buy from Nene Valley potters.

During the third and fourth centuries major pottery industries in Roman Britain were more likely to be rural in location but sometimes an industry was so successful that a major town grew up around the kiln sites, and became more than just an appendage to the industry. The best-known example of this in Roman Britain was the Nene Valley pottery industry which became centred on the town at Water Newton just to the west of modern Peterborough, known as *Durobrivae* (**71**). A pottery industry had existed here since at least the beginning of the second century and possibly earlier but it was only of local significance. Throughout this time the fine ware market in Roman Britain was so dominated by the Gaulish samian ware industry that other sources of pottery had only limited success. By the end of the second century the samian ware potteries had entered a period of steep decline and their products gradually disappeared from the Romano-British marketplace over the next 20 or 30 years. A few industries in Britain stepped in to fill the gap and the Nene Valley was one of them. They supplied colour-coated bowls and dishes which matched some samian forms and also a series of drinking beakers, sometimes decorated with appliqué figures of animals known as 'hunt cups' (see **60**). Mortaria were also made, and on one unique example illustrated here the potter signed his work (**72**).

The Nene Valley potters were well placed. Although their various kiln sites straggled along the banks of the Nene for several miles, the main road from London to the north (Ermine Street) passed through the area and the town of *Durobrivae* had grown up along it. The river Nene would have almost certainly served for transporting the products to the North Sea where they could be shipped to the northern frontier and southwards to London. Whatever the routes used, they were effective, for Nene Valley products are found almost everywhere in Roman Britain.

While *Durobrivae* grew to be a place of some consequence very few potteries are associated with the civitas capitals or *coloniae* in the third

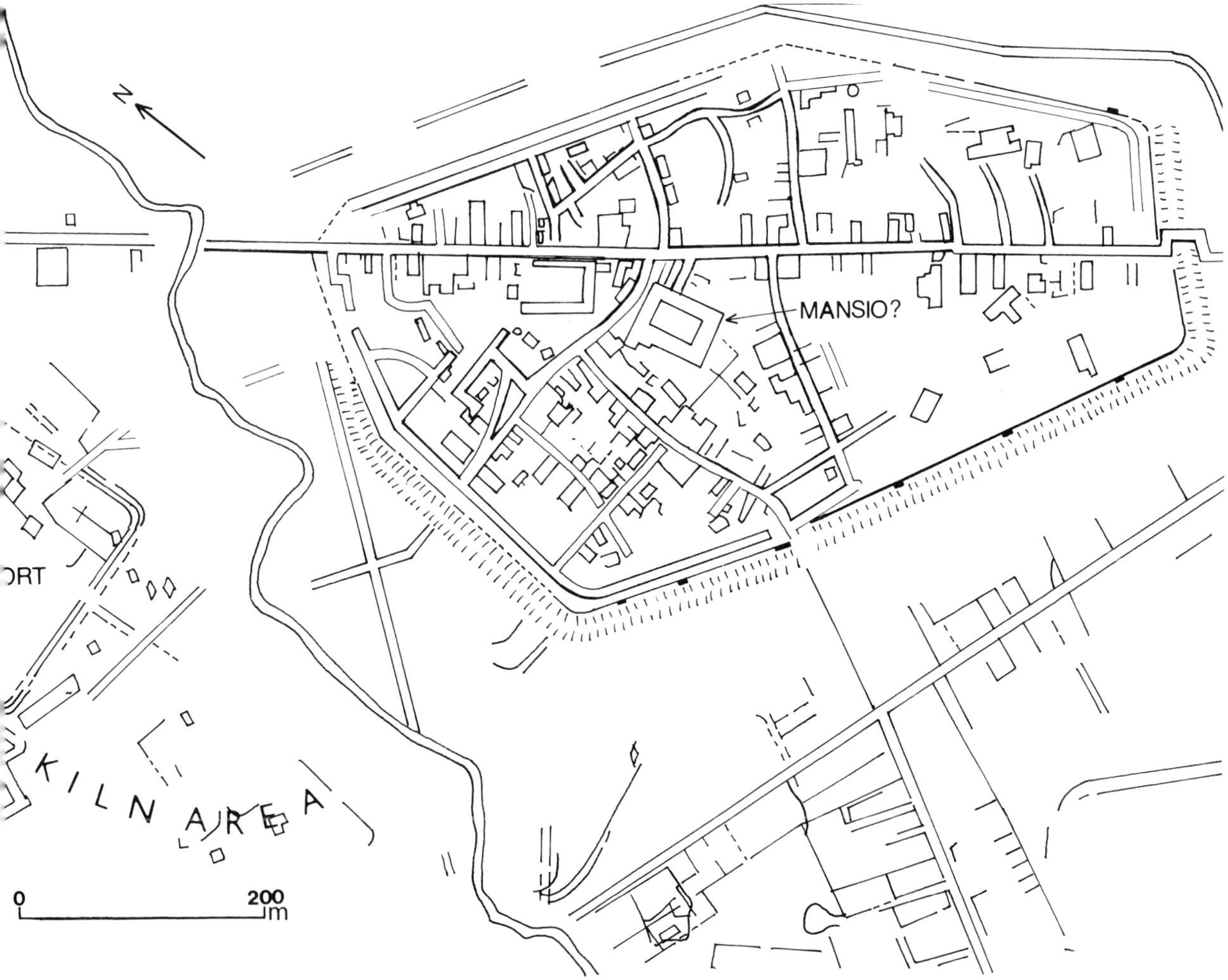

71 *Plan of the town at Water Newton* (Durobrivae) *which grew up largely as a result of the pottery industry in the area, capitalizing on its location on a major road and access to water transport. The sites of what may have been a* mansio, *and an earlier fort are marked. (After Mackreth.)*

72 *Painted inscription on a* mortarium *from Water Newton. This exceptional example records that Sennianus the potter fired (*VRIT*) the piece at* DUROBRIVIS *(Water Newton). Probably third century and a very useful reference for other sherds.*

and fourth centuries. Instead many important pottery centres seem to be almost as far away from towns as possible. The Oxfordshire, New Forest and Alice Holt industries consist of regional groups of kiln sites quite unconnected with the major towns one would have assumed to have been their principal markets (and indeed were). Why? There are all sorts of possibilities and no facts. For example, did the élite in the *civitates* tend to stifle local production (of whatever sort) through their control of movements and taxation? Or, alternatively was access to the Thames (and therefore most of the province) of greater importance to the Oxfordshire and Alice Holt industries? As we know nothing of taxation in Roman Britain or pottery distribution controls it seems rash to make assumptions and generalizations based on the hypothetical effects of hypothetical systems. Instead we must content ourselves with the observation and remember that these kind of possibilities may also have affected other industries like food production, which are much more poorly represented in the archaeological record.

The important point here is the development of the town. Like London, *Durobrivae* was not an official foundation but unlike London it was not apparently elevated to formal status (though we should not ignore the possibility that it was, and that we simply do not know about it). It is clear from aerial photography that the town was never laid out in a regular fashion and probably had no building which served as a basilica or forum though there was probably an official inn. It was clearly a product of local commerce and industry. Nevertheless the town could afford to provide its own earth fortifications consisting of a bank and a ditch. Little is known about the town, but a group of people were wealthy enough here to endow a probable Christian church with a substantial amount of silver plate in the fourth century. It seems that the concept and convenience of towns was an idea sufficiently well established in the minds of the local community for them either to develop a town, or to put it another way, not to obstruct its natural growth given the local circumstances. *Durobrivae* is an example of a different kind of Romano-British town and we need to recognize that the idea of a town was flexible enough to accommodate it.

Glass manufacture

Glass was widely used in Roman Britain (**73**) but unlike pottery the fabric of the glass cannot be definitely associated with a specific place. Manufacture could take place in towns or in a rural location, depending on availability of fuel and reasonable access to markets. These considerations, and the risk of breakage, would favour a town-orientated industry but it is clear that glasswares were used widely in the countryside, perhaps made by itinerant craftsmen. At the Lullingstone villa in Kent, some 25km (16 miles) from the nearest town fragments of several hundred glass vessels were found.

At Caistor-by-Norwich a glass manufacturing workshop consisted of a main L-shaped

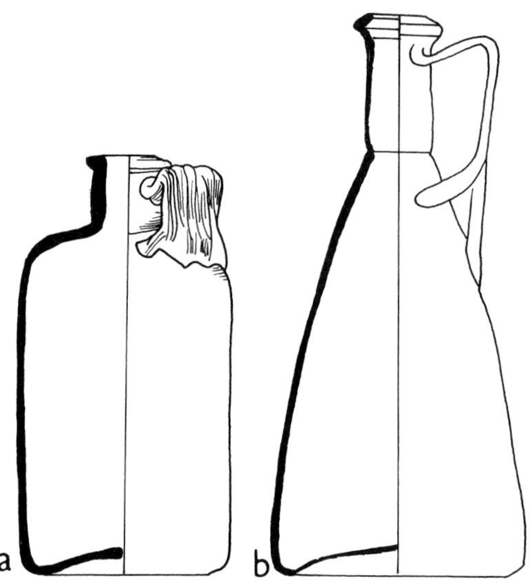

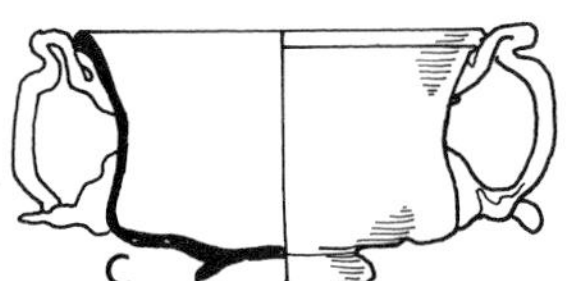

73 *Some of the principal forms of glass which are found on Roman town sites;* a *bottle, usually blown square in shape with drawn handle;* b *handled bottle of a more elaborate variety;* c *moulded cup with handles made from separate rods;* d *pillar-moulded bowl.*

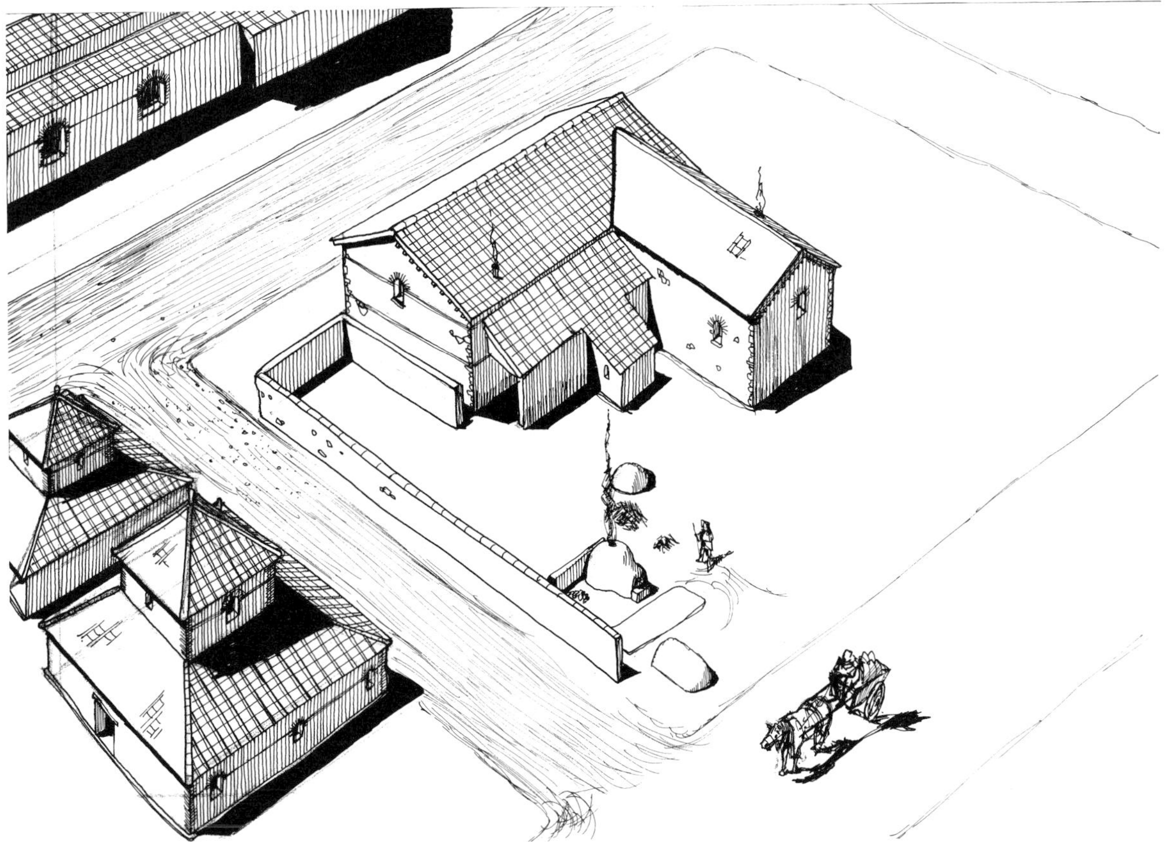

74 *Reconstructed view of the glass factory at Caistor-by-Norwich (*Venta Icenorum*). A number of hearths were found along with debris from glass manufacturing.*

building divided roughly into two, with an access corridor from a partially enclosed courtyard. In the courtyard were the glass furnaces, presumably to minimize the risk from fire (**74**). Of course we have no idea of where the products were sold but we might assume that this took place on the premises and perhaps in the forum, with a certain amount being re-sold locally by merchants. Other furnaces are known, for example at Wroxeter and Mancetter but owing to the nature of the product it is virtually certain that all major towns would have had a glass production factory at some time.

The mosaic industry

The mosaics which were laid in Romano-British country houses in the fourth century belonged to what was by then a well-established tradition. As early as the mid-first century some exceptional country houses, particularly Fishbourne, were having mosaics installed, probably by mosaicists brought in from Gaul or even Italy. In time, a domestic industry would have developed and studies of mosaics have usually concluded that regional industries and traditions grew up centred on major towns, called 'schools'. This is based on the distribution of mosaics in similar styles in rural villas clustered around towns. It has been generally assumed that these distribution patterns, for example the Orpheus-type mosaics around Cirencester (*Corinium*), may be evidence for individual workshops in the towns in this case attributed to the period 300-20. In other words a master craftsman, or men, with assistants, worked from a town where he would be commissioned by villa owners to work in their houses, possibly preparing complex panels in the workshop and then transporting them. However, there is no satisfactory way of distinguishing style-copying from original work.

In fact, the number of mosaics attributed to any one 'school' is fairly limited, about 14 being associated with the Corinium Orpheus 'school', of which one is in London, one in Silchester, one in Dorchester and at least one in south Wales. While the workshops may have existed as 'schools' there is no convincing evidence for this being a town-based industry and it is hard to see what the advantage of a town location would have been. We may be looking at regional fashions as much as school styles and even if there were 'schools' with master mosaicists working from towns they would actually have done most of their work in the villa sites. As with many aspects of Romano-British archaeology good ideas and theories have a habit of turning into facts: no actual town workshops have been identified.

The 'small' towns

There were many 'small towns' which defy easy categorization because despite their size little is known about them except that they were not towns with formal status. The civitas capitals and the colonies were relatively early foundations; most seem to have been in existence by the end of the first century. The small towns took rather longer to develop and apart from their relatively small size the only consistent feature is that a major road usually ran through the centre. Buildings were laid out in a haphazard fashion resembling medieval villages and towns with winding streets, except that they even lacked the equivalent focal point of a church. Very few, for example Dorn (Gloucestershire) and Kenchester (Herefordshire), had defences. There are exceptions, Alchester, for example, lies a little way from a major road and also had a regular street grid.

Some may have grown up around forts, for example at Wall (*Letocetum*) in Staffordshire (**75**) but it is just as likely that the forts were sited close to traditional gathering places so it is perhaps more likely that the majority had some basis in pre-Roman Britain. This was

75 *The baths at Wall as they appear today. They almost certainly formed part of the* mansio *complex and would have been the central feature of the small town, earning much of its revenue from passing trade. (English Heritage.)*

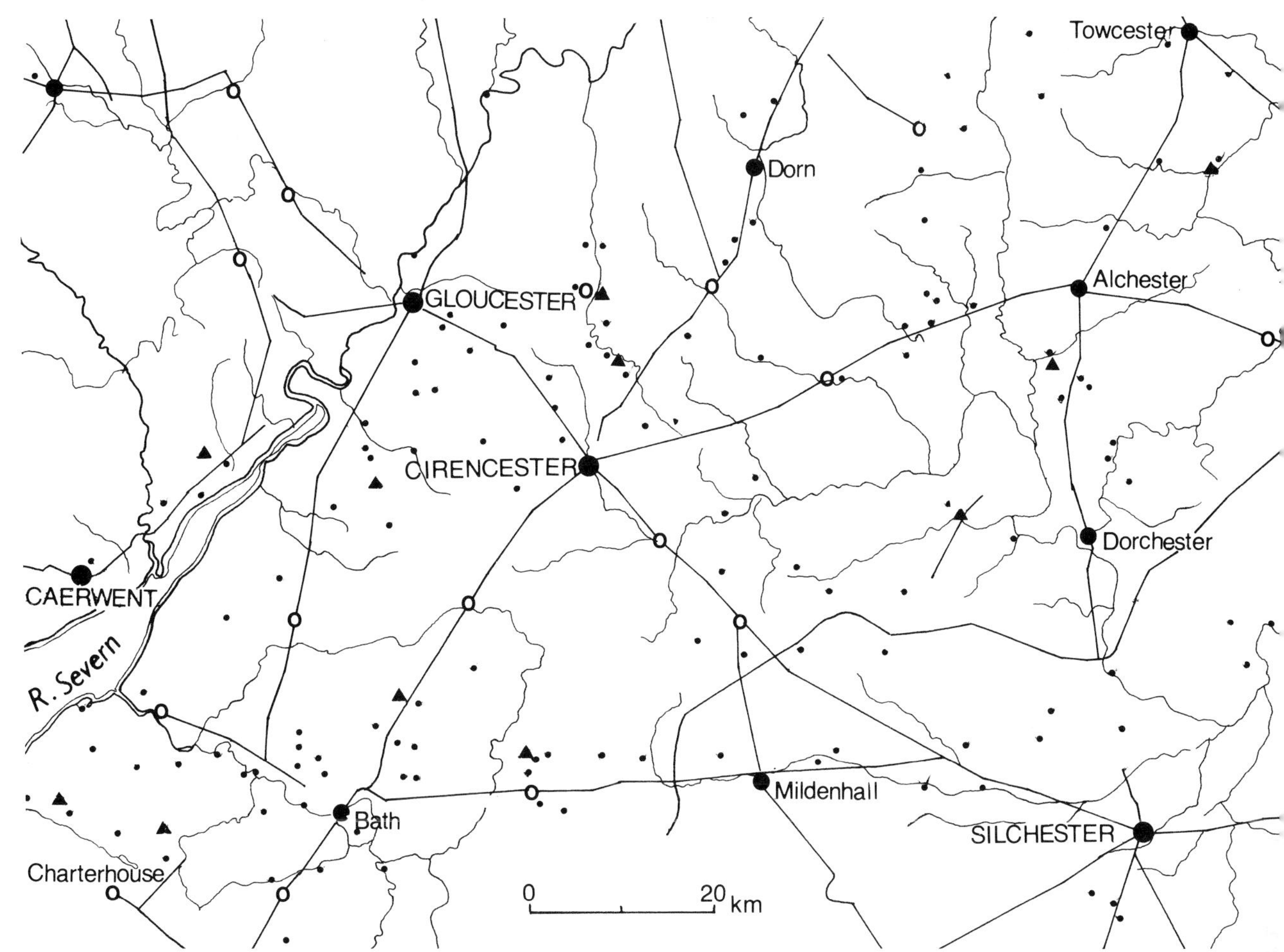

certainly the case where towns like Baldock and Great Chesterford were concerned. Even where the small town developed close to, rather than on, the site of a late Iron Age centre this was likely to be where the latter was not located in a place suitable for a road to run through. It had therefore been by-passed and thus the nucleus of settlement was likely to drift. Like the civitas capitals the reasons were likely to be more than one in any individual case.

It can hardly be coincidence that the small and major towns generally lie in places between 16 and 32 km (10 and 20 miles) apart along roads. This sort of distance was roughly equivalent to a day's journey. Passing trade would have therefore influenced the development of small towns at sites in an appropriate location, such as Crayford and Springhead which lie between London and Rochester, at a day's journey or thereabouts from a major town. A map of the

76 *Map of the Mendips and Cotswolds area in Roman times showing the relation between major towns, minor settlements, temples (▲) and villas (·) and the system of roads. This was probably the most densely populated part of the province. The distribution of the villas is biased towards proximity to the towns, roads and rivers, for example the roads running from Dorn and Alchester to Cirencester. It seems that the villas were dependent on access to the towns, but it would have been equally true that the towns were dependent on produce coming from the villas. (Based on the Ordnance Survey Map of Roman Britain, Crown copyright reserved.)*

Cotswold area in Roman times also shows this sort of distribution very clearly (**76**). Local self-sufficiency was probably even more important because long-distance traffic and trade was almost certainly confined to a period between April and October. During the winter small settlements would have played a vital role in serving the needs of outlying farms and houses whose occupants would have been unable to travel far.

There were a number of small towns which seem to have depended on the existence of local specialist industries or the extraction of resources. In the Roman world the majority of mines were owned by the imperial government and administered on its behalf by a procurator who acted like a kind of small-scale governor. He controlled all activities on the site even to the extent of restricting services like shoemaking to approved concessionaires. Mines were also controlled by the army in the initial phases of a conquest and subsequently could be leased to private entrepreneurs, though a fixed proportion of metal remained government property. Naturally mines required a considerable amount of labour and this was usually slave or forced. Can we really call a mining settlement a town? In the true sense of the word, probably not but the communities themselves would have come to resemble small straggling villages with many of the various activities associated with town life.

At Charterhouse in the Mendips lead mines were in operation as early as *c.*50. Lead was a vital commodity because it was the only substance known at the time which could be readily manipulated and hammered into a variety of shapes; in other words it served some of the functions which are now fulfilled by plastics. It was essential for the manufacture of piping and waterproofing, and was also the main component of pewter. Pewter became particularly popular in the fourth century and as we saw above the small settlements at Camerton and Nettleton on the Fosse Way both became manufacturing centres. Lead in an impure form contains silver and this was an added attraction of its exploitation. We know that British lead was considered valuable enough to be exported: a cistern found at Pompeii seems to have been made of British lead. Charterhouse was an extensive settlement though very little is known about its buildings. These however included a small amphitheatre, perhaps more accurately a cock or bear pit, constructed simply out of raised earth banks.

The small town at Brampton in north Norfolk appears to have developed as a result of specialization in pottery and production of iron and lasted from the first century at least until the end of the third. It is particularly interesting that the settlement had a wharf giving it access to the river Bure which meets the coast in the vicinity of the Saxon Shore fort at Burgh Castle and a minor coastal settlement at Caister-on-Sea. This makes it virtually certain that the settlement's products were traded over some distance. The presence of iron-works is proved by the large quantities of slag found, with some buildings apparently being used by metalworkers. Pottery production was mainly in the form of straightforward kitchen wares though some potters seem to have concentrated on making flagons and mortaria which require more skill, and were generally made by specialists. Between London and Verulamium the small settlement at Brockley Hill, *Sulloniacae*, was a major production centre for mortaria and flagons. The mortaria potters stamped their names on their products which have as a result been identified over a wide area, but especially in the south-east. Sited on a main road it was well placed to make the most of the main markets in London and Verulamium both of which were only a day's journey away (see **77**).

There are many other examples of small towns that seem to have more or less entirely depended on the existence of specific specialist industries. They included Droitwich in the west Midlands which was called *Salinae* indicating its connection with salt. A considerable amount of evidence in the form of buildings, storage containers and by-products has been found for the extraction of salt from salt-bearing springs. The town at Middlewich in Cheshire seems to have had a similar industrial base. The one consistent factor is that these small industrial towns never really developed into anything particularly significant. Largely anonymous in the ancient record we often do not know their former names and they rarely produce evidence for anything other than elementary buildings – though they have in the past been the subject of minimal archaeological attention.

The perceived slow development of small towns has been linked to a hypothetical change in taxation from gathering of tax in cash to a more localized collection of goods in kind, such as crops. This would have reduced the stimulus to obtain cash by selling produce or services in a market; but we should be wary of such a sophisticated explanation when the available

77 *Stamped impression of a potter called Marinus from a* mortarium *made in the Verulamium area, perhaps at the Brockley Hill settlement. The stamp reads 'MARINUS FECIT' – 'Marinus made [this bowl]'. Late first, early second century.*

evidence is so limited. Alternatively, we could see the *civitates* reaching a maturity in the third century, having benefited from early investment and therefore exhibiting less evidence for development at this time. The small towns may have benefited from the development of the countryside, perhaps supplying services and markets to the increased number of more affluent villas in the third and fourth centuries, though even at the largest and most developed the small towns were hardly impressive expressions of Roman urban life. Of course, the small towns in reality consisted of many dozens of different settlements each with a unique set of factors lying behind both beginnings and sustained growth; we have to recognize this and accept that only in a very few cases can we suggest reasons for their existence. Water Newton was one but there were also the towns which grew up around the site of a shrine. Bath is the best known but there were also others such as Springhead. These are such special cases that they are discussed in Chapter 6.

The *vici*

Earlier on we saw how the presence of forts may possibly have played a role in promoting the development of towns, but in all the cases mentioned the forts were given up at a relatively early date, leaving the civil settlement to survive on its own merits. The northern and western part of the province remained a military zone throughout Romano-British history with a number of forts being consolidated in stone and becoming permanent features. In these cases the civilian settlements remained suburbs of the forts around which they had grown up. Whether we can really regard them as towns is a problem but it is likely that they functioned as local centres and markets of a sort. Most are known from aerial photography, for example at Old Carlisle in Cumbria, or outside many of the forts on Hadrian's Wall, and probably date from around the middle of the second century.

At Vindolanda, where the fort *vicus* is one of the very few to have been excavated, the circumstantial evidence of coin loss suggests that the *vicus* may have fallen out of use long before the fort was abandoned by the end of the fourth century. However, it is probably safe to assume that the *vici* would have continued to exist in some shape or form so long as the fort existed. Unlike the *vici* in southern Britain it is not so easy to see an association between an existing native settlement and a fort; in the north they were rather more likely to be a direct consequence of the fort alone and as such, considerably more dependent. Even so we have an altar of second- or third-century date from near Vindolanda which records a dedication to a goddess called Sattada by the senate ('*curia*') of the 'Textoverdi'. These were almost certainly the inhabitants and government of the immediate area, with a centre in the *vicus* at Vindolanda (**colour plate 15**) or more probably a few miles away at Corbridge. So even if Vindolanda's *vicus* was a consequence of the fort there may already have been something of an established tribal community in the area.

We have little evidence of the nature of the people who came to live in these *vici* but in one instance we know that a trader called Barates from Syria married a Catuvellaunian woman, a former slave, called Regina who was buried in the *vicus* cemetery outside the fort at South Shields. However, it is equally likely that people were also drawn from the general vicinity of a fort, attracted by the obvious captive demand.

Most military *vici* consist of fairly simple buildings straggling along the roads leading to the fort though in the most elaborate instances an independent street pattern grew up. Like more conventional small towns these are usually irregular. The buildings tend to resemble the early commercial strip-house properties found in the major towns of the first and second centuries though occasionally more elaborate courtyard structures resembling inns have been identified. In a number of instances, Old Carlisle and Housesteads being two of the most conspicuous, field boundaries and terraces can also be seen and this creates an impression of forts which, together with their civilian annexes, were probably largely self-sufficient though obviously we do not know to what extent agricultural land was farmed by the soldiers. This would have had obvious advantages – the unique collection of writing tablets from Vindolanda's late-first-century fort shows that supplying an outpost with food and goods was a complex and arduous task. By the third century there may not have been a clear distinction between military and civilian interests and it is probably better to see these forts and their *vici* as single units, especially in the third and fourth centuries, soldiers living with families in the civilian settlements. Their sons probably went on to join the unit while the fathers retired to the *vicus* to carry on an established family business or small-holding.

6

Religion in towns

Introduction

One of the most mature features of Roman government was the ability to accommodate provincial religious beliefs and customs. This was all part of ruling by exploiting existing ways of life. The basic practice of attributing good and bad events to the actions and whims of gods was common to Celtic and classical cults in any case. People sought to influence a god's behaviour by offering gifts at shrines, almost a kind of contractual arrangement based on a promise, 'if you will do me this service, then I promise that I will offer up such and such a gift at your shrine', though much of this was probably part of day-to-day casual superstition rather than devoted faith (**78**).

For Roman Britain the merging of existing cults with classical gods meant that the abstract deities of the Celtic world were represented as humans and were often associated with a similar Roman god; Mars, for example, became allied with a number of Celtic hunter-warrior gods like Cocidius. Celtic cults were not usually centred on temples but instead the focal point was more commonly a tree, a spring or a hill. These often had temples built on or

78 *Altar from the* colonia *at York recording a dedication to the god Arciaconus (an obscure local divinity) and the spirit of the emperor (N.AVG[V]ST[I] in the third line) by a centurion called Mat... Vitalis. The letters V S L M in the fifth line are a stock abbreviation for* votum soluit libens merito. *This means that a vow was being freely and deservedly fulfilled. In other words Vitalis had promised the god an altar if he was granted a favour; as the latter was a private arrangement with the god there was no need to mention it.*

near the site in the Roman period, for example at Harlow, but temples in towns were unlikely to have such origins for obvious reasons, unless the town itself grew up around the centre of a cult. The most famous example is Bath, *Aquae Sulis*, but there were several smaller settlements with similar backgrounds. Temples have been found all over Roman Britain but it is only in towns that we find examples of all the different aspects of Romano-British religious life including state cults, individual temples, which we might regard as centres of social or community cults, and domestic religion.

State cults

Despite religious tolerance provincial communities across the Empire were obliged to pay lip-service to official religion. In about AD 12 or 13 the townspeople of Narbonne in southern Gaul dedicated an altar inscribed with a record of their vows to worship the spirit of Augustus for ever. Pliny the Younger, as governor of Bithynia and Pontus, wrote to the Emperor Trajan in 112 to confirm that he and the provincials had fulfilled their annual vows to pray to the gods for the emperor's health and safety.

Similar events took place in Roman Britain though with so few inscriptions the evidence is not widespread. The town senate of Chichester recorded a vow for Nero's health and safety in the year 59, interesting not just because of early date for an imperial dedication but also because it states the existence of a formal local government body (Appendix 2). A fragmentary and undated inscription from London may record a dedication to the emperor cult (*Numeni Caesaris* or *Augustorum*) in the name of the province.

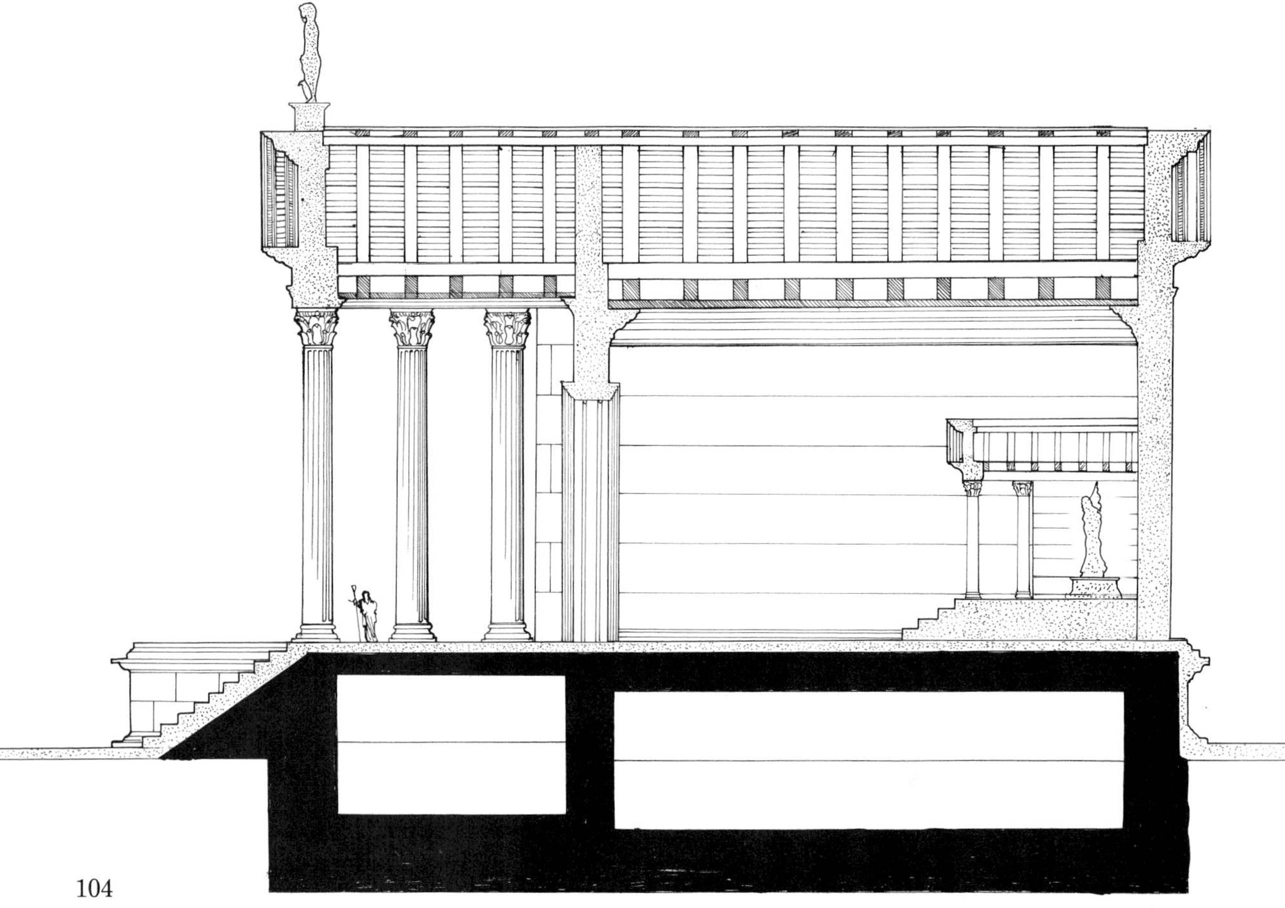

79 *Reconstructed cutaway elevation of the Temple of Claudius at Colchester. The solid black part represents foundations and vaults visible today beneath the Norman castle keep though these are in fact divided into two pairs on either side of a line running through the middle of the temple. See also* **11**.

80 *Section of frieze from a classical-style temple at Corbridge and probably dedicated to Jupiter Dolichenus (Dolichenus was an eastern god associated with Jupiter). The mounted figure is Apollo and the figure leading another horse is either Castor or Pollux. Third century.*

The London emperor cult inscription suggests that the centre of the imperial cult was based there – an obvious location. If so, it had been transferred from Colchester. As we saw above (p. 29-30) one of the earliest developments in formalizing the province was the building of a temple to the deified Claudius in Colchester. By 60 it was sufficiently far advanced to act as the centre of the colonists' resistance to the Boudican Revolt. The temple foundations were used in the eleventh century as the base for the Norman castle keep and what remained of the superstructure was cleared away. However, it is certain that the temple was an impressively-sized building in classical style (**79** and see **11**). It lay inside a substantial walled precinct and a large altar stood in front of the temple (see cover). The building's dedication to Claudius had probably made much of his successful conquest of Britain, perhaps in the form of carved reliefs. In Canterbury an irregular *insula* facing the theatre on one side and the forum (?) on the other seems to have formed a substantial temple precinct. The building itself has not been located but its central location and imposing precinct make it very likely that this was an important classical temple which was almost certainly associated with a state cult.

Most Roman towns elsewhere based their local state cults in temples which formed integral parts of the forum. The Romano-British forums and basilicas are largely distinguished by the absence of these temples except for Verulamium and a small temple added to the forum at Caerwent. The Verulamium temples would almost certainly have been dedicated to the Capitoline Triad made up of Jupiter, Juno and Minerva. Many more examples are known on the continent and in North Africa (see **9**) so it is curious that Roman Britain seems to have had so few. It may simply be that after the Boudican Revolt state cult temples were considered by the government as unnecessarily provocative – in the decades following the revolt (which was when many of the forums and basilicas were being built) there must have been a very real fear of a re-emergence of armed rebellion. This is no idle speculation, Britain was very nearly lost in 60. Of course this does not explain why the civic authorities in Verulamium built what they did unless either the structure was already under construction before the change of policy, or it was because the Catuvellauni felt it was an appropriate gesture of solidarity.

Classical temples of any form were always rare in Roman Britain (**80**), and the cults of purely classical deities just as scarce. In later years we do have some instances of dedications to Jupiter Optimus Maximus ('the Best and Greatest') on what we call 'Jupiter columns'. These were columns normally erected in a public place, such as a forum, with a plinth recording the dedication to Jupiter by some local worthy, or a provincial governor. Examples are known from Cirencester (see Appendix 2) and Great Chesterford.

Celtic, synthesized and oriental cults

The majority of urban temples were built in a simple style called 'Romano-Celtic', consisting of a square central chamber, the *cella*, and a surrounding square ambulatory (**81**). The only structural evidence that we have for their form (a well-preserved example at Autun in France) suggests that the central chamber was tower-like and the ambulatory had a lean-to roof. Variations on this theme include circular and octagonal examples, but all retain the principle of concentric chambers. No Romano-British urban examples survive above their footings so we know nothing about internal decorations. Like the Temple of Claudius at Colchester they were generally sited in a precinct, the *temenos*, which was either surrounded by a wall or possibly a covered (?) colonnade. The precinct could take any form and this usually depended on the layout of the town. At Verulamium the so-called 'Triangular Temple' occupied an awkwardly shaped *insula* created by the entry of Watling Street from London at an angle at variance to the grid (**82** and see **7**). On the other side of the town a much larger, rectangular, *insula* acted as a precinct and was much more symmetrical and conventional as a result. At Silchester a small trapezoidal precinct beside the town walls and containing three temples made up a whole *insula*. Urban temples were not always within the main area of settlement. Recent excavations in London revealed possible traces of an octagonal Romano-Celtic temple just to the west of the city walls. However, the temple seems to have been built about 170, roughly fifty years before the defences were erected. It may therefore have lain within a suburb which was subsequently excluded from the enclosed area.

81 *Reconstructed elevation across the temple and precinct in* Insula *XVI at Verulamium. This was a large complex in a style known as 'Romano-Celtic' and stood adjacent to the theatre with which it was probably associated (see* **7***).*

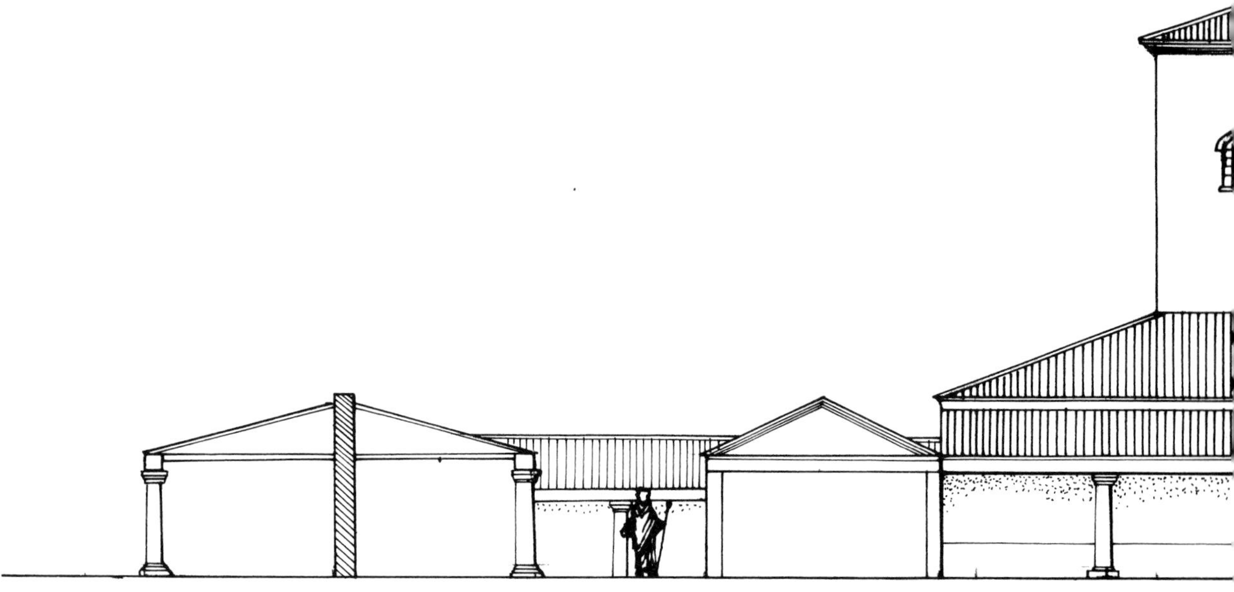

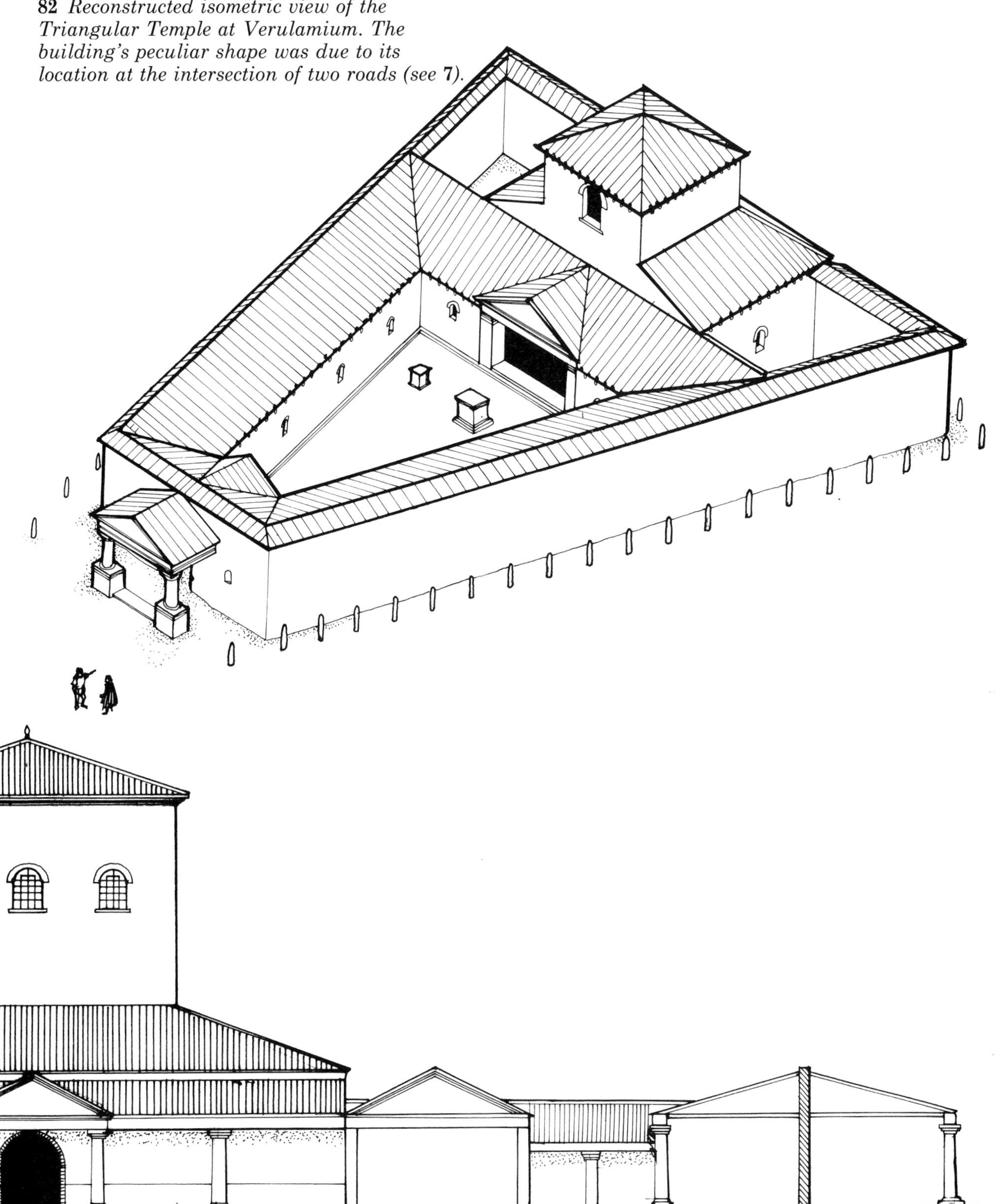

82 *Reconstructed isometric view of the Triangular Temple at Verulamium. The building's peculiar shape was due to its location at the intersection of two roads (see* **7***).*

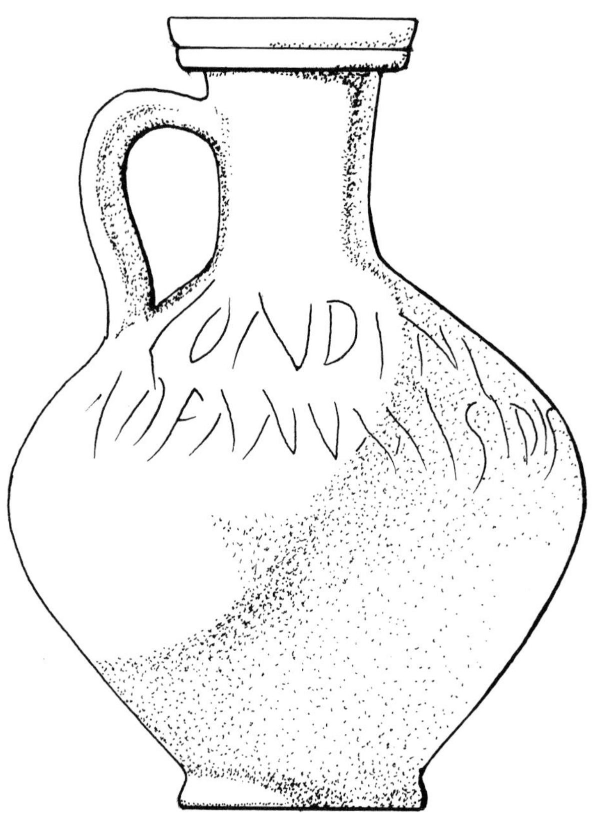

83 *Flagon from Southwark, London, bearing a graffito recording an address 'London, by the temple of Isis'. First century, though of course the inscription could be later.*

Even small towns could have room for temple precincts, perhaps as many as two or more. At Godmanchester, a minor town on Ermine Street with a possible military origin, a small temple precinct was established at least as early as the first half of the second century beside a building identified as the *mansio*. The temple, which had at least two structural phases, was probably dedicated to Abandinus – a votive feather found in a filling refers to the god. The town also had another temple precinct which occupied a prominent position beside Ermine Street, but little is known about it. Interestingly a substantial Neolithic complex of banks, ditches and wooden obelisks dating to the third millennium BC has recently been discovered in the area. It has been identified as a temple connected with astronomical predictions. If so, there may have been something of a local religious significance and tradition about the place though of course coincidence is just as plausible an explanation.

Throughout the first four centuries AD the Roman world became increasingly susceptible to the appeal of cults originating in the eastern part of the Roman empire. Quite why we cannot be sure, but there seems to have been a widespread desire to seek more spiritual explanations for life and its meaning, especially as Roman power waned. The towns were crucial to the spread of these religions because they were centres of communications and trades and therefore new ideas. So it was here that people already familiar with the cults were likely to establish temples.

Not surprisingly London, as a major port, has produced the most evidence for such cults. As early as the late first century we know that London had a temple to the Egyptian goddess Isis because a flagon has survived bearing a graffito which refers to it. The cursive inscription says simple *Londinii ad fanum Isidii*, which means 'At London, by the Temple of Isis' (**83**). In a way the inscription is of more interest than an otherwise unidentifiable building; unless it is fraudulent (anciently) we can be sure that there was an Isis sect active in early Roman London. It, or another like it, was functioning nearly two centuries later when a governor called Marcus Martiannius Pulcher arranged for a temple to Isis in London to be repaired (**84** and Appendix 2). Artefacts found in London show that other Egyptian deities, for example Cybele and Atys, enjoyed the attentions of Roman Londoners.

The cult of Mithras was concerned with a complex myth based on good versus evil and centred around the killing of a bull. Exclusive to men, the cult had attractions to the military and is best known in military areas. However, it was also popular in ports or towns with a military presence (London had a fort and soldiers were seconded from the legions to the governor's staff). Unlike more conventional temples where ritual was enacted outside the building a Mithraeum acted as a stylized 'cave', emulating the cave in which Mithras had killed the bull. The buildings were either subterranean or had sunken floors and would not have had windows. Inside the devotees could proceed with their initiation rites and other ceremonies in an atmosphere suitably heightened by darkness and skilful use of artificial light. These conditions made the cult a self-contained and unobtrusive one.

London has the only certain Romano-British urban example of a Mithraeum (**85**). Its discovery in 1954 was accompanied by the finding of a number of cult statues which had been concealed by the followers (see below). Like most Mithraea it was built in basilican form because this suited the congregational aspect of the cult, something equally applicable to Christianity so it is no coincidence that both used the same existing building type. It was put up some time between 200 and 250 on the banks of the Walbrook stream on top of nearly two centuries worth of urban rubbish and spoil. Despite this downmarket location it contained marble and limestone sculptures of considerable quality. It is certain that a Mithraic relief found in the vicinity in the nineteenth century came originally from the temple (**85**b). It was dedicated by a veteran of the II legion and had been carved from marble at Orange in France. The temple's proximity to the stream seems to have resulted in flooding and this caused structural problems. In the fourth century the temple appears to have become a focus of local hostility for it was seriously damaged and left to become derelict. However, the sculptures and ritual equipment were all carefully buried beforehand, which suggests that the cult was being deliberately suppressed. By this time London was one of the Romano-British towns with its own bishop (see below) and it is reasonable to suppose that the London Christians were directly opposed to the presence of a cult which had features they regarded as insultingly similar to their own.

84 *Altar from London recording the rebuilding of a temple to Isis by Marcus Martiannius Pulcher, governor of* Britannia Inferior, *some time during the third century.*

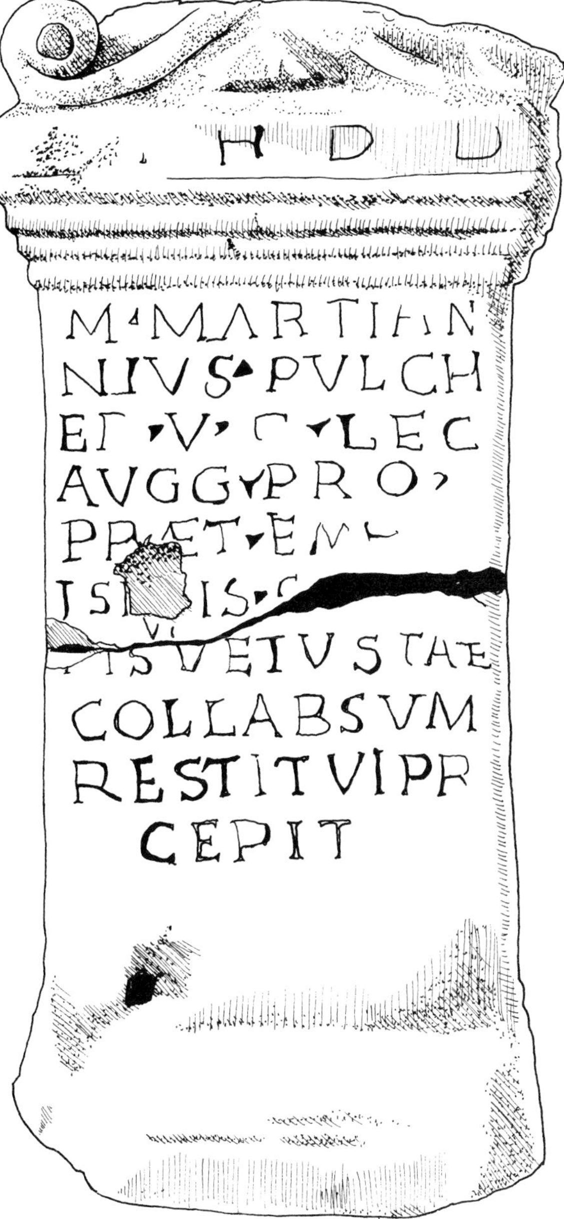

It is unfortunate that we have no similar building that we can certainly associate with Christianity. Christianity was an established urban cult by the fourth century. At the Council of Arles in 314 bishops from London, York and possibly Lincoln were present. These bishops would have had churches but where those were is another problem altogether. At Water Newton the chance discovery of a group of silver pieces marked with Christian motifs and slogans dating to the fourth century is certain evidence of an active local Christian fellowship which may have had a church in the town; however, the fact that they secreted away and never recovered their valuable goods suggests that the group was not popular (**86**). The 'church' at Silchester is an enigmatic building which cannot be attributed to any religion with certainty (**87**). That Verulamium's Christian activity was centred on the *martyrium* of Alban is more definite, but the building lies somewhere under the Abbey church. At Colchester recent excavations have revealed a church-like building in the middle of an extramural cemetery. Here the east-west orientation of the

85a *Cutaway reconstructed view of the Mithraeum in London in its first phase with nave and aisles. In the far corner was a well. The Walbrook stream lay just beyond the apse. The building, reconstructed from original materials, is visible today in Queen Victoria Street.*

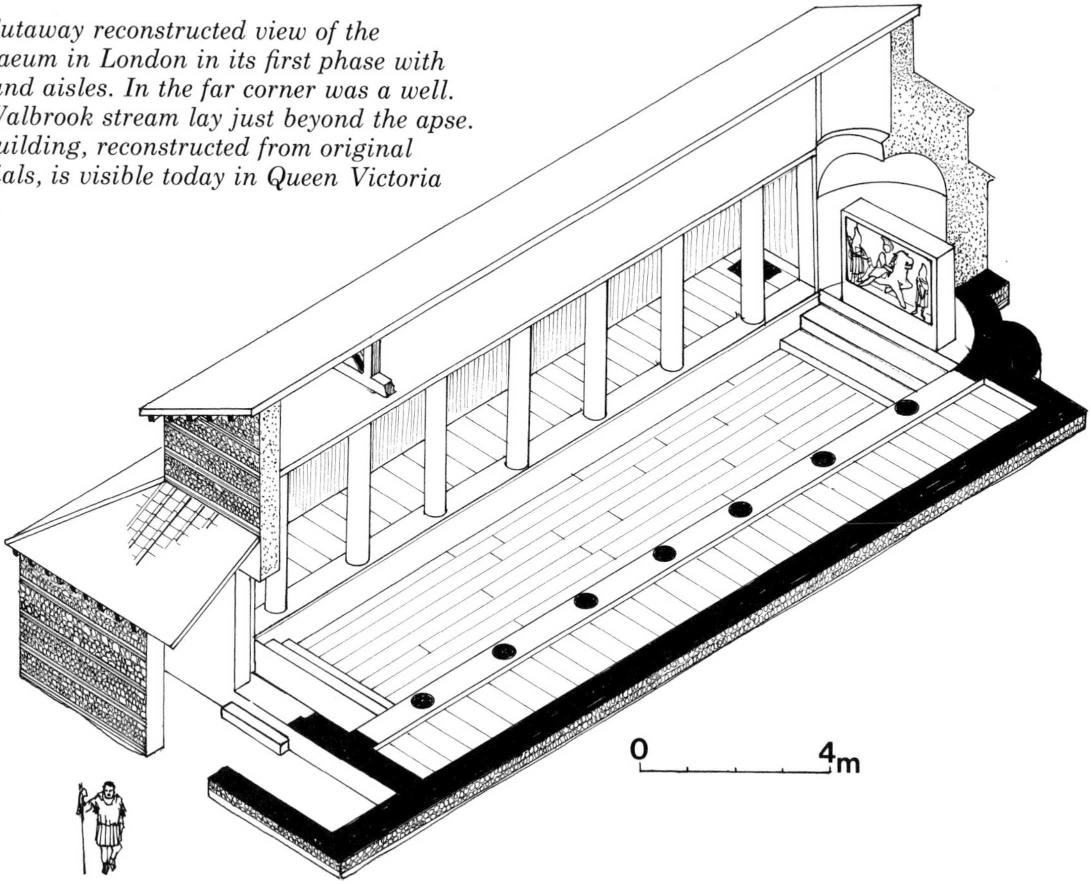

b *Marble relief from near the London Mithraeum site recording its dedication by Ulpius Silvanus, a veteran of the II legion* Augusta. *It was made at Orange (*Arausio*) in France.*

86 *Part of the Water Newton treasure. Some time in the fourth century a small Christian sect in the town buried a cache of silver plaques and vessels, some of which bear unequivocal references to Christianity. The larger plaque (height 15.7 cm (6 in)) bears a simple 'Chi-Rho' monogram while the other bears a pagan style record of a fulfilled vow by someone called Amicilla (width 10 cm (4 in)). The use of such plaques was traditionally a pagan custom and the find is an interesting conflation of conventional religious practice with what was still a relatively new cult.*

graves makes it likely that this was a church for the use of mourners, perhaps on or near the site of the grave of a particularly notable local Christian, maybe a martyr (**88** and see below p. 118). However, none of these examples have either revealed artefactual evidence like the Water Newton treasure or wall-paintings like those from Lullingstone. So while we know that Christianity was followed in Romano-British towns we have no idea of the extent or exactly where.

Romano-Celtic temples were occasionally associated with theatres. The theatre at Canterbury is known from traces of walls and was almost certainly accompanied by a temple of unknown style within a substantial colonnaded precinct across the main street. But such an association was not necessarily confined to large towns. At Wycomb the central feature of the small town seems to have been a temple precinct, probably containing a temple of Romano-Celtic style. Finds indicate a range of gods, including Mars and the *genii cucullati* (an obscure Celtic triad of unnamed hooded figures). Close by, traces of a curving masonry wall have been tentatively identified as remains of a theatre but there are problems because apart from the curve there is nothing else to confirm what it was. Wycomb is interesting because the temple's prominent location suggests that the town itself may have grown up around the shrine, rather than vice versa. This is a particularly interesting theme and is worth exploring in closer detail

Shrines that grew into towns

In most cases the temples and their precincts were products of the town. The larger temple at Verulamium lies on the same axis as the

87 *Reconstructed view of the 'church at Silchester'. No artefacts of any Christian association were found when it was excavated though the small square foundation at the front may have supported a baptismal font. The building faces east but churches usually face west.*

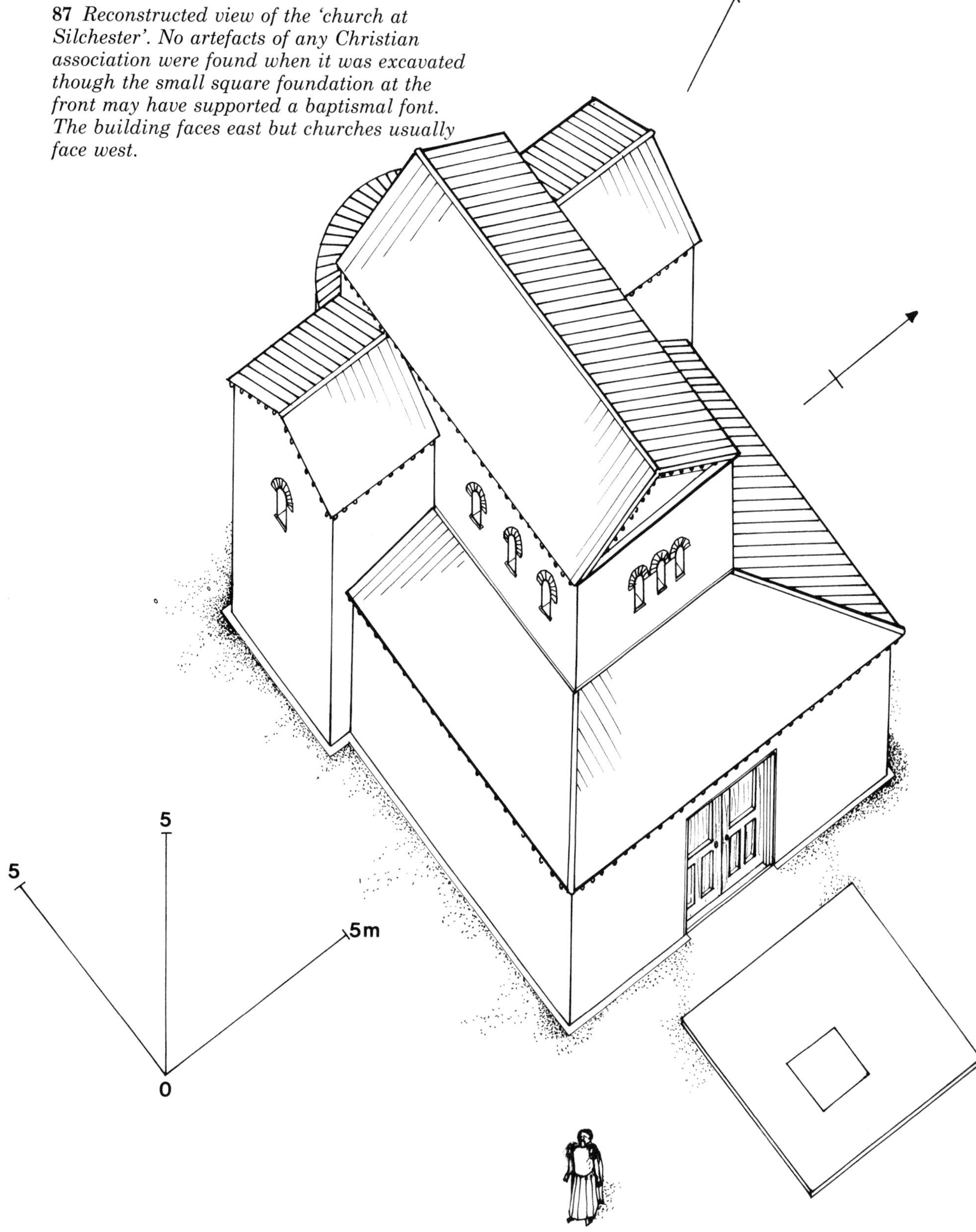

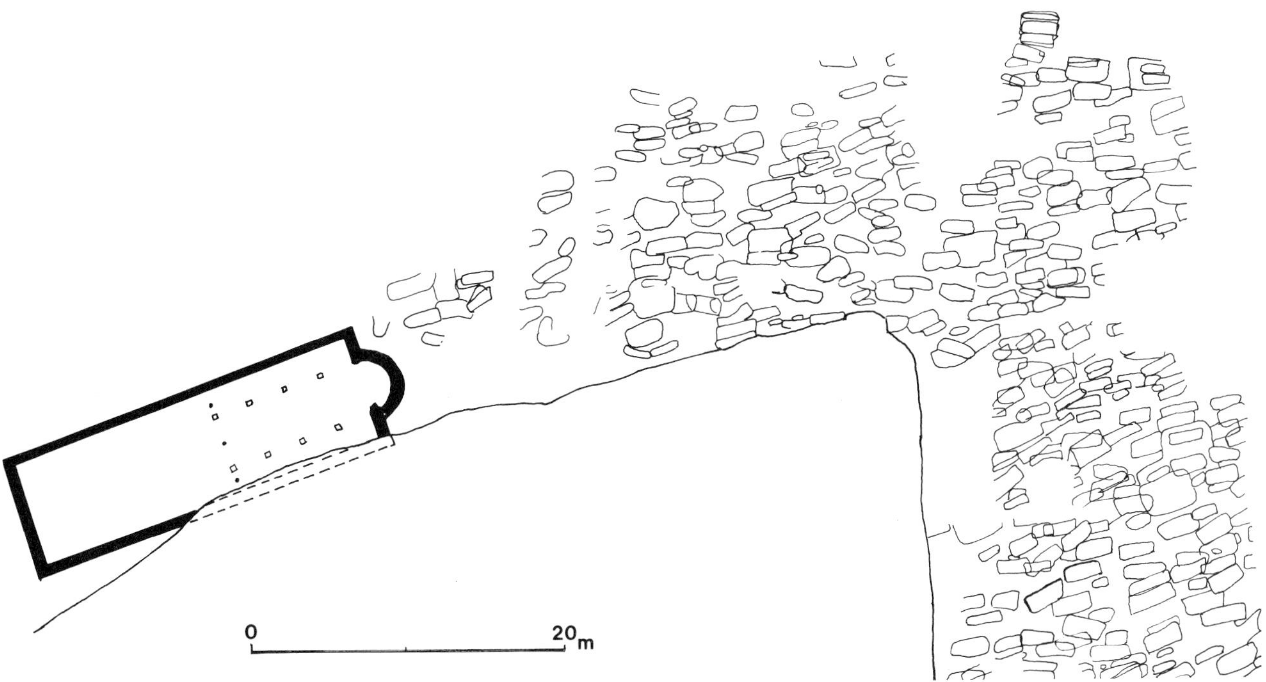

88 *Plan of the Police Station site 'church' and cemetery outside the south-west corner of the walls of Colchester. Note the orientation of the graves. (After Crummy.)*

theatre in an adjacent insula and both lie close to the centre of the town. The town's layout was probably designed with them in mind – in other words a kind of religious zone where myths and rituals could be acted or carried out before an audience or congregation.

In a few cases a town, or at least a town-like settlement, grew up around a sacred place. Wycomb is certainly a possibility but in the best known cases, at Bath and Springhead, a Celtic cult already existed on the site. After the invasion of 43 temples were built, and settlements grew up around them. Springhead was always modest in size and almost nothing is known about the several temples that existed during the Roman period other than that they were Romano-Celtic in form. The place was probably regarded as sacred because of the spring, but at the site today it is clear that a small perfectly-formed hill immediately to the north is a very dominant and pronounced feature which may have had some importance. Perhaps rather more crucial to the settlement's development was its prime location on the main road up from the Kent coast to London and therefore to the rest of the province also.

Lying on a major route seems to have been a feature of most town-like settlements which grew up around shrines and suggests that town-like services were provided there. Quite what the process of development was we cannot know but we could envisage an important Celtic shrine attracting a military presence to a place traditionally associated with gatherings of the local population. In places where it was both appropriate and desirable the subsequent or contemporary laying out of roads would then 'put the shrine on the map'. Thereafter its custom was more or less guaranteed, especially if it had a reputation for healing. While there are plenty of places where this didn't happen, for example the unsuitable hill-top temple at Lamyatt Beacon, it can hardly be coincidence that the Fosse Way has a number of settlements which seem to have developed around shrines. For travellers this would have made the site convenient as a place to make vows, offer sacrifices and stay a night. These shrines were also bound to have had appeal as recreational and interesting places to stay.

At Nettleton, on the Fosse Way, a small fort of uncertain date overlooked the narrow valley, suggesting that there was a good reason to be there. This may have been the presence of a Celtic shrine to a little-known god called Cunomaglos which needed policing (shrines might act as focal points of local resistance), and a possible Late Iron Age settlement. The fort was probably disused by the early second century at the latest and by the third century the valley came to contain not just a magnificent octagonal temple built in Romano-Celtic style (though by an architect of dubious competence) but a significant number of other buildings which included other temples and a water-mill. It is obviously difficult to form a conclusion about a settlement like this. Unlike Springhead the physical geography makes the site very restricted and it is unlikely to have spread far beyond the area covered by the archaeological excavations. However, the impression is of a self-contained settlement with an obvious source of income sited on a major route. Of more significance is the way in which, following the temple's collapse, the site remained in occupation by people who were engaged in the manufacture of pewter. This suggests that Nettleton's population had not been entirely restricted to those concerned with administering the cult(s).

Unlike most of these places Bath was identified early in the province's history as a cult centre of such major importance that it was swiftly developed into a site which earned a reputation across the Empire. It would be naive to assume that this was purely based on devotional considerations. The 'healing' waters which emerged from the ground and were associated with the Celtic deity Sulis were just as obviously a profitable commodity. For people visiting Bath the experience must have been exciting and enormously entertaining and it would be quite wrong to imagine that custom was confined to morose individuals with severe problems or grudges.

Bath was developed in the 60s and 70s by erecting a retaining wall around the spring to create a pool. The pool acted as a focal point for the cult centre by giving pilgrims somewhere tangible into which they or the priests could (and did) throw their offerings. It also created a head of water which was run off into the bath complex built immediately to the south. To the north, the main cult altar was sited in a temple precinct. The temple itself was a simple tetrastyle structure in classical form but with sculptures which were a mixture of Celtic and classical motifs. In the early fourth century the whole complex was radically altered by enclosing the spring pool in a vaulted cover building, and adding some sort of ambulatory to the temple (**89** and **colour plate 16**). The cover building was balanced by the erection of a little known structure to the north. Not very much is known about the rest of the settlement but on the site of the medieval abbey there may have been a further religious complex possibly built in the second century under Hadrian. This appears to have included a circular classical temple known as a *tholos* and may even have had a theatre.

It is evident from the enormous number of finds made in and around the baths and temple complex (including the partial excavation of the sacred spring) that the site was very popular and attracted visitors from all over the province and from other parts of the Empire. Does this make it a town? In many respects the settlement resembled a town, albeit a small one even if it was much larger than a place like Springhead: it had substantial buildings, houses, walls and extramural cemeteries. However, it apparently had no public administrative buildings and the dominant feature was the cult centre which was about a third of the width of the whole site. It was also not a civitas capital. But it is difficult to imagine that Bath did not serve many of the functions of a town, and may even have had some sort of delegated administrative role. It would have acted as a market for people who lived in the outlying countryside and it lay on a major route (the Fosse Way). So for practical purposes it can be regarded as an unusual town which grew up from an unusual origin, even if it did not enjoy official status.

Communicating with gods

Bath's particular appeal to pilgrims must have been a combination of many things: the marvellous natural setting of the site, surrounded by hills; the mystical appeal of a natural hot spring; and its location on a major route. Visitors sought the services of Sulis-Minerva and these ranged from healing to arranging for some disreputable person to have his or her come-uppance. Sulis-Minerva was contacted by throwing inscribed lead sheets into the spring and these tell us what the various 'customers' wanted. If the deity fulfilled their wishes, or simply needed encouraging gifts were donated to the spring as well, such as jewellery, plate

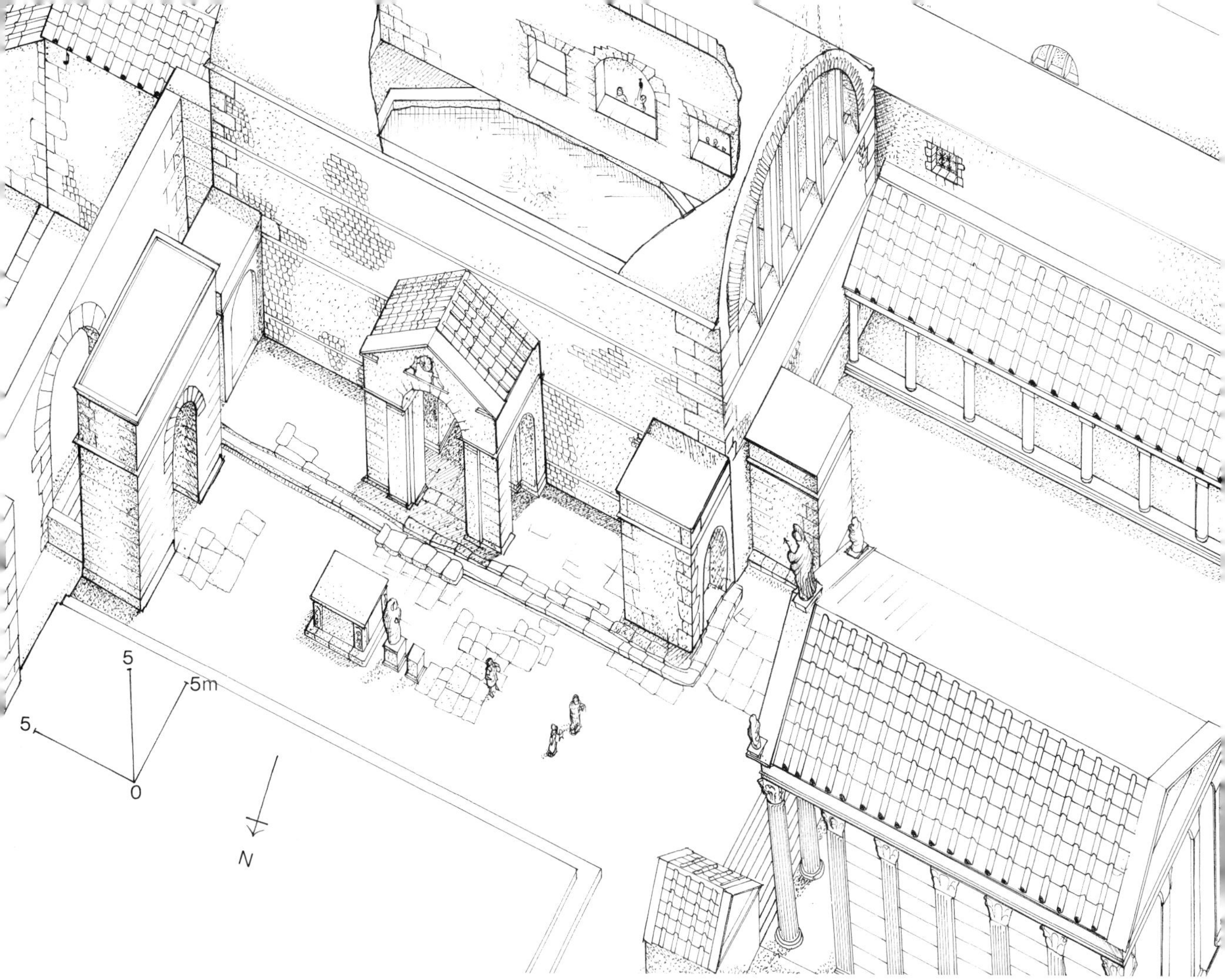

89 *Reconstructed view of the congested Temple precinct at Bath as it may have appeared during the fourth century. In the foreground the Temple of Sulis-Minerva overlooks the precinct with its altar. Behind the altar is the sacred spring enclosed by its vaulted cover-building. The cutaway roof shows pilgrims throwing offerings to the spring through three special windows. (Based on views by S. Gibson but adapted.)*

and coins. We do not have the same kind of written evidence from Bath at other town sites but we do have a number of instances where offerings were obviously being made over long periods of time (**90**).

At the 'Triangular Temple' in Verulamium the modest enclosed precinct surrounded a number of small pits containing animal bones, presumably sacrifices. There was also a large number of miniature pots which may have

90 *(Below) A small bronze ansate plaque (diameter 81 mm (3 in)) from Colchester bearing an inscription recording the fulfilment of a vow by Cintusmus the coppersmith to a god called Silvanus.*

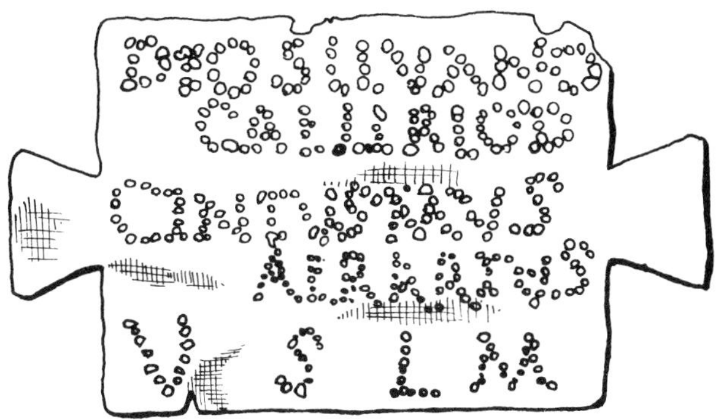

contained liquid offerings or libations. A recently discovered classical-style temple in York was also associated with pits containing animal bones and there were also a number of coins found in the ground around the building. Coins were a very common gift at sacred sites probably because they were cheap (the vast majority found at sacred sites are very worn examples of low denominations). The few places where we know, or assume, that state cults were observed are not accompanied by such finds and this is an interesting feature of Romano-British religious life on a day-to-day basis.

Death and burial in Romano-British towns

All towns had burial areas which were set aside specifically for the purpose. These were outside the area of settlement, something which was enforced by law, and were demarcated by some sort of boundary. An extensive cemetery to the east of London seems to have been defined by ditches, some of which created zones within the cemetery. In cases where cemeteries are located within a Roman town this is usually because they belong to an earlier and smaller phase in the town's history. Where a cemetery has been extensively examined it sometimes appears that graves were grouped according to different burial practices, such as the type of grave good, alignment of the body or the use of chalk packing in the coffin. These may represent extended family groups, or ethnic groups, though we cannot associate any one practice with any particular social sub-division apart from the nominal 'Christian' practices of orientating the body east-west and not using grave goods.

In general, cremation was customary during the first two centuries AD, thereafter inhumation became normal but not exclusive. In a cremation burial the burnt ashes of the deceased were placed in a container, usually a pottery or glass urn, and buried along with several other vessels containing libations and offerings. The group of vessels was occasionally enclosed in a miniature chamber made out of tiles or stone. Usually a pipe of some sort was inserted into the covering soil through which further offerings to the deceased could be passed. The individual graves were marked either with some sort of timber structure, which only survives in post-hole form, or a tombstone.

When inhumation became customary the wealthiest families paid for expensive decorated stone or lead coffins buried in mausolea. Those less well-off probably used wood coffins or constructed cists out of tiles or slabs of stone whilst the poorest were probably buried in nothing more than a shroud. Wood coffins naturally rotted away and traces are hardly ever found except for the iron nails used in their construction. In exceptional instances, for example in a cemetery to the north-east of Winchester, lead lining was used for a wood coffin. Shrouds present similar problems but the gypsum graves at York (where the bodies were surrounded with a gypsum packing) preserve the impression of the shrouds and sometimes fragments of the cloth.

Sometimes there is evidence for different ritual practices. In London, up until *c*.160, a number of skulls of young males were thrown into the Walbrook stream (a tributary of the Thames which passed through the town) and other waterlogged locations. This has been linked with the Celtic cults based on the decapitated head. The head was thought to retain the spirit of the deceased and to have special powers such as foretelling the future, especially if the person had been held in great esteem. Certainly the London heads show evidence of having been left out on view before they were thrown into the water. The rest of the body was probably cremated in the normal way.

Cemeteries are particularly interesting because they are the only source of factual evidence for the nature of the urban population (assuming, possibly incorrectly, they were confined to the urban population). Cremation burials give us little physiological information for obvious reasons but tombstones can supply some statistical material about the kind of people who lived in any one place. The trouble is that tombstones usually belong to people who are otherwise unknown and hardly ever carry information which allows them to be dated. Instead we have a name, age, possibly town of origin and sometimes further details of kin who were either buried there too or who were responsible for erecting the stone (**91**). They can be useful for identifying the presence of a fort and the nature of its occupants, of particular interest where a town is thought to have developed out of a fort *vicus*, for example the tombstone of Sextus Valerius Genialis, trooper with the *ala* I *Thracum* at Cirencester in the 50s or 60s. Sometimes the grave was

91 *Tombstone of Flavia Augustina, aged 39 years, 7 months and 11 days, her son ...nius Augustinus aged 1 year and 3 days, her son (name weathered) aged 1 year, 9 months and 5 days. The stone was erected by her husband Caeresius Augustinus, a retired legionary from the VI legion based at York. As the children are portrayed as much older than they actually were and the inscription does not fill the available space the stone was almost certainly one of those bought from a tombstone mason's stock and inscribed to order. From York. (Height 1·73 m (6 ft).)*

marked by a more elaborate monument. The sphinx from Colchester and a stone bust from York may have come from two which were subsequently broken up (**92**, **93**).

If the cremation is accompanied by datable grave goods, such as samian pottery or coins, then an estimate of its date can be made, but unfortunately it is extremely rare for a tombstone to be found in association with its burial, and in any case it is almost certain that the majority of graves would only have had a timber marker. Usually tombstones survive because they were removed for reuse as masonry elsewhere. Occasionally a cremation container carries an inscription. A particularly explicit hand-inscribed one on a lead urn from York says that it contained the ashes of Ulpia Felicissima aged eight years and 11 months, though another from the London/Verulamium area on a jar says simply 'SATTONIS', meaning '(the ashes) of Satto'.

The tombstone problem is just as relevant to inhumation cemeteries but it is at least possible to gain some sort of idea about the genetic characteristics of people from the same community, the reasons for, and age at, death and the various conditions from which they suffered during their lives. Two of the best known cemeteries are at Cirencester (Bath Gate) and at Poundbury by Dorchester. The archaeological effort involved in systematically examining hundreds of graves is enormous and not surprisingly very few such cemeteries have been paid such attention. At Poundbury a small number of mausolea were located in amongst the surrounding inhumations, at least two of which were decorated with painted wall-plaster (**94**). It has been suggested that, as the bulk of the graves are east-west orientated, indicating that the population was primarily Christian during the time that the cemetery was in use, these may mark the graves of local martyrs or local Christians with a reputation. Equally they may simply be an example of how even in death some are more equal than others, and represent people whose families had more money to spend on the afterlife.

The Bath Gate cemetery at Cirencester was in use throughout most of the fourth century and showed an interesting bias towards adult male burials – of 337 skeletons where the sex could be determined 241 (71 per cent) were males. One suggestion is that perhaps the population of the town contained a large number of

92 *Stone sphinx from Colchester, probably from a funerary monument. (Height 84 cm (33 in).)*

93 *Life-sized stone female head with a third century hairstyle from York. It may well have come from a mausoleum.*

retired soldiers and retired government officials though there is nothing specifically to confirm this. A number of the skeletons exhibited evidence for gout, apparently a unique concentration for Roman Britain, and it has been noted that amongst the modern local flora is a plant which contains a chemical called Colchicine, traditionally used to treat the condition. However, the London cemetery mentioned above produced a similar proportion of male burials so it may be for more general reasons that urban cemeteries had a male bias – perhaps men were more likely to gravitate to towns looking for work in government service, in household staffs or as labourers.

At Colchester more than 700 burials from a single cemetery were examined in the late 1980s at the Butt Road site, just outside the south-west corner of the town walls (see **88**). A small proportion were aligned north-south and were generally accompanied by grave goods, normal for pagan burials of Roman date. By the early fourth century, however, a change seems to have taken place: burials were now orientated east-west and far fewer had grave goods. These later burials were associated with a rectangular structure with an apse at its east end. This has been plausibly interpreted as a cemetery church though nothing was found which bore any kind of Christian motif.

Examination of the Colchester skeletons showed that most were buried in wooden coffins on their backs with hands crossed and wrapped in some kind of simple shroud, one of which

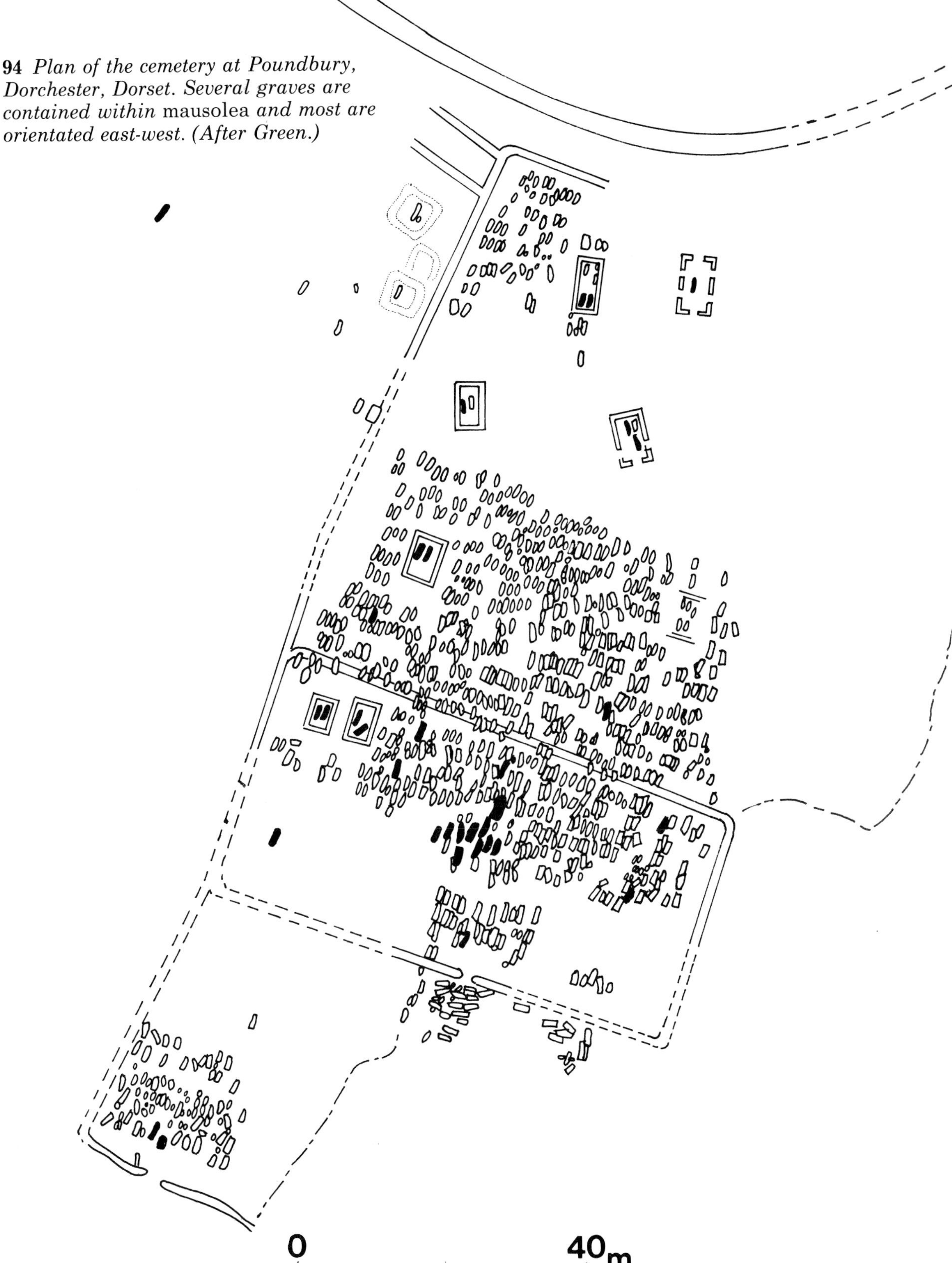

94 *Plan of the cemetery at Poundbury, Dorchester, Dorset. Several graves are contained within* mausolea *and most are orientated east-west. (After Green.)*

seems to have been made of Chinese silk (a remarkable instance of long-distance trade). Grave goods were mostly everyday personal ornaments such as hair-pins, brooches, necklaces and armlets though occasionally they were also equipped with sandals and pottery or glass vessels containing food and drink for the journey. It is interesting that the latter were found in some of the 'Christian' graves, which shows how a long-established tradition can endure even when its ostensible purpose has disappeared (this of course assumes that the 'Christian' interpretation is correct).

One of the most interesting features of these inhumation cemeteries is that they form the most comprehensive evidence for an urban population in the fourth century. This was a period for which archaeologists have tended to argue for diminished urban populations on the basis that the density of housing was reduced in favour of more widely-spaced buildings. The evidence is really inconclusive but it is possible that arguments about urban populations based on perceived distribution of housing may be based on false assumptions. As pointed out in Chapter 3 it is quite impossible to tell how many people might have occupied what appears to be a single house. The evidence can also be interpreted in opposing ways – the male bias at Cirencester could be argued as showing that the population was likely to be a stagnant one and sustained only by the artificial influx of retired soldiers, rather than by a thriving and prosperous population reproducing itself.

7

The collapse of Roman towns

The latter part of Roman Britain's history is even less well known than the earlier part, and this makes the fate of the towns one of the most difficult and obscure features of the period. We know that between about 342 and 370 tribal incursions from northern Britain and across the sea from northern Europe created a climate of insecurity. The Roman government was also showing further signs of disintegration. A number of Roman military commanders attempted to take power by force, for example Magnentius who involved Britain in his bid to become emperor in the West between 350 and 353. There were similar rebellions by Magnus Maximus (383-8) (**95**) and Constantine III (407-11).

Unfortunately none of this can be directly linked to the towns because there are no useful literary references and urban inscriptions have not survived (if they existed). We know that after the major barbarian incursion of 367 the general Count Theodosius was sent to Britain by the Emperor Valentinian I (364-75) to reconstruct the province. He based himself in London which he 'restored', according to the historian Ammianus Marcellinus. After various military reorganizations and withdrawals of troops, Britain's *civitates* were finally told to take care of their own defence in 410 by the Emperor Honorius, though it is evident that this was only formalizing a break that had already taken place. Even this latter reference is not certain, and may not even refer to Britain at all.

During the first and second centuries all the evidence gives us a reasonably clear impression of major towns being developed in fairly homogeneous form: London, the civitas capitals and colonies were all equipped with the various facilities required to fulfil their functions as administrative, economic and social centres. These varied a little from place to place and the time scale was also protracted and not necessarily contemporary but it appears that a broadly similar pattern of development was taking place. This was certainly guided at the very least by official provincial administration, rather than being purely local in instigation and planning, and backed by motivated and wealthy high-ranking members of the communities. Even the small towns show a common and gradual, albeit modest, degree of romanization based on their location or some kind of local industrial specialization.

In the third century, apart from the building of town defences and widely spaced stone houses, there is less impression of provincial urban regularity. Instead regional factors seem to have played a more influential role, with some towns showing signs of sustained investment, for example Canterbury's theatre or the reconstruction of the temple precinct at Bath, others a change in circumstances manifested in the different functions of public buildings like Silchester's basilica, or industry-based towns capitalizing on the change in the economy in favour of domestic production – Water Newton is the best example.

The changes in urban economies during the Roman period are hard to understand, and particularly so in the fourth century. London has provided the largest quantity of evidence for urban occupation even if its individual buildings have only been traced with difficulty. This has been due to the enormous numbers of small-scale rescue excavations since the 1960s. Much has been made of the widespread occurrence of a dark humus in levels dating to the third and fourth centuries: it has been used as a basis for arguing that the intense commercial

95 *Bronze coin of Magnus Maximus (383-8) who took control of Britain, Gaul and Spain. (Actual diameter 22 mm (1 in).)*

activity of the first and second centuries was an artificial situation, subsidized by cash injections from government and wealthy individuals. When this gave way to the developed provincial economy, London had less of a role to play and instead became a primarily residential area with large areas of land given over to farming by the fourth century.

This is an interesting idea, especially if it can be extended to other towns as well, and some of the evidence certainly makes such an interpretation seem plausible. The houses in Cirencester, which may have actually been farms, have already been mentioned in Chapter 4. Some of the towns have also produced evidence for a change in the way in which they were administered in the latter part of the period as shown by the demolition of London's basilica in the early fourth century and the occupation of Silchester's basilica by metalworkers from the mid-third century on. But what this really means is less clear because we can hardly accept the notion that if a basilica ceased to function then civic justice and government of the tribal cantons also ceased. The result would have been urban anarchy or collapse during the fourth century and this is not something there is evidence for in the archaeological and historical record. London, for example, was issuing coins in the name of Constantine I, the Great, until at least 325 (**96**) and may also have been used by Magnus Maximus to strike gold between 383-8. It was known as *Augusta* throughout most of the fourth century which implies that it was still functioning as the provincial capital.

In some other towns the basilicas appear to have remained in use, for example at Caerwent and Cirencester. The latter's forum was altered during the fourth century by having a dividing wall built across the piazza. This has been linked to the town's late status as a provincial capital, perhaps making provision for a governor's residence. Certainly the forum seems to have endured considerable wear on its flagstones during this time which makes it likely that civic activity of some sort was still going on, though this may have been commercial rather than administrative. The extensive fourth-century extramural cemeteries, discussed in the previous chapter, are surely proof that there was still an organized urban society.

Some late-fourth-century repair work on Hadrian's Wall seems to have been performed by gangs working in the names of several of the *civitates*. One from Cawfields milecastle (no. 42) credits the *civitas* of the Durotriges at *Lendiniensis* (Ilchester) (**97**), another from the fort at Carvoran credits the *civitas Dumnoniorum* whose tribal centre was at Exeter while the Brigantes were also named on a stone now lost from Blea Tarn. These are very interesting because if they have been correctly attributed to the late fourth century then it appears that the various provincial authorities were working in concert (perhaps at Theodosius' behest) to encourage or oblige the tribal communities to contribute to the reconstruction, a vital part of Britain's security.

The implication from this is that the tribal governments based in towns were still quite capable of mobilizing their communities and must therefore have had the motivation, resources and facilities to do so. If they could do this then it is equally likely that they could maintain their towns in a centralized way, in

96a *A bronze coin of Constantine I (307-37) struck at the mint in London* c. *309-13. The legend* ADVENTUS AUG *means 'The arrival of the Emperor' and may refer to an otherwise unrecorded visit to the city by Constantine. Similar coins from other parts of the Empire have been shown to coincide with testified visits by Constantine. The mint-mark is* PLN, *an abbreviation for* Pecunia LoNdinii, *'money of London'.*
b *bronze coin of Constantine I also struck in London,* c. *314-17. (Actual diameters about 22mm (1in).)*

so far as it was necessary. This may be a great deal to conclude from three brief inscriptions but there are no parallels from earlier periods. The finds of late metalwork in Germanic style in town cemeteries, for example at London, Caistor-by-Norwich and Dorchester-on-Thames were traditionally taken to be evidence for the presence of Germanic mercenaries, the *foederati*, employed by towns for their own defence (**98**). This is an ambitious assumption to base on the evidence of buckles which were also standard issue for the Roman army; they might be evidence merely for the presence of individual soldiers in transit or residence. However, whether the buckles are evidence for garrisons of Roman soldiers or for mercenaries makes no difference to the implication that civic government was still operating and that there was something worth protecting.

If the evidence for late urban administrative activity is ambiguous so is that from other public buildings. None of the amphitheatres of Roman Britain seem to have been repaired or specifically maintained during the fourth century. At Silchester extensive robbing of the arena wall took place but this may have been post-Roman activity (see **29**). Structural alterations at Cirencester limited access to the arena though what this means in terms of function is not very clear. At Wroxeter the public baths seem to have been largely ruinous by the end of the fourth century and the same fate had befallen Verulamium's theatre which had become a rubbish tip. Yet even at Wroxeter the collapsed columns and other stonework in the baths exercise hall bear ruts worn by wheels which suggests a considerable amount of day-

97 *Stone from Hadrian's Wall (near milecastle 42 at Cawfields) recording a section of wall repaired by the Durotriges tribe from Ilchester in Somerset. The C in the first line stands for* Civitas *followed by* DVRTRG *for the tribe. The town name of* Lindinis *is written as* L|ENDINESIS. *Its very crude style indicates that it is likely to be of late date, recording repair work in the late fourth century.*

to-day traffic (**99**) – hardly a sign of a dead town.

Many urban defences were strengthened during the fourth century by having external bastions added to them (see **46**). This may have been part of Theodosius' programme of reconstruction, a quite plausible scenario in terms of the time-honoured tradition of preparing for the war that has just finished but the evidence is only circumstantial. In a few cases, like Verulamium, they were apparently part of the original late-third-century design but for the most part bastions seem to have been built during the second half of the fourth century. They may represent a change in style, reflecting

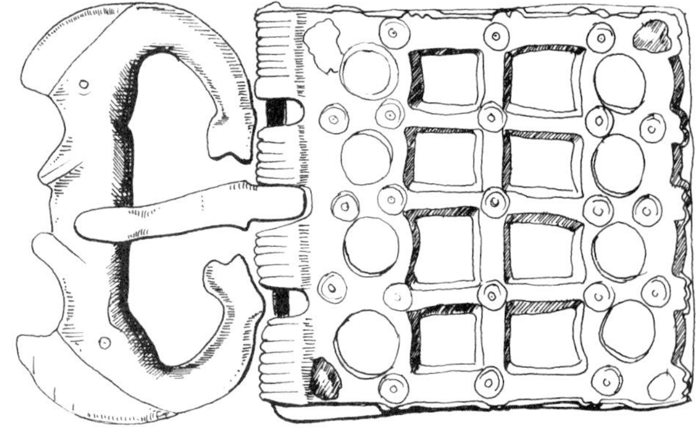

98 *Buckle from Dorchester-on-Thames of a type sometimes associated with the presence in towns of mercenaries of Germanic origin in the late fourth century. However they are now considered to have been just as likely to be standard military issue for the period. (Length 10 cm (4 in). After C.S. Green.)*

99 *A very worn statue from the baths at Wroxeter. It had ended up as part of a floor but the wear indicates that there was still a considerable amount of wheeled traffic. (English Heritage.)*

the preference for defensive artillery mounted on external bastions, but many show signs of having been erected with reused stonework.

This may have followed a 'crisis' leading to hasty demolition of convenient structures, but it is equally possible that if some public buildings and temples had been allowed to run down then there would have been reasonable quantities of stone lying around on derelict sites. Cemeteries were favourite sources and several bastions in London have been found to contain sculptures and inscribed stones from tombs including parts of that belonging to the first-century procurator Classicianus. At Kenchester, a remote town possibly acting as a subordinate *civitas* centre for the Dobunni, an elaborate fourth-century gate and tower were built partly out of stone taken from a building of some architectural pretensions. Considering that the Saxon Shore forts were built in this style it is more likely that the urban authorities took it upon themselves to 'up-date' their defences. A late-fourth-century gate in the lower part of Lincoln contained one piece of temple entablature upside down in its plinth suggesting that it was a handy block, rather than that the temple had been demolished for that express purpose (see **47**).

But by the end of the fourth century, and more particularly during the early part of the fifth it becomes clear that what we regard as the archaeological definitions of a town site being 'Roman' had very largely disappeared. While life of a sort was evidently going on in the towns it is much harder to define because there is, literally, very little *to* define – coins had ceased to be either imported or imitated locally and pottery production in any kind of organized form ceased. Even building in towns, apart from occasional traces of timber structures and possible churches, had apparently stopped.

Understanding what happened after about 400 is much more difficult for these archaeological reasons. The existence of a fifth-century water-pipe in Verulamium, overlying a demolished hall which itself overlay a house which was not built before 370, is often quoted as evidence for sustained organized community life though this does seem rather a lot to read into a single pipe. St Patrick, who lived during the fifth century, had a father who was a decurion, which implies that the political and administrative organization of some towns was at least nominally intact. On the other hand the Lower Thames Street bath-house in London fell into ruin during the first half of the fifth century. A Saxon brooch was dropped amongst the roof-tiles and while this could be argued as evidence for a ruined city with scavengers rooting through the derelict remains it is also evidence for people still living there.

Continuity of sorts is much more likely than termination. In London a number of excavations in recent years have shown that there was an extensive seventh- to ninth-century settlement to the west of the former Roman capital, centred on a part still known as the Aldwych (literally 'old *wic*', *wic* being an early English corruption of *vicus*). Finds from a site in Covent Garden showed that the settlement was engaged in trade and industry. In 731 the monastic historian Bede described London as an international trading centre. It seems unlikely that it could really have ceased to exist in this sense for a long period in between, though for the moment the fifth and sixth centuries have yielded few finds in London. Another reference of his, this time in the *Life of St Cuthbert*, describes the saint's visit to Carlisle in 685 where he saw a fountain in working order.

Much the most convincing evidence for the existence of a fifth-century urban community (as opposed to isolated instances of occupation evidence) has been found at Wroxeter. The town is now in largely open fields and this has made systematic examination of late- and sub-Roman levels possible. Towns which were built on in the medieval period have almost invariably had these levels so damaged that building up any kind of accurate general picture is impossible, though recent work at Canterbury has identified the presence of circular huts with sunken floors containing Saxon-style pottery thought to belong to the mid-fifth century. The same area yielded an exceptionally rare Visigothic gold *tremissis* struck in South Gaul about 480, and a burial has also produced a gold *solidus* of the Byzantine emperor Zeno (474-91).

Other Roman towns which are still unbuilt upon have usually suffered from early excavation work. This tended to ignore the minimal traces of building activity in the fifth century. Silchester is the best (or worst!) example while Verulamium has yet to fulfil its archaeological potential. At Wroxeter an extensive range of timber buildings were erected in and around the baths exercise hall (**100**). These included what have been identified as shops and a larger structure similar to a winged corridor town-house in plan. These buildings were erected in and around the ruins, in a manner still to be seen in a number of the former classical cities in Turkey and Greece where ruined buildings of Roman date contain modern shops built into ancient vaults.

It is interesting that so many Romano-British town defences evaded wholesale demolition even if their buildings did not. This suggests that the wall circuits still had some sort of defensive role to play. The sixth-century chronicler Gildas describes them as fearful places where the population indulged in pagan ritual activities, which implies that they were not wholly abandoned. The Wroxeter instance has been argued as evidence for a sort of chieftain's stronghold rather than an urban community. This may be much closer to the truth for many town sites once the centralized influence of provincial government had disappeared. The tombstone of Cunorix, found outside Wroxeter's walls, probably belonged to an Irish warrior chief who lived there during the fifth century (**101**). However, it is impossible to tell whether he was there at the invitation of the local community, or was part of a group which had taken control of the settlement by force.

Perhaps the best evidence for urban continuity in a form which went beyond the mere presence of individuals lies in Christianity. There are extremely few instances of structures which can convincingly be argued to have been churches. But there are a number of cases where churches of later date were almost certainly built on or out of churches which had been founded in the Roman period, even if the earlier structure has not been identified. Bede says that St Augustine established himself in Canterbury in a church built during the Roman period on the east side of the town. The most likely candidate is the church of St Pancras, the ruins of which are still visible.

At Verulamium, the settlement moved away from the former Roman town and gathered around the *martyrium* of St Alban which probably lies under the medieval abbey church. There are also instances of medieval or sub-Roman churches being built in the ruins of a forum or basilica. At Lincoln a sub-Roman church with burials of possibly fifth-century date has been found in the forum, while at London it is interesting that the medieval church of St Peter on Cornhill lies in the middle of the basilica. At York the headquarters building of the legionary fortress attached to the colony, which survived intact for several centuries after the Roman period, now lies under the medieval Minster. If Roman buildings were

100 *A reconstructed view of the fifth century timber house built in the ruins of the baths* palaestra *at Wroxeter. (Painting by Ivan Lapper; English Heritage.)*

being reused this was only sensible. We know that the practice could extend to using old temples as churches because Pope Gregory advised this in a letter written in 601 to avoid presenting Christianity as a destructive force. This in itself suggests that a number of urban pagan temples were both intact and functioning and that communities still existed.

Towns were of course a product of trade and a thriving economy. The rich villa estates which were such a conspicuous feature of the fourth-century countryside in central and southern Britain must have relied on urban demand for their produce. By the fifth-century the villa houses seem almost without exception to have been given up, though circumstantial evidence in a handful of cases, like parish boundaries and church estates, is thought to point to the survival of the estates as single units (for example at Withington in Gloucestershire). At Orton Hall Farm near Peterborough and Frocester (Gloucestershire) there is some evidence for continuing cultivation on into the fifth-century, though as yet there is no evidence for the earning of the significant surplus wealth which financed the fourth-century villas. The disappearance of wheel-made pottery and coinage points to a denuded economy which was much more likely to be based on small-scale self-sufficiency. If so this must have had a significant effect on the capacity for towns to maintain populations of any size, let alone large ones.

101 *Tombstone of Cunorix from Wroxeter. The base Latin inscription* CUNO RIX MAQUS MAQUI COLINI *means 'Hound king, son of the son of the Holly' and appears to refer to a chieftain of Irish origin. If so he may have been a warrior employed to help defend Wroxeter or he may have been part of a group which actually controlled the settlement. It has been attributed to the fifth century and was found outside the north-east town wall. (English Heritage.)*

Although the traditional name for this period, the 'Dark Ages', is now regarded as a little old-fashioned it is none the less true that we cannot accurately discern the nature of society in post-Roman Britain. Such evidence as has been gathered in recent years and described briefly above shows that we cannot draw any kind of general conclusions. Instead it seems likely that local circumstances were far more influential and the fate of each town was dictated by them. This may have been as simple as the presence of, or lack of, a single dominant individual. A place like London was very unlikely to be abandoned and instead its nature probably changed gradually over a number of generations, though it would have remained a trading centre. At other places like Silchester or Caistor-by-Norwich the Roman settlements were eventually more or less given up but the presence of medieval churches within both may point to a low level of, and consequently archaeologically undiscernible, continuity.

By the early years of the fifth century Romano-British towns as components of a unified complex trading, economic and governmental framework had disappeared from the record available to us. This tantalizing state of affairs is unlikely to alter but some of the evidence discussed above suggests that the process of decline need not have been especially protracted. But ultimately the towns, as Roman towns, faded into obscurity because they no longer served their purpose as extensions of the Roman government, and because the insecurity following Roman rule prejudiced the economic surplus on which they depended. The world had almost turned full circle for Britain but as so many Roman towns re-emerged as major settlements in the medieval period we cannot assume they entirely ceased to function, even temporarily.

Appendix 1: Where to visit Roman towns

Most of Roman Britain's major towns have some sort of visible remains but these are mainly confined to fragments of the walls. This list refers to the most significant examples of buildings that can be seen. Would-be visitors are advised to check in advance that sites are accessible, especially during the winter. The most satisfying sites are Bath, Lincoln, Verulamium and Wroxeter.

Aldborough, North Yorkshire
Sections of wall and two mosaics *in situ*. Defences accessible any time, mosaics summer season only.

Bath, Avon
An outstanding site. The baths and sections of the Temple Precinct are accessible from the Pump Rooms in Stall Street along with a museum containing some exceptional finds (open daily).

Caerwent, Gwent
The town defences are particularly striking on the south, including the gate. Town-houses in Pound Lane (western part of the town off main road). Temple on north side of main road in the middle of the town (Cadw). The basilica is currently being consolidated for display. Access at any time.

Canterbury, Kent
The city wall forms part of north wall of St Mary Northgate. Disappointing fragments of theatre in hotel in St Margaret's Street. Town-house in Butchery Lane. Royal Museum in High Street (weekdays).

Chichester, West Sussex
Cogidubnus' inscription on view outside Assembly Rooms in North Street. Amphitheatre off Whyke Lane, a turning from the A259 just east of the city wall.

Cirencester, Gloucestershire
Defences visible in Corinium Gate off London Road just by junction between A417 and A429. Amphitheatre: leave town centre to south-west up Querns Hill, amphitheatre visible off Cotswold Avenue. Corinium Museum in Park Street is outstanding (closed Sundays, and Mondays as well during the winter).

Colchester, Essex
Most of the city walls visible on west, north and east. Balkerne Gate at west is accessible, as is Duncan's Gate in the north sector. The excellent museum is in the Norman Castle, including the vaults to the Temple of Claudius (weekdays, and Sunday afternoons in the summer). The 'church' has been exposed for display just outside the SW corner of the town defences a short walk from the Balkerne Gate.

Corbridge, Northumberland
A former fort which grew into a town close to the northern frontier. A street with granaries, temples and former fort buildings is accessible on a large site to the west of the modern town along with an excellent museum. Open all year.

Gloucester
East gate visible outside Boots store in Eastgate. Museum in Brunswick Street (closed Sundays).

Great Casterton, near Stamford, Leicestershire
Only the defences on the northern side can be seen off a lane signposted to Ryhall.

Leicester
Museum and Jewry Wall (part of the baths) accessible from St Nicholas' Circle on the inner ring road. Jewry Wall accessible any time, museum closed Fridays.

Lincoln
Gates visible in the north and east of the upper town, and at the south-west in the lower town. Basilica rear wall 'Mint Wall' behind hotel in Westgate and forum well-head nearby. Museum in Broadgate (daily).

London
Various sections of wall, best on north side of Tower Hill and within the Tower of London. Fort wall junction with town wall visible in Noble Street close to the Museum of London which contains the most outstanding collection of finds from a Roman town (closed Mondays). Some also at the British Museum in Gt Russell Street (daily). Temple of Mithras visible as a reconstructed display of original material in Queen Victoria Street.

Silchester, Hampshire
Town defences visible almost in their entirety but the gates are not well preserved. The cleared and consolidated amphitheatre is accessible outside the walls just north of the church in the eastern sector. Finds in Reading Museum (closed Sundays).

Verulamium (St Albans), Hertfordshire
Verulamium Museum with its excellent displays of finds from one of Roman Britain's premier towns lies close to the theatre which is the only example visible in Britain (daily). Parts of the defences in the southern part of the town can still be seen and a mosaic is visible in its original location a short walk from the museum (daily).

Vindolanda (Chesterholm), Northumberland
The *vicus* settlement is laid out just outside the fort's west gate. Various buildings can be seen and an extensive range of displays are on view in the museum (daily).

Wall, near Lichfield, Staffordshire
The only small town of Roman Britain where the *mansio* and baths can be seen. There is also a small site museum (daily except Monday and some Tuesdays).

Water Newton, Cambridgeshire
Accessible from junction of A1 and A605. Defences visible as mounds, and the agger of Ermine Street from London on its way to Lincoln.

Wroxeter, Shropshire
The 'Old Work' and the baths complex, along with the *macelleum* have recently been renovated and it is now possible to walk around the site comparing the surviving remains with reconstruction paintings placed at strategic locations. There is a site museum (daily).

PROVINC NAR
RBONENSIS
ORDINIS RES
SILVRVM

Appendix 2: Inscriptions

There are very few inscriptions from Roman towns in Britain which tell us anything factual about their history. Some of the most important, also referred to in the text, have their full restored texts given here in chronological order along with a brief commentary.

c.50-80 (CHICHESTER, *Noviomagus Regnensium*)

[N]EPTUNO · ET · MINERVAE
TEMPLUM
[PR]O · SALUTE · DO[MUS] · DIVINA[E]
[EX] · AUCTORITAT[E · TI]· CLAUD·
[CO]GIDUBNI · RE[G · MA]GN · BRIT·
[COLLE]GIUM · FABROR · ET · QUI · IN · EO
[SUNT] · D · S · D · DONANTE · AREAM
[.....]ENTE PUDENTINI · FIL

This inscription has provoked much debate over the precise status of the client king Cogidubnus, who ruled over the Regnenses in southern Britain following the Roman invasion. The restoration shown here is that of J.E.Bogaers. However, in this context the most interesting point is that a local guild of smiths (*collegium fabrorum*) had donated funds for the building of a temple to Neptune and Minerva with Cogidubnus' permission. It was built on a site dedicated by someone whose name is missing, but was a son of one Pudentinus. (*RIB* 91; see *Britannia*, 10, 1979, 243-254).

102 *Inscribed base from Caerwent recording a dedication to the legate of the II legion, stationed at nearby Caerleon, by the* civitas *of the Silures. About* AD *213. The base can be viewed in Caerwent church porch.*

59 (CHICHESTER, *Noviomagus Regnensium*)

NERONI
CLAVDIO · DIVI · [CLAUD
AVG · F ·] GERMANI[CI
CAES · N]EPOTI · TI · [CAES
AVG · P]RONEPOTI · DIV[I · AVG
AB]· N · CAESARI · AVG ·[GERM
T]R·P·IV · IMP·IV · COS·IV
S·C·V·M

A dedication slab recording vows of loyalty by the local town senate (abbreviated to S in the last line) to the Emperor Nero. This shows that Chichester had been established as a town with its own government at a very early date. The imperial titles in the last line allow the inscription to be precisely dated. (*RIB* 92.)

c. 61-69 (LONDON, *Londinium*)

DIS
[M]ANIBVS
[C · IVL · C · F · F]AB · ALPINI · CLASSICIANI
(at least two lines lost)
PROC · PROV · BRITA[NNIAE]
IVLIA · INDI · FILIA · PACATA · [INDIANA]
VXOR [F]

Tombstone of the procurator Classicianus found in two parts (1852 and 1935) reused in a bastion on the city wall. Tacitus mentions Classicianus as playing an instrumental part in the reconstruction of Britain after the Boudican Revolt (*Annales*, xiv.38) and the tombstone's location suggests that the provincial government was now working from London. (*RIB* 12.)

79 (VERULAMIUM)

[IMP·TITO·CAESARI·DIVI·]VESPA[SIANI·]F·VES]PASIANO·AVG]
[PM·TR·P·VIIII·IMP·XV·COS·VII·]DESI[G·VIII·CENSORI·PATER·PATRIAE]
[ET·CAESARI·DIVI·VESP]ASIAN[I·F·DO]MI[TIANO·COS·VI·DESIG·VII·PRINCIPI]
[IVENTVTIS · ET ·] OMN[IVM·COLLEGIORVM·SACERDOTI]
[CN·IVLIO·A]GRI[COLA · LEGATO·AVG·PRO]·PR]
[MVNICIPIVM·]VE[RVLAMIVM · BASILICA·OR]NATA]

or:

[CIVITAS·CATV]VE[LLAVNORVM · FORO·EXOR]NATA

or:

[RESPVBLICA·]VE[RVLAMIVM · LATIO·DO]NATA

Records the dedication of the forum or basilica at Verulamium in 79 during reign of Titus and the governorship of Gnaeus Julius Agricola. Its restoration is an interesting exercise in the standardized formulae of imperial Roman inscriptions.

129-30 (WROXETER, *Uriconium Cornoviorum*)

IMP CA[ES] · DIVI · TRAIANI · PARTHI
CI · FIL · DI[VI] · NERVAE · NEPOTI · TRA
IANO · H[A]DRIANO · AVG · PONTI[FI]
CI · MAXIMO · TRIB·POT·XIII[I] · COS·III·PP
CIVITAS · CORNOV[IORVM]

This inscription records the dedication of the forum of the town in 129-130 to Hadrian by the community of the *Cornovii*. The building is not specified but the inscription was found near the main entrance to the forum. (*RIB* 288.)

140-44 (BROUGH-ON-HUMBER, *Petuaria*)

OB · HONOR[EM]
DOMVS · DIVINAE
IMP · CAES · T · AEL · H[ADRI]
ANI · ANTONINI · A[VG · PII]
PP · COS·I[II]
ET · NVMINIB · A[VG]
M · VLP · IANVARIV
AEDILIS · VICI · PETV[AR]
PROSCAEN·****·DE·SVO·[DEDIT]

Records the dedication of a new stage (*proscaenium* by the *aedile* (magistrate) of the town of Petuaria, Marcus Ulpius Januarius, about 140-4 during the reign of Antoninus Pius. Januarius' names indicate that he received his own citizenship during the reign of Marcus Ulpius Trajanus (Trajan, 98-117) (*RIB* 707.)

c.213 (CAERWENT, *Venta Silurum*)

[TI · CLAUDIO]
PAULINO
LEG ·LEG·II
AUG · PROCONSUL
PROVINC · NAR
R BONENSIS
LEG · AUG · PR · PR · PROVIN
LUGDUNEN
EX · DECRETO
ORDINIS · RES
PUBL · CIVIT
SILURUM

Inscription from a statue plinth recording that the government of the *civitas* of the Silures decreed that a statue of Tiberius Claudius Paulinus be set up. He was legate of the II legion at nearby Caerleon but subsequently became governor of *Britannia Inferior* (see Chapter 4) in about 220. (*RIB* 311.)

221 (YORK, *Eboracum*)

[I·O·M·D] · ET · GENIO·LOCI
[ET · N·A]UGG · L·VIDUCIUS
[L·F·PLA]CIDUS · DOMO
[CIVIT]·VELIOCASIUM
[SEVIR · N]EGOTIATOR
[CRET · A]RCUM · ET · FANUM
[D·D·L·D]·D·[D] · GRATO · ET
[SELEUCO · COS]

Inscription recording the erection of an arch (*arcum*) and temple (*fanum*) by Lucius Viducius Placidus, son of Lucius from Rouen (*Veliocas[s]ium*). They were dedicated to Jupiter Dolichenus, the spirit of the place and the spirits of the emperors. The man concerned, who was a priest (*sevir*), is known from another inscription at a shrine on the mouth of the River Scheldt and the two give some indication of the extent of the pottery trade he was engaged in as a merchant (*negotiator cret[arii]*). The consulship information in the last two lines makes it possible to date the inscription exactly. (*Britannia*, 8, 1977, 430)

c.250 (LONDON)

I N H D D
M * MARTIAN
NIUS ▶ PULCH
ER ▶ V ▶ C ▶ LEG
AUGG ▼ PRO *
PRAET ▲ TEMP[LUM
ISIDIS ▼ C.....
TIS VETUSTATE
COLLAPBSUM
RESTITUI PR[AE
CEPIT

Altar from Upper Thames Street, London found used as filling in the late riverside wall. It records that Marcus Martiannius Pulcher, possibly governor (or deputy governor) of Upper Britain in the middle of the third century rebuilt a temple which had collapsed. The name of the deity is severely damaged but is probably Isis. (See 84 and *Britannia* 7, 1976, 378)

c.350 (CIRENCESTER, *Corinium Dobunnorum*)

I O [M]	**SI]GNUM ET**	**SEPTIMIUS**
L·SEPT[IMIUS]	**[E]RECTAM**	**RENOVAT**
V P PR B [PR]	**P]RISCA RE**	**PRIMAE**
REST[ITUIT]	**LI]GIONE CO**	**PROVINCIAE**
CIUIS RE[MUS]	**L]UMNAM**	**RECTOR**

The three surviving sides of the Jupiter column base from Cirencester record that L. Septimius, governor of B(ritannia) Pr(ima) and a citizen of Rheims, restored the column dedicated to J[upiter] O[ptimus] M[aximus]. It had originally been dedicated under the old religion (*prisca religione*) which suggests that the work was done during a period of revived paganism, perhaps during the reign of Julian the Apostate (360-3). (*RIB* 103.)

Fourth century (Old Penrith)

D M
FL·MARTIO·SEN
IN·C·CARVETIOR
QUESTORIO
VIXIT·AN·XXXXV
MARTIOLA·FILIA·ET
HERES·PONEN
[DUM]·CURAVIT

Tombstone (now lost) dedicated to Flavius Martius, senator of quaestorian status (i.e. had served as a quaestor) in the *civitas* of the Carvetii. He died aged 45 and the stone was erected by his daughter Martiola. Martius is an exceptionally rare instance of a Romano-British *civitas* councillor whose rank and name we know. He will have worked in the *civitas* capital of the Carvetii at Carlisle (*Luguvalium*). (*RIB* 933.)

RIB is a reference to the catalogue of inscriptions: *The Roman Inscriptions of Britain*, 1965, Collingwood, R.G., and Wright, R.P., Oxford. Other references are to the annual journal *Britannia*, published by the Society for the Promotion of Roman Studies, London (see Further Reading).

Further reading

General

There are a number of modern books which cover the history of Roman Britain, for example Sheppard Frere's *Britannia* (1987), and Peter Salway's *Roman Britain* (1981). More recently Martin Millett has summarized much current thought about the history of Roman Britain in his *Romanization of Britain* (1990) while a great deal of factual material has been covered by Barri Jones and David Mattingly in *An Atlas of Roman Britain* (1990). All include sections concerned with towns and their history and development. The major sources mentioned here can be easily found in the Penguin Classics series, including Tacitus' *Annals*, and Suetonius' *Lives of the Caesars*.

These provide an excellent background to the whole subject but a more detailed general look at towns can be found in John Wacher's *Towns of Roman Britain* (1974) and *The 'Small Towns' of Roman Britain* (1990), the latter written in association with Barry C. Burnham. Both books follow the same pattern of considering different types of town by examining individual examples in detail. Graham Webster's *Fortress into City* (1988) contains a number of chapters written by excavators recording some of the more recent work in major towns with a distinctive military history. These are mainly the colonies, but Cirencester and Wroxeter are also included.

Alan Sorrell's *Roman Towns in Britain* (1976) provides a number of artistic reconstructions of Romano-British urban life. The present author's *Buildings of Roman Britain* (1991) contains many reconstruction drawings of buildings in Roman towns, and *Finds of Roman Britain* (1989) includes many illustrations of finds from Roman towns.

Individual towns

Books concerned with the Roman history and archaeology of individual towns are frustratingly limited. Probably the most comprehensive are George Boon's *Silchester: the Roman Town of Calleva* (1974), Peter Marsden's *Roman London* (1980) and Ralph Merrifield's *London, City of the Romans* (1983). A more up-to-date and very useful survey of work done in the capital is Dominic Perring's *Roman London* (1991) in Seaby's Archaeology of London series. Barry Cunliffe's *Roman Bath Discovered* (1984) covers the recent excavations in a very special case of urban development. Alan McWhirr's *Roman Gloucestershire* (1981) provides useful summaries of archaeology in Gloucester and Cirencester. Unfortunately most of the other major towns have not yet been the subject of the kind of book which usefully brings together old and new material.

Apart from these, the other books which are directly concerned with individual towns are the archaeological reports prepared by excavators. The most recent to have appeared are Michael Fulford's reports on new excavations at Silchester. The forum and basilica are covered in the *Antiquaries Journal*, 65 (1985), 39-81, and the amphitheatre in a monograph published by the Society for the Promotion of Roman Studies (*Britannia* Monograph No. 10, 1989).

'Standard' excavation reports include a number published by the Society of Antiquaries in London in its Research Report series. The most important are M.R. Hull's *Roman Colchester* (1958) which includes an examination of the defences and the Temple of Claudius, and Sheppard Frere's three volumes of *Verulamium Excavations* (1972, 1983, 1984). The first volume covers the *Insula* XIV shops, the second includes sections on the basilica and houses while the third contains detailed catalogues of finds. Earlier excavations by Sir Mortimer Wheeler were covered earlier in the same series in *Verulamium: a Belgic and two Roman cities*, published in 1936.

Information about current excavations often appears first in abbreviated form in the pages of *Current Archaeology*, published at 9 Nassington Road, London NW3 2TX and available bi-monthly on annual subscription. Working through back issues of this magazine is an extremely useful way of reading preliminary summaries of very recent excavations, excavations which may not reach final publication for a decade or more. The Society for the Promotion of Roman Studies at the Institute of Archaeology, 31-34 Gordon Square, London WC1H 0PP includes a more comprehensive survey in the 'Roman Britain in 19-' section of its annual journal *Britannia*. It also contains specialist articles on all different aspects of Romano-British archaeology, including for example Tom Blagg's survey of inscriptions referring to buildings (*Britannia*, Volume XXI, 1990, 13-31). Membership of the Society grants access to its comprehensive library.

Economics and industry

Kevin Greene's *The Archaeology of the Roman Economy* (1986) is a very useful introduction to understanding something of how production and trade functioned in the Roman world. The excavations on the site of the New Fresh Wharf in London produced a wealth of evidence for the extent and sources of traded goods which entered Britain through the province's busiest port (Dyson, T.(ed.), *et al.*, *The Roman Quay at St Magnus House, London*, Special paper no. 8 of the London and Middlesex Archaeological Society (1986). For coinage see Richard Reece's *Coinage in Roman Britain* (1987) or Chapter 9 of the author's *Finds of Roman Britain* (1989).

Religion

Romano-British religion is a popular subject amongst academics and there has been much lively debate about how Roman and Celtic cults were synthesized by Romano-British culture. Martin Henig's *Religion in Roman Britain* (1984) covers most aspects while Graham Webster's *The British Celts and their Gods* (1986) discusses the nature of beliefs. Both incorporate discussion of how religious practices were followed in towns. Three of the most useful surveys of death and burial are: the Royal Commission on Historical Monuments for England's volumes on *Roman London* (1928), and *Eboracum, Roman York* (1962), and Alan McWhirr *et al. Romano-British Cemeteries at Cirencester* (1982). The first two contain extensive catalogues of burials, tombstones and grave goods while the third is a comprehensive survey of an inhumation cemetery with discussions about the make-up, ages and diseases of the buried population. See also Ann Woodward's *Shrines and Sacrifice* (1992) in the same series as the present volume.

This is only a very brief survey of some of the literature available concerned with Roman towns and related aspects of Roman life. Many are 'popular' works which can be found in large bookshops, at major site museums or local libraries, and most contain extensive bibliographies which can guide the reader further. The more academic excavation reports are sometimes available at academic bookshops but are more usually only found in university libraries or occasionally at specialist second-hand bookshops.

Glossary

ala A body of auxiliary cavalry (auxiliaries were provincials attached to the Roman army; their units served alongside the legions).

amphora The universal means of transporting perishables in the ancient world. There were many forms of this heavy pottery container, but almost all had handles and could be stacked against one another. The neck was usually plugged with wood and a painted inscription recorded the nature, quantity and owner of the contents.

as Small denomination base metal coin, struck in copper or bronze. There were 4 to a ***sestertius*** (see below).

axonometric Form of projection used to show buildings by drawing vertical lines directly from a plan. In this way the absolute dimensions are retained to scale.

basilica A kind of town hall. Rectangular in shape with a nave and, usually, a pair of aisles. The building type has remained in use for churches.

canton A tribal area within a province

civitas capital The town from which a tribal canton was ruled, and sometimes called a cantonal capital. It was not legally distinct from the canton.

colonia A town founded for the use of retired military veterans and their families as a way of granting them land and assisting in the control of provinces. Its inhabitants were normally Roman citizens. Britain had at least four: Colchester, Gloucester, Lincoln and York. London also may have been elevated to colony status.

decuriones Members of the town council, *ordo* (see below).

forum An open piazza or market square in front of the basilica. The other three sides were usually made up of rows of shops and covered colonnades.

isometric Form of projection similar to **axonometric** but the plan has its angles altered to create an illusion of perspective. The dimensions are retained to scale.

macellum A kind of miniature forum, probably associated with a specific trade.

magistrates The *decuriones* on the town council competed for annually elected magistracies. The two most senior were the *duoviri iuridicundo*. They were in charge of the council and justice in the canton. *Aediles* dealt with public services. In the *coloniae* there were *quaestores* to administer finances.

mansio An official inn or staging post.

martyrium A chapel attached to the tomb of a Christian martyr which often developed into a major church or cathedral.

mithraeum Temple dedicated to the worship of Mithras. Although similar to the **basilica** the temple was windowless and often partly subterranean in order to emulate Mithras' cave.

municipium A civitas capital (usually) which had been singled out for special treatment. Its citizens were elevated to 'Latin status' which meant more than just provincial but was not as prestigious as Roman citizenship. After 212 and the edict of universal citizenship this ceased to be of significance.

oppidum The Latin word for a town. It was used by ancient authors like Julius Caesar to describe large low-lying native settlements in Britain and northern Gaul. It is still used to describe such settlements which are generally defined as zones demarcated with lengths of ditches.

ordo The town council, made up of 100 men who fulfilled a property qualification and had successfully competed for annually elected magistracies.

samian ware A fine red-slip ware manufactured mainly in what is now central and southern France. There were many forms, plain and decorated, and they were shipped into Roman Britain in enormous quantities during the first and second centuries. Production had ceased by the mid-third century.

sestertius The largest denomination base metal coin, struck in brass. There were 4 to a *denarius*, the standard silver coin. Around the year 100 a legionary soldier was paid 300 *denarii* a year.

terminus ante quem Literally 'time before which', a term used by archaeologists when a dated feature lies over another, earlier, feature. Suppose the occupation debris of a gatehouse on a city wall contains a coin dated 212 AD then it is clear that the gatehouse, and probably the wall must have been built before 212.

terminus post quem The opposite of *terminus ante quem* and means 'time after which'. Suppose a building is undated but lies over a filled-in ditch which contains a coin dated to 100AD. The house must have been built after 100AD.

territorium Land associated with a colony, divided up amongst the colonists.

tetrastyle Form of classical temple where the triangular pediment was supported by four free-standing columns.

vicus A small settlement or town. Normally used now to refer to the civilian townships which grew up around forts.

Index

(Page numbers in **bold** refer to illustrations.)

Please note that towns are referred to by their modern names except Verulamium and Vindolanda which are distinct from modern settlements and which are conventionally published under their ancient names. The ancient names for other towns are given where known.

Index of places

General index